The Mother of All Jobs

How to have children and a
career and stay sane(ish)

Christine Armstrong

GREEN TREE

LONDON · OXFORD · NEW YORK · NEW DELHI · S

GREEN TREE
Bloomsbury Publishing Plc
50 Bedford Square, London, WC1B 3DP, UK

BLOOMSBURY, GREEN TREE and the Green Tree logo are trademarks of
Bloomsbury Publishing Plc

First published in Great Britain 2018
This edition published 2019

A catalogue record for this book is available from the British Library

Library of Congress Cataloguing-in-Publication data has been applied for.

ISBN: PB: 978-1-4729-5625-5; eBook: 978-1-4729-5623-1

2 4 6 8 10 9 7 5 3 1

Typeset in Minion Pro by Deanta Global Publishing Services, Chennai, India
Printed and bound in Great Britain by CPI Group (UK) Ltd, Croydon, CR0 4YY

To find out more about our authors and books visit www.bloomsbury.com
and sign up for our newsletters

With deepest thanks to the parents, teachers, social workers, therapists, academics, carers and friends who have generously shared their stories: you know who you are and I will always be grateful.

Contents

Contents

The parent crunch – why I've written this book

This is a book about how work is eating family life.

In the last 20 years, the average working day in the UK has increased to almost nine core hours, the longest average working week in Europe. But, on top of that, the smartphone has added another two hours, for those who stay connected. Even on holiday, more than a third of us keep up with email. In the same period, commutes have got longer, now standing (usually literally) at over an hour and 20 minutes per person, per day in London, and an hour a day outside the capital, with 3.2 million people having to commute more than two hours each day. Meanwhile, over the last 20 years house prices have almost quadrupled (ironically, a change many attribute to women's salaries being included in mortgage calculations), so most adults need to work to contribute to the rent or mortgage. It's no surprise, then, that during this period over a million more mothers have entered the UK workforce. Since 1975 the number of working mothers has increased from half of all mothers to 72 per cent.

The challenge is that more mothers are joining the workforce at exactly the same moment that the working 'day' has become the working day, evening, night, weekend and holiday.

Meanwhile, our societal structures – schools, childcare, workplace, routes to promotion – remain largely designed for the era of *The Tiger Who Came to Tea*, when mummy was at home cleaning up, doing the shopping and giving Sophie her bath. Not only that, but we also live further away from our extended families who, in times past, might have stepped in to care for our children while we were working. Plus, our family structures are more varied with more single parents, same-sex parents and blended families.

Health and Safety Executive data shows that the most stressed group at work is professional women aged between 35 and 44: for reasons often attributed to sexism, lack of support, home/work imbalance and family needs. When I tried full-time working motherhood, I could just about manage it, but only at the expense of my own happiness and my engagement with my family – and that despite having taken on board all the good advice about marrying a man who shoulders more than his fair share of the domestic load. Assuming this 'failure' was down to my own incompetence, I started interviewing hundreds of working mothers about their lives to try to find some answers. This book shares their stories, their pain and what they have learned.

What they have shared won't be relevant to everyone. If you live on the same street as your mum, sister and aunt and don't have a job that tethers you electronically, you probably won't find all their experiences resonate. That could lead you to the conclusion that this book explores first-world, middle-class problems that impact only those lucky bitches with 'career' jobs and kids. And that would be largely true. Which could be reason enough not to explore the subject at all. Except... except that if we truly want to understand why we don't have more gender diversity at the senior/decision-making levels of business and politics then we have to fully understand what drives women to step back or out of work before they are in a position to make more of an impact. And, what I have come to understand from listening to these mums is it isn't just that our workplace was never designed for women – let alone the 80 per cent of us who have children by the age of 45 (ONS data) – it's that the other big changes going on in the workplace and society are making many modern jobs more stressful than a screaming baby. Before you even have a screaming baby.

Some argue that this stressful period is a necessary step on the way to a more inclusive society. That if one generation sacrifices itself and women get into senior roles at scale we will be able to reorganise society so it better meets the needs of families and future generations. If that were working, it could be a worthy effort. But it doesn't seem to be going so well. Because, despite their huge numbers at the entry level of many jobs, too many women step off or are pushed back long before they get their hands on the controls. After decades of women trying to smash the glass ceiling, most top jobs remain filled by men, notably 94 per cent of the CEOs of the FTSE 100 in 2016. It remains staggeringly true that there are more men called David (eight) or Stephen (seven) among the top CEOs than there are women. Financially, it's not working either: male chief executives of the UK's biggest publicly listed firms earn on average 77 per cent more than their female counterparts. But the pay gap starts much earlier in our careers. By the age of 30, when the average woman has her first child, the gender pay gap is 9 per cent. But, in the first 10 years of our children's lives, it grows to 17 per cent. Mothers of teens earn 33 per cent less than their male and childless peers.

Even as I write, gender pay reports are causing media uproar, showing that, among the ten thousand plus companies who have shared their data, in almost eight thousand, men are earning more than women, based on median hourly pay. Which is particularly interesting when you bear in mind the suspicion many statisticians report about how exactly the numbers have been arrived at. Many companies have come out to defend their large gaps, explaining that it's because the men have more senior roles despite in many cases a 50/50 gender split at entry level. Well quite! The question then is how the lived experience of working – specifically working parenting – impacts on both genders and why it deters too many capable women before they get to these senior roles.

A big part of the problem is that, as work has expanded and more women have joined the workforce, the needs of our children haven't changed. Neither the length of school day, usually six or seven hours, nor the long holidays designed for an agrarian calendar. Nor the amount of sleep children need. Nor the incredible number of questions that small children ask in a day: four-year-old girls apparently top the charts with 390, which, as a woman with a four-year-old girl, strikes me as a conservative estimate. Or the one thing children consistently say they want: more time with their parents. But what *has* changed is the dramatic rise in the incidence of child mental health disorders. In 2018 it was estimated that 800,000 children have mental health disorders, a figure that includes a significant rise in self-harm, including reports of it occurring in children as young as three. Yet, somehow, we've designed an average working day of 11 hours, which meets the edges of our little boy's or girl's need for 13 hours of sleep.

When my sisters and I were young, growing up in a very ordinary family in Bournemouth, my dad was an estimator at a construction company and our mother taught English as a foreign language. He worked from 8.30am until 5pm. During his lunch break every day, he took a drive to a viewpoint, ate his sandwiches and had a snooze before returning to work an hour later. My mum worked mornings or perhaps did one lesson after lunch so she could pick me up from school at 3.15pm. I don't ever remember either of them taking a work call at home. Or staying late for work. Even my dad's Christmas party was lunch at the pub (this was on the cusp of everyone noticing that drinking and driving was a bad idea). We, like most of my friends, had family dinner at about 6pm, and then rocked around at home until bedtime, uncluttered by any great drive to accomplish educational or developmental goals. After that, one or other of my parents often went out to our local sports club – my mum to swimming or yoga and my dad to play bridge or squash. When they both went to a dinner or a party, a babysitter came. And, when we sold our four-bedroom, semi-detached house with a normal garden I seem to remember we got £36,000 for it. I'm not telling you this in order to set up my childhood as any rose-tinted perfection or even to say that I wished we lived like that now, but simply to remember that, until very recently, working left space for children to be children and adults to be adults.

That isn't how it is for most people I interview, be they mums, dads, non-parents, people who can't pay the bills or people who can and still worry about it. But it's mums who get the pointy end: the pregnancy, birth and feeding, the guilt of being shit mothers (going back to work early, working too much, never at the gate) and the dawning realisation that society lied when it was suggested that this was all possible. It is why almost two-thirds of new mums say they want to retrain or change roles. It's why the word 'Mumpreneur' has entered our vocabulary, as more and more mothers set out to escape their frustrations and define their own ways of working.

There are other challenges too. Many of us have children later than our mothers did, and we often come to babies well trained in the ways of work but poorly attuned to the needs of our children. Many of us have got our buzz from work for so long we don't know how to get energy from home life. We get bored, anxious, frustrated, lonely, angry, resentful of our partners and lose who we are. Some of us adjust. Others slink back to work as soon as possible and hope it gets better. Only to find that we can no longer give what we once did to our careers, because we're always bloody exhausted and people make 'part-timer' gags when we try to leave at 5pm to get to the nursery and cook tea and put the children to bed and sort out the house and then work so late on screens that we sleep very badly and never catch up at the weekends. So, we run and we run and we run. As Australian psychologist Steve Biddulph says: 'The enemy of love in modern life is not hate, but hurry.' Which reminds me of one mum who told me that her catchphrase is 'Hup hup', as if she doesn't have time to tell her children to hurry up.

And then there are the judgements. Those that hit us hardest are from our children. Not perhaps when they are babes in arms, but when they get funny and cross and really good at expressing what they want. Like the seven-year-old who wrote her accountant mother a letter saying 'Yor not my mummy eny mor bcos I never see you'. She didn't write the same letter to her dad who works a lot too. Or the marketer whose sons call her a 'bad mummy' if she goes out in the week, even though their dad often stays for beers after work. Their little friends can also twist the knife: one of my daughter's nursery mates insisted that I couldn't be her mum because she never saw me. And, to check my credentials, demanded proof by asking if I knew the name of my daughter's sister!

But the judgement comes from adults too. The celebs, glossy magazines and Instagram mummies who implicitly or explicitly tell us that you just have to work really hard to be happy. The Katie Hopkinses and Nigel Farages who say we must 'work like men' and 'be prepared to sacrifice family life' if we want to be successful. The friends and family who can't understand why we don't step back from work and 'enjoy our kids' as if there were indeed a magic money tree to pick from. Working extremely hard, still feeling behind on the bills and being judged by our kids and others in our life is a tough gig.

That is before we consider the era of hyper-parenting – a syndrome that has caused our ideals about the role of parents to be set higher than they've been at any point in human history. Many of us are (or are surrounded by) tiger parents, pushing kids academically; helicopter parents, trying to guide all their decisions; parents of 'little emperors', buying them everything they want; or overschedulers, who hope that learning to play Mozart at four will provide advantage. This is very involved parenting that still has to go on top of the working day. Even if you try hard to resist these trends (I would describe my own parenting inclination as more 1970s-style benign neglect) it adds extra pressure and guilt if you wonder whether your non-Mandarin-reading, non-Kumon maths and phone-less child might end up less than mediocre.

This book seeks to understand this stressful world and its impact on all of us through the stories of those who live in it. Because people are shy of revealing their parenting problems, the names and supporting details have been changed to protect the innocent. They are mostly told from the perspective of mothers, with input from partners and their kids, as well as lots of other people observing these changes: teachers, psychologists, nannies and childminders, GPs and so on.

While each of these stories explores individual decisions, the big questions are really about the kind of society we want to live in. What equality means; it simply can't be that women have won the right to do everything men have done, plus everything women have done, all at the same time. What values do we really value: those that take seriously the needs of our children or those that view the world through the lens of our earning power? What does 'work that works' look like, how do we achieve it, who needs to change to make it real? When will we stop to look at the impact of modern life on the next generation – their sleep, their anxiety, their self-harming, their eating disorders – and say, 'we know why we needed to break away from the discrimination of the seventies, but was this the very best we could come up with?'

The Mother of All Jobs is about the battle to make modern working parenting actually work. If not for our own wellbeing and sanity, then perhaps for our children's.

CHAPTER ONE

My story

This is the book I wish someone had given me the day before our oldest daughter was born and I became a mother.

As I drew her out of the birthing pool and on to my chest, she looked up. Our eyes locked and I fell in love with her, as mothers have since the start of time. I floated through the next weeks in a bubble of happiness. I lay awake smiling and watching her breathing. My usual cynicism was lost to the joy of our baby. My life of 'busyness' at work was forgotten, as I focused all my attention on this perfect, little being.

Before that day, as I worked in communications and then at a London advertising agency, it had never occurred to me that a baby would ruin my career. She'd change things, of course, but it didn't cross my mind that I'd want to stop work or even work part time. When my wise, father-of-three, CEO advised me to make no plans for after the baby because I might change my mind, I was indignant. I said that I'd be going back because working was what I did and I loved my job, I loved travelling the world to present insight reports. I loved running research projects into what was cool for 20-somethings, or how people changed their spending habits through the 2008 downturn, or the rising green agenda.

I know now that I saw our baby as another project, in a similar category to getting married and setting up a home – another thing to get on with. It was what the senior women I worked with appeared to have done. So I didn't worry when, around the time of her birth, my husband said he wanted to accept a redundancy payment and plan a new business. And I didn't worry when my CEO resigned to take up a new role while I was on maternity leave.

Six months later and feeling mostly ready to go back, I was staggered to realise that everything had changed. A new boss suggested I might want to come back three days a week. That he would be 'happy' to 'take on responsibility' for my team. That maybe I could focus my energy on 'some PR'. What I heard was that he was taking away my role and my team as a kindness to me and my baby. I was furious and bewildered. I remember leaning against a wall outside the office struggling for breath.

I called HR, lawyer friends and my ex-CEO in a frenzy. A day later HR called back to say that I'd completely misunderstood the conversation. It was an exploratory chat, not constructive dismissal and, anyway, going to tribunal was very time-consuming and I only had a case if I couldn't get another job at the same or better salary. For the first time in my life, I felt the rage and impotence of being discriminated against. It was perfectly clear that he and I could not work together, and he was going nowhere.

Panicked and needing an income, I threw myself into a job search and did something very stupid. I accepted the wrong job for the wrong reasons. Having moved from a communications background into research at the ad agency, I'd always felt a bit of a fraud, without 'real research credentials'. To address this, I accepted an offer from 'a proper research agency', a company that did surveys about what people thought of everything from banking charges to mobile phone masts. They said that they wanted to do more of the kind of research that I enjoy, listening to people rather than asking them to click yes/no answers but, even then, in the interviews, I had an inkling that wasn't wholly true.

The day before I started, with an overwhelming sense that I'd made a crap choice, I called the search person and told her I didn't think it was right and didn't want to go. She smoothed it over: I was going to be perfect, it was going to be perfect. I wanted to believe her, I was worried that finding another job would take a lot of time when our income had for months been just statutory maternity pay of about £130 a week.

At lunchtime on the Friday at the end of my first week, I left my grey basement office and made three calls from a park bench. The first was to a management coach my company had used to help our team a year or two before; the second to my ex-CEO; and the third to my husband. I told them all I'd made a mistake and wanted to resign and go home. It wasn't that I couldn't cope with being at work when I had a baby (although I found it harder than I expected), it was that I didn't like the culture or feel I had the right skills to do well.

The former management coach told me to leave then and there and find another job. My former CEO and husband said it was too early to call. So, I went back to the office and tried to make it work.

It felt like fighting my way out of quicksand. The more effort I exerted, the worse it got. I felt very isolated. No other women there had children and I wasn't connected into my established professional network because I went home every evening. I slept very badly. Partly because we had a baby. But more because, once awake, my mind churned with endless, anxious worries about work. I remember at night, pressing my heart to my husband's sleeping back and following his breathing pattern in the hope of absorbing his tranquility.

To get into the office in town, I was dashing out of the house just as our daughter got up and arriving home anxious and depressed just as she needed to go to bed, while my husband was managing the majority of the childcare. Yet still leaving work many hours earlier than my new colleagues did. As much as I wanted to get to know some of them better, I felt I was out so much already that I couldn't stay for drinks. I also didn't have time for the things I'd always done that help keep me calm, like a bit of exercise or an evening of roaring with laughter with friends. I tried a few lunchtime options but, since colleagues used to joke about my part-time hours anyway, taking a proper lunch break wasn't going to work. At worst, I was failing at everything: a listless and ineffective employee, a distracted mother and wife.

Soon after I joined, they sent me to Austin, Texas for a couple of meetings. It was two flights and 18 hours' travel each way. I arrived at the Four Seasons Hotel late at night, with my tits like cannonballs, bursting with milk. I plugged in my breast pump and it did nothing. In panic I tried every socket in the room. I ran sobbing to the reception where a man with decades of hotel experience smiled kindly. He seemed like a guy who'd seen it all: snakes in the bath, trigger-happy drunks and the odd popstar driving a Lamborghini into the swimming pool…. But I'm not sure he'd ever dealt with a hysterical British woman in the middle of the night trying to resuscitate a breast pump.

The poor man tried so hard to help, using every adaptor he could find. Finally, in a tone in which one might break the news of death, he said, 'Ma'am, I've called the 24-hour drugstore, there is a lady there called Linda waiting with a pump for you, your taxi is outside now.' We sped through town at 2am to snatch from poor Linda (who in my mind now resembles a traditional white, haloed angel complete with wings), a hand-held pump of the kind I'd never seen. I had to build it in the back of the taxi ('put the flange into the joint') returning to the hotel to spend the rest of the night sitting in the hotel shower weeping inconsolably and swirling pumped milk down the drain.

The truth was that, aside from having a job I wasn't well suited for, I didn't know anything about children and how to organise my life with them in it. I'd read books of course. Lots of books about pregnancy, birth and the psychological development of babies and toddlers. But little about actual motherhood. I had a niece and nephews I adored from a few hundred miles away. Despite being a keen reader who'll pick up any lifestyle newspaper article or magazine column I can get my hands on, I couldn't or didn't find the advice I needed.

I was slow to realise the damage this was doing to my relationship with our daughter. She and I seemed to live in different worlds and when we met we shared mutual incomprehension. I had no idea what babies and children did. I'd get home jangly with stress and try to indulge her, based on a highly idealised view of babies and what they were supposed to be like. When that failed, as it always did, I got frustrated. As did she. I interpreted her behaviour as irrational and disruptive and took it personally. Then I gave up and did more work.

Having failed to identify the real problems, I didn't know how to resolve them. By then I'd defined my role as to keep the household going financially and thought that, if I kept on going, she'd grow up a bit and things would get easier. I couldn't see that my overreactions to her emotional outbursts encouraged more of them. I didn't think that her terrible sleep pattern was driven by her need to get my attention. She would howl when I put her to bed and at 15 months she learned how to climb out of her cot and would rampage around the house. And I would chase her around and bundle her back and she'd get up again and again and again and again. In the morning, I'd get up and go to the office with the taste of vomit in my mouth that comes from exhaustion.

At some point, I correctly realised something needed to change. Much less promisingly, the answer I came up with was to have another baby. At least I'd be able to escape my basement life among the worn grey carpet tiles. I didn't need a pregnancy test to tell me I'd succeeded in getting pregnant: I caught the smell of a colleague's trainers during a meeting in a small glass office and it made me sick.

Our second daughter was born in a panic. In the final stages of delivery, there was meconium in the pool water. This is a bad sign because it can show that the baby is in distress and needs to come out quickly. I was dragged out of the pool and led to a bed as a senior midwife held my chin and directed very, very clearly 'PUSH, PUSH NOW'. The baby arrived blue and not breathing, and alarms rang as medics ran in. As they took her away to resuscitate her I howled and begged them to bring her back to me. When they finally did – I think it was all of about 10 minutes – I was determined I'd never let this child go. And I pretty much didn't let go of her for the next seven months.

With the intention of respecting her stability and routine, we kept our oldest daughter in childcare while I was on maternity leave. I don't remember at the time considering it might not be the right thing to do. I thought that changing her routine would be bad for her; that she might be affected by her mother being dedicated to another child didn't register. That period at home, however, did show me we had an unhappy toddler on our hands and that we had work to do to sort things out.

The problem was that I still didn't know what. So, I did what I thought I was supposed to do, and – don't laugh – went back to work, even more full of resolve to make it better for myself and the others in the team. I remember forcing myself back through the glass door. I wore bright pink in the hope it might fool myself or anyone else. But things felt much worse. While away, I'd actually fallen back from the very small bits of progress I'd made before I had the baby. My biggest client was in the office on the first day I was back. I said I looked forward to joining the meeting to catch up on what I'd missed, but was told there wasn't a chair available for me.

Finally, I came up with an idea to break out of this misery and find some answers. Before I had kids, I'd written for *Management Today* magazine. I emailed the editor and asked if I could go and interview some mums with big jobs and small children. My plan was to learn from their experience and use it to fix my world. He agreed (without, it has to be said, any enormous enthusiasm) and I set off to talk to mums who were CEOs, MDs, board members, law firm partners, management consultants, entrepreneurs and many more.

On-the-record, they had loads of answers, which I diligently wrote up. They all looked inspiringly in-control. One gently suggested I pulled off the Cheerios stuck to my sleeve before we started. Over the course of a few months, the interviews went from an inconsequential and unpaid blog to the cover of the magazine. The advice in them was sensible: plan really, really well; live by Excel spreadsheets; hire excellent childcare; and just focus on work and home and nothing else. All of which I could follow, but none of which made any difference.

Many flashed glimpses of troubles but ultimately said they were thriving. Which some, of course, were. But over time I came to realise that some were not. They, too, were struggling with their kids or their marriage or their job. They felt excluded by their colleagues. They wondered if it was all worth it. They despaired of really being recognised for what they contributed. They wondered if they should quit and buy a hayloft in the Hebrides. My process was to invite them to be as honest as possible and then remove anything too personal before it was shared publicly. Very early on I started to see the patterns in what they asked me to remove. I understood why they were so careful: their interviews would be read by their bosses, peers, competitors, junior colleagues and their own families. A few became quite anxious about saying anything at all and one, when she read her own words back, couldn't bear for it to published and asked me to pull the whole thing.

But it still took a while for me to cotton on to the scale of the gap between some of the on-the-record conversations and what they said privately. Strangely, it was in one of the least interesting conversations – when someone treated a pre-interview call purely as a PR exercise and gave formal, pre-planned answers about her perfect family life – that opened my eyes. Afterwards, someone who knew her socially said: 'Oh she's totally miserable, her husband's been shagging the nanny for years and she knows it and so does everyone else'.

I still don't know if that was even true (I didn't interview her) but the potentially huge disconnect between her words and her reality made me look much more closely at and engage more with women – not just for formal interviews, but socially – who were inclined to be more honest. Stories emerged. Crying in board meetings, coping with professional bullies, postnatal depression, anorexic children and, finally, one confided that her husband had left forever shortly after we spoke. These darker, messier stories reflected what I was seeing among my friends. At about this time, I met a lawyer friend for 'a glass of wine' on a Saturday night, which turned into two bottles, plus a cocktail and a whole baked Camembert, as she told me how she left work by the fire escape to try to see her kids before bed without her colleagues noticing she was 'leaving early'.

Their troubles told me that I wasn't the only one who couldn't make this work. And that I wasn't struggling only because I'd made a crap job choice. I was hearing the off-the-record accounts of working mums who are finding it hard. The things they say quietly to each other when no one else is listening. The words that are never designed for the wider world. That is what this book is. The honest account of dozens of mums that they wouldn't tell you unless you were a friend and they wanted to confide in you. But in among the struggles, I also found mums who were doing well and enjoying life. They have insight we can all benefit from, though the answers are really personal and complex: choosing good childcare and being well organised isn't enough.

The interviews gave me the confidence to finally resign from my job without a role to go to. In a café over lunch, a great friend listened to a torrent of angst for 45 minutes before saying what even I was coming to understand was true: 'You're utterly bloody miserable Christine. Go back to the office, resign, get your coat and go home.' I went home that evening and shared her advice with my husband and he wholeheartedly agreed. The spell was broken. The next day, terrified and lacking any sort of financial plan, I resigned with no job to go to. HR were very unsure of how to announce the news, asking if they could tell people that I wanted to spend more time with my children. I said no, noting that no one would have demoted my husband because he'd had a baby, no one would blame his resignation on wanting to spend more time with his children, and he'd never have to pump his tits in a hotel room in Texas.

After a year with virtually no income I co-founded Jericho Chambers, which is a consultancy structured around flexible work. We had a third daughter, who we've had a chance to really enjoy as a baby and toddler. We don't always get it right, but we get it right enough of the time that everyone in our house now sleeps perfectly well in their own beds. If anyone achieves that by reading this, then I'll feel it was worth it. But my real hope is that you are able to enjoy your transition into motherhood far more than I did.

Even if you didn't, there is still time to catch up. Last night I came home from work and I found our eldest daughter jiggling on the front doorstep waiting for me. Now eight, she was bursting to tell me about a competition she'd won and what she'd done in her gymnastics class and to show me the fairy gardens she and her sisters had been making. I was struck by how much our relationship has moved on since those early dark days. I am very grateful to all of those whose honesty and wisdom has helped us find this happier, easier, more content place.

This book has come out of these experiences and what I've learned since. I've applied some of what I've discovered to my own life. Without making foolish claims of supermum bullshit, it has transformed me and our family in positive ways. So much so that I sometimes wonder whether, at its heart, it is one very long apology letter to our oldest daughter for making such a bloody mess of her first few years.

A note on how to read this book:

If you're reading this book then there's a good chance that you're feeling time-poor, totally knackered and rarely get much peace to read alone. Quite possibly you have a stack of books and magazines by your bed that you really want to read but never quite get to the final page of. I know that, so this book it set out in very approximate chronological order of what happens to working families, from getting pregnant to having a baby or two or more, through the toddlers, school years, teens and so on. It's designed so you can read it from cover to cover or dip in and out of whichever bits are of most interest. If you haven't been to the toilet on your own for four years then you're probably not in need of a chapter on the choices you might make before you have kids, so just skip it. Each chapter ends with some thoughts that sum up the learnings for anyone who is too tired or wired to read the rest in any depth. But, just to be clear, these are the views of people I have interviewed. Of course, everyone's situation and worldview is different. Don't get cross if it doesn't suit where you are, and don't feel judged if it's different to how you do it: whatever works for you and your family is the right answer.

Finally, as my editors will confirm, I've struggled to finish this book because almost every day I hear a new story or detail that builds on my insight so, for my latest thoughts, visit christinearmstrong.com/more.

CHAPTER TWO

I love my job but is it time I settled down and thought about kids?

MY PARTNER MATT AND I have been together for five years and live in a small one-bed we bought last year. We both work full time – he's in IT and I'm a Project Manager, and while we work pretty long hours at times, our careers are important to us and we love what we do. His company offers really steady progression and I'm in line for a promotion and pay rise this year. A friend has also recently called me about a more senior role at her company too, which I'm considering. We have lots of friends, mainly through work, and spend a lot of our spare time out socialising, usually ending up at a gig or club a couple of nights a week.

Lately though, the 'baby' conversations are starting to become more frequent. Friends are starting families and birth announcements are taking over my Instagram feed. I've always thought I wanted two or three kids but now that it's becoming more of a reality, we just don't feel like we're ready yet. There is still a lot we want to do before children. We've only just started to earn decent salaries that will hopefully grow over the next couple of years so we can finally start saving for a wedding, furnish the flat and clear some long-overdue credit card debt.

Ultimately, we both want kids but not anytime soon. But realistically how long can we wait? Is there ever a good time? And is there a way of having kids that doesn't take away everything that matters to us…: our friends, our jobs, our way of life?

Navneet, 33, Project Manager

****

Navneet's situation, so familiar although it comes in many guises, started me thinking about the advice the women I interview would give her at this point.

Just hearing her talk is a reminder of that time of life about which parents of small kids are hopelessly gooey eyed: the magical bit 'Before Children'. When you're in it, it can feel really quite pressured with lots of competing issues about work and home and money. But later, looking back, you're blown away by your capacity to be fabulously selfish and not even notice. To work hard, sure, but also to eat, drink, sleep, do as you please and then sleep some more. To spend your money on pretty things that catch your eye.

People lament, 'If only I'd known how precious the time was … I'd have read more books, learned Italian, taken up amateur dramatics, rafted the Grand Canyon, watched dawn rise, climbed the Himalayas, traced our family tree, gone to more parties, had more sex, done more drugs….' After the baby, some parents feel the loss of this freedom like a missing limb. Others cling to their wild times, trying to party even with a baby and small kids, becoming more and more ragged. The happiest seem to accept the change and shrug. When they're trapped at home with a rampaging two-year-old on a Friday night they content themselves with the knowledge that they've been to enough parties. And that they won't have a monster hangover.

At the risk of totally putting Navneet and Matt off, Lou, 35, an events organiser who is working four days a week, describes the difference in her lifestyle before and after having her two kids like this:

Before:

'It was him and me and impulse trips, weekends away, eating out, drinking out, partying. Shopping – having disposable income and not having to think about childcare. Enjoying our friends' kids and being able to give them back. Eating out was what we used to do the most! All other content is explicit – getting it on, all-nighters, spooning with your best friends, holding their hair back in the loos, putting them in taxis so you can carry on your night! Outfit swapping with friends – when does that happen once you've got wobbly baby tummy?'

After (and do note that this only gets her from dawn to the bit when she starts to drive to her office):

'Up after four or five hours' sleep on a good night. Dressed, cup of tea, shower, make-up, bag packed, kids' bags packed, husband's bag packed (half joking): am fully ready by 7am. Kids' 7am wake-up – milk, dressed, teeth, wash, shoes, coats, blend juice (yes, I know I'm a wanker but I can't have breakfast at the office for free if I arrive after 8.30am). And get out the door. Navigate getting to the car with two flight-risk toddlers. Get them in the car with various tantrums about them wanting to climb in themselves, which seat they want, not wanting to get in. Strapping one of them into the car while making sure the other one isn't standing in the traffic. Getting into car after they've been dropped off at nursery and having 30 seconds to sit before I speed off to work (juice in hand) to face another day….'

She also throws in how it changes the dynamic between her and her partner:

'Mostly we agree on the big stuff but when getting the kids out of the house we have a different approach so it's actually better on the days that he leaves ahead of me. I rush and shout as loudly as possible and get them thinking the house is on fire and we have to move RIGHT NOW. His is to gently engage them with the reasons why we are getting ready and how it would be good for them not take off the shoes and coat we have just helped them put on and not unpack their rucksacks on the carpet while mummy is running back upstairs for her phone. This clash means I can only think of a handful of occasions when we've left the house talking.'

And she is someone who, having paid for two nursery places and some babysitting for work events is worse off at the end of the month than when she started. Yet, even in her darkest moments, Lou says that not having the kids would have broken her. Just talking about that possibility – it took them longer than she hoped to get pregnant and she had a traumatic miscarriage a few months before they conceived their eldest – brings tears to her eyes. She says she watches her kids sleeping and chokes with her love for them. She inhales their pillows and believes that her reason for being is to be their mother.

Time to make decisions?

We can't know how Navneet and Matt will feel about their children if they have them. But we do know about the rage and agony that people who want kids and can't get pregnant suffer. Couples who have tried to conceive for lonely months and years before seeking help and then spent their savings on fertility treatments, would implore them to think seriously about having the baby soon. It isn't for me to add to the cacophony of 'news' about the decline in fertility rates after 35, but a dad who met his partner when they were both in their late 30s and went through six rounds of IVF before having a baby describes it like this:

'Being in Infertility Club is awful. It's like a bereavement without having had the life but with the tantalising possibility that it might all end one day if you do the right things. It makes you wary of being around children and happy families. We basically stopped being asked to go out with friends because I think they found it too awkward, and we didn't mind that. When our daughter arrived, one of our friends said, "Oh great, you can come out with us and X and Y, and A and B now" – i.e. them and two other couples with six kids between them. I knew what he meant, it was fine. So, you resent friends with kids. The worst bit was resenting strangers – who you didn't think deserved kids – you get a bit Darwinian about it: "How come their genes get to jump on a generation but mine don't?" The capacity for self-pity and bitterness is enormous. One of the worst parts was thinking that other people felt sorry for us – which I'm sure they did. Of course, the flipside is that everyone was vastly and genuinely delighted when we had our daughter.

'And the things people say to you…. I tended to have an almost American attitude to it, wanting to talk about it all the time. But the downside of that is that everyone has an opinion on it, far more than with other medical conditions. I mean, I bet no one has an opinion on endometriosis or leukaemia or lupus. There are some staples that so many people said without thinking, either because they didn't know what to say or because they were idiots. Things like: "Can't get her pregnant? I'll have a go if you like", to "Just go on holiday and forget about it and relax", to "Everything happens for a reason" (baffling!), to "Just go and get drunk", to "My sister couldn't have kids, she got three dogs, she's never been happier", to "If only you'd got on with it sooner, eh?"

'And of course, let's not forget: "You want kids? Just you wait till you've had a couple, you'll wish you'd never bothered, we never get any sleep!", to "You can take a couple of my kids off me, if you like, they're a nightmare". Then there were the sincere but odd bits of advice to go and see some nun in County Carlow or to light a candle in such-and-such a church. It's well meant, but honestly….'

When I pose Navneet's dilemma to the IVF dad above, he has no hesitation in replying: 'She's 33? Get on with it.'

That said, I regularly interview women who conceived naturally much later, including in their early 40s. So, I share the thoughts of my sister-in-law, Dee Armstrong, who happens to be a fertility coach at The Natural Fertility Centre in Edinburgh:

'When women come and see me, there is generally help we can offer but I get nervous after 40, at which point conception rates fall more sharply and miscarriage rates rise more steeply. In an ideal world, I would definitely advise Navneet and Matt to get on with it sooner rather than later. If she is ovulating regularly that's a good sign. She should definitely get to grips with her cycles and I recommend all my clients read *Taking Charge of Your Fertility* by Toni Weschler – the fertility bible. Something very basic to learn is all about your cervical fluid, which appears a few days before ovulation – if women have been using hormonal contraception for years they may not have seen it since their teens and it may all seem a bit of a mystery. Matt should also pay attention to his side of things, of course. Especially if he's been enjoying a party lifestyle he may well have given his sperm a bit of a caning and they may need some time and TLC to get back to full strength. In particular, we are concerned about men who have been regular users of weed in the past – marijuana can have a long-lasting detrimental impact on sperm and if men are in that category they would be well advised to have a sperm DNA fragmentation test sooner rather than later – the bog-standard semen analysis offered by your GP won't cut it. The bottom line is I would advise Navneet and Matt, from a purely biological point of view, to crack on with it. They might need three months to get in shape from a fertility standpoint – all diet and lifestyle stuff – but after that they shouldn't wait.'

For the sake of clarity, I have to tell you that she is only saying 'cervical fluid' because this is a book. In person, she says vaginal slime. After I got married, she initiated a fascinating/slightly awkward chat about what to look out for.

She also has advice on how women can check on their fertility:

'The other thing that some women consider is a "fertility MOT", which they think might give them some idea of how much time they've got to play with. The crucial part of the MOT is a hormone test called the Anti-Müllerian hormone (AMH) test, which gives an indication of egg reserve or roughly how many eggs you have left in your ovaries. The results tell you what your egg reserve is compared with fertile women in your age group. The test used to only be offered in hospitals prior to embarking on a round of IVF and typically cost a few hundred quid by the time you had factored in a consultation with the doctor to explain the results. However, these tests are now being offered online for as little as £60. Proceed with caution, however, for two reasons: one, because fertility experts advise that the results of these cheaper tests may be questionable because of the lack of standardised lab facilities and two, because while your egg reserve might tell doctors a lot about how your ovaries will respond during IVF, that doesn't necessarily mean much in terms of how your body is going to behave if trying to get pregnant naturally.'

Money, money, money

Money is the subject on which there is no grey area and no doubt from those who have gone before and decided to have children: pay off those debts and squirrel away every penny you can. What no one ever seems to say quite clearly enough is that you reach your peak disposable income for the next gazillion years *before* you have kids. Even if your earnings do go up afterwards, your disposable income dries up like an open packet of wet wipes. The wisest woman I ever interviewed on this subject said her mother told her she had to save 50 per cent of her income until she settled down and had kids, and she did.

But no one else does this. As one mum put it: 'You can't ever afford to have a baby.' But Matt and Navneet can't see that yet. The baby is a hypothetical concept – I mean how expensive can nappies be, right? – and the stuff they're spending money on now (seeing friends, buying regular stuff, going out) is just what life is about. It's not unreasonable for them to feel complacent. They've both done well at work and their incomes have gone up. Their costs went down when they combined two rents into the flat and they expect to earn more money in the future. It all feels like it's going in the right direction. But, if and when they have kids, they will wince at the memory of buying their lunch at Pret a few times a week or dropping the equivalent of a week's food shop into a cocktail bar on a Friday night.

Their current sense of progress will come to a wailing halt as they lose income for maternity leave. Assuming both return to work, they then will gain a huge childcare bill. If one or both of them chooses to work part time they both will lose some income and probably still gain some childcare costs. If one or other stays at home full time, they will lose up to half of their income – more if that person is Navneet as she'll earn more than him after the promotion. What's more, the very act of having a baby may damage Navneet's prospects. My apologies, because this really is depressing, but *Normative Discrimination and the Motherhood Penalty* (Harvard University, 2010) reports that *both men and women* discriminate against women for having children. It found that both women and men held mothers to higher standards than non-mothers and dads and that this damaged their chances of promotion, being hired and pay. Specifically:

'Mothers were offered a salary that was, on average, $7,000 less than the salary offered to childless women. On the contrary, fathers were offered a salary that was, on average, $6,000 higher than the recommended compensation for men without children.'

What I particularly love about this stat is that the benefit for the dads doesn't even compensate for the losses to their partners. The point is that, whatever they do as a couple, they are likely to be significantly worse off financially if they have a baby.

Is this a good time for Navneet to change jobs?

A lot of women would advise Navneet to bag any promotion possible that she can get before she has kids. There is some evidence that being more senior can actually help you get more flexibility at work when you need it, but this of course depends on how senior and where you are working.

Looking at other jobs in other companies now *could* be smart, but there are three critical factors to bear in mind.

The first and perhaps most important question is whether she is happy and well established where she is. Babies can make you feel vulnerable at work, so if she's enjoying her colleagues and feels secure, that may be a good reason to stay on. But if she's unhappy – feeling undermined, bullied or unsupported – then looking for somewhere happier now could be transformative and actively thinking about her options is a good idea before she gets pregnant, when moving may seem too risky and arduous. Moving jobs between kids – as I did – is hard. You start feeling exhausted because you have a new baby and a massive additional mental workload as you get to know everyone, their systems and the new role as fast possible. Figuring out who is going to be a brilliant ally and who's an untrustworthy little shit on three hours' sleep isn't easy. You're also less likely to get the benefit of the doubt if and when you need to leave early or arrive late than if you've put in 10 solid years and have a reputation as a workhorse.

The second consideration is salary and maternity benefits. Navneet and Matt need to turn their brains to doing a competitive review of her pay: remember that it is usually around the birth of our first child that the pay gap between men and women starts to gape. But it's not just about the salary. Does her company offer enhanced maternity beyond the statutory minimum? If it's a good package, that is an important pull to stay in the company. If, though, she would only get statutory minimum, she may want to look at what competitors do. The evidence is that most of us don't do this research before we start new jobs for fear of triggering alarm bells about our professional intentions. For example, Glassdoor, a website that allows employees to review their employers, spoke to 1,000 women for its 2014 Maternity Benefits Survey. While happy to ask about holidays, pensions and healthcare, the survey found that 78 per cent of women would not question a potential employer about maternity benefits at interview stage, for fear that it would jeopardise a job offer. Given that she has friends in the sector, it should be possible to do some quiet digging on- and offline. And, while she's tarting up her CV she might as well also pop into a few recruitment agencies or have a look online to see what other options may also be out there.

The point here is to run the actual numbers: 'If I get this pay rise and no benefits versus if I get that pay rise and good benefits it will come out as….' Be hard-headed. Don't be one of those women who later say, 'I didn't really think much of it' as they look in the kitchen cupboards and count the meals they need to find until the end of the month. Also, look at it longer term if more kids are a possibility: even if enhanced benefits aren't offered until she has two years of tenure in a new company, they could make a big difference for a second or third child.

The third factor is the working culture and how working parents are treated. Can she see role models who are able to combine their work and home lives happily? Mothers who have done well professionally have often stayed with one employer through their baby years. Ideally at a place in which they are known and supported by a good network. Many do choose to work flexibly after the baby and it is well worth looking to see if those options are available. One mum who'd worked with the same company since graduation was amazed to be offered a big promotion when she got back after her first maternity leave. She'd asked for a job-share role and the only person they could match her with was far senior to her. They took a risk, it worked brilliantly, and it jumped her up her career. She has stayed with the company ever since: she now has three children, still job shares at the same company 10 years later, and her and her job-share partner were recently promoted again.

As Navneet considers these choices, she and Matt might also want to step back and think about an alternative approach that some parents say they wish they'd given more attention to before 'getting trapped in the city'. This could be the time to move out of town, cut back their costs significantly and change to a different pace of life. A mum who works at a bank told me she is already counselling her kids to think about professions that are not dependent on city living, such as nursing, teaching, dentistry and medicine. Even if some salaries might work out lower than those in in the city centre, the quality of life, housing and education could be better. This relocation might also include moving closer to their families – India possibly isn't the place for them right now – but could they be nearer to his family? It may not be the big professional/career jump Navneet had in mind but, depending on their real priorities, it may be a path to greater long-term contentment.

Boundaries

One specific thing both should consider is the boundaries between work and home life. When you are young and lacking the big responsibilities of kids or failing parents it's easy to fall into working very, very hard and socialising through work. We talk about 16-hour days or working all-nighters, often with pride. But those patterns can be hard to break. Many say they wished that they'd started to learn to manage their hours rigorously and turn off digital devices before they had kids and had no choice. It takes practice to learn to be one of those annoying but productive people you sometimes work with who always seem to be able to deliver on target without tanking their own weekends. Later, you will be glad you had set up new work patterns before people around you mutter about 'baby brain' while you fantasise about smacking them in the mouth.

It is also time to consider broadening their social lives beyond work. Being on maternity leave when all of your friends are in the office can feel like you've been banished. You really want to have local, non-work friends whose company you enjoy. This is especially important when so many of their friends are younger, which means they may not connect quite so well when their conversation drifts into whether the baby is constipated again and the shocking price of formula.

Do they need to move?

Having a baby in a one-bedroom walk-up isn't ideal long term, so looking at other places is smart. However, bearing in mind the advice above, fixing your budget at a point that won't destroy you later is crucial. Given the cost of houses (whether rented or bought) this will feel like an impossible conundrum, especially as with small kids you need the shortest possible commute as you could end up paying for childcare every minute you're stuck in a car or on a train.

A social media marketer said she and her partner went all out and bought a five-bedroom house before they had kids. It needed a lot of work and they mortgaged as far as they could possibly go in the area in which they wanted to live. Meanwhile, her friend, who earned more than her, moved into a two-bedroom flat in a shit area. She thought her friend's decision was weird, but now they both have a one-year-old. Her friend is loving working two days a week and has very little financial pressure, while she is back full time, starting work at 7am so she can leave at 4.30pm to see their daughter, and is hysterical with exhaustion and besieged by their mortgage and nursery bills. She would swap the big house, with a never-ending list of renovations they can't afford and have no time for, for the flat in a heartbeat. Another mum told a similar story. They invested in a big period fixer-upper before kids, which they thought would be their dream family house. Two years later they sold it for a smaller, less fancy place with modern plumbing and no leaking roof. Amanda MacKenzie, now CEO of Business in the Community, has specific advice for anyone ambitious: 'You have to have focus. We didn't get distracted by moving or doing up houses or anything else. When my kids were little it was about work and home and that was it.'

As they look at houses, there is one more factor that I hesitate to even raise, as it might just tip this into madness. Schools. I know, I KNOW. But if they want to go ahead and buy 'the family house' then looking at schools now makes sense so that they get it right; they don't want to pay ridiculous moving costs twice. Of course, when we were kids, your mum signed you up to the local primary and that was that. My own mother says that her brother took her in on her first day of primary with a note from my gran. These days, someone would call social services if you tried it.

The point to bear in mind is that if they go ahead and have kids, the school decision will come sooner than they think: it is a cliché-because-it's-true that the early years screech past. When your oldest hits three you feel you've barely started but are confronted by a form to choose a pre-school (if that's what happens in your area) and then a primary. So, before they move, and especially if they get the money together to buy – I'm sorry, because this is bananas – they have to look at the school entry criteria. There is no point in paying over the odds to move next to the best local school and find out later that they had to have been attending a particular church since before conception to get on the sodding list for it. I hardly dare to mention secondaries but if you are the kind of person who wants to settle for the next 20 years you may as well take a peek.

What about all that spending?

If they do decide to have kids, the advice on buying anything at all is clear: spend very slowly and very wisely for the long term. This isn't the moment to decide you always wanted a fabulous beige sofa set or long, dangly gold earrings or anything at all that isn't indestructible. My pet theory is that brides wear frilly white dresses because, after kids, you never get to have anything pale or delicate again. Delete from your view Kelly Hoppen interiors, spiral staircases or anything with 'fine' in its description (art, china, knit, dining).

It's all very dull and probably what your mum would have told you. Live with the working-but-a-bit-crap TV, dining table or sound system. When you do have to fix or replace them, research something that will last 20 years. If your coffee machine saves you £3.50 in Starbucks every day then fine, but get one with pods that cost less than a flight to New

York. Better still, get a cafetiere or one of those indestructible pots that sits on the stove. If your bike is knackered, get a decent one but one that isn't so flash it'll get nicked every three weeks. Similarly, with cars, save your midlife crisis version until the kids leave home. Just before pregnancy number one was the moment my husband decided to buy the convertible he'd always wanted. It lasted six weeks with a baby in the tiny backseat; we now drive a knackered Ford S-Max that we call the skip-on-wheels.

On Navneet's wardrobe, women I've interviewed advise against buying anything cheap, trendy or fitted. After the birth, you won't have the disposable income to spend on new clothes, even though everything you have will seem dated and, quite possibly, too tight due to your, ahem, evolved body shape. One elegantly dressed PR exec – who is not yet 30 – told me she binned her entire wardrobe of Reiss clothes after her second child because they suddenly looked like they belonged to a younger and shinier version of herself. She has evolved – slowly – into a softer, more grown-up look. She would advise her younger self to buy fewer, better-quality clothes with a conscious thought that they would last 10 years rather than 10 weeks.

If you're too tired and wired to read the above

- Be neither dozy nor overly hysterical about your fertility: read, inform yourself, make active decisions. If you are reading this and don't have a partner yet, then open your mind to other options. Egg freezing is best done when you are younger.
- If you don't yet have a partner, remember that who you choose will impact on your ability to be successful at work. Research

from America shows that 'people with extremely conscientious spouses are 50 per cent more likely to get promoted than those with extremely unconscientious spouses'. Conscientious spouses take on household tasks and create a satisfying home life, enabling employees to focus more on work; they also 'display pragmatic behaviors that their mates emulate.'

- If you do have a partner talk, talk, talk to each other about what you want and if it will include kids. If you do want them, discuss how you will parent, who will step back at work, how you will make decisions and everything else that may happen. Gay adoptive dads told me that the homework essays and questionnaire their adoption agency made them complete about parenting have proved a great base for a stable relationship and calm parenting. This was a role traditionally taken on by religious leaders in the run-up to marriage, but which can be replicated in any relationship.

- Relish being the absolute centre of your own world. Give yourself time generously to read mags, loiter at the gym, drift around the shops, volunteer at a food bank. Do enough stuff that you won't look back and regret wasted opportunities. That includes going to every party, every leaving do and every opening of a paper bag. When you next go to a party, people will have forgotten what Aperol spritz was. It also includes relishing spending time alone.

- Adjust mentally to the idea of growing up. Having a baby is for many of us the first real acceptance of 'adult' life. So, start to come to terms that this high-living life is a great phase but it will end if you have kids – and usher in another important and exciting phase.

- Choose your employer. If you stick with the one you have, make it an active decision: look at the other options and feel confident it is the right place for you for the next few years. Consider your own feelings about your role, your pay, the maternity leave policies and the culture for working parents. If you decide to move, remember that the difference between statutory maternity leave and paid maternity leave could be half a year's salary or more. Most mums I spoke to counsel against moving jobs during the baby years if you can avoid it.

- Get real about money. Pay off your debts and minimise your cost base – even though you may feel that currently you're better off than you have been before. Now isn't the best time to start throwing cash at fillers and botox, high-end face creams or appointing a chi-chi hairdresser. One mum decided to go blonde when she had three kids under five and then horribly regretted the time and money that maintaining it ate up.

- Don't tie yourself in knots about the secrecy that is spun around getting pregnant. A woman who works in a business dominated by women says she has a whole routine going about colleagues who suddenly start wearing floaty scarves that 'drift' over their tummies. She immediately puts bets down on them being pregnant. The thing is that this seems like a big deal to you but it's likely that almost everyone around you – when you are 33 and appear to be settled down – may be wondering when it'll happen. They could think this even if you say you are Never Having Kids. And when they do find out, don't expect them to collapse to the floor in astonishment.

- This is not the best time for either of you to decide put all your cash and time into launching a risky, fledgling business.... Save that adventure for later.

- Plan your housing. Don't consider just the cost, but also the amount of work you may need to do and how you pay for that, the commute, the neighbourhood and access to good schools. Also think about who else lives there: is this an area in which you could meet people and make friends and where your kids will be part of the community? Living in the hipster quarter is ace at the right moment, but a deeply uncool modern housing estate that's close to good schools may serve family life better than you expect.

- Start bedding into the local area as soon as you get there. Even before you have kids, see if you can join a local club or class (maybe an exercise class, given that having a baby is, ahem, a bit of a workout, being reasonably fit can help). Having friends very close to where you live will help more than you imagine.
- Don't buy beige. Or glass. Or get a place with a spiral staircase.
- Do ask for advice from friends and relatives with kids who are growing up. They know stuff. As with secrecy above, if you trust one or two senior women at work with kids it may be worth having an informal chat with them. You may be surprised by how supportive they are. One amazing woman I worked with fought really hard for me to get decent maternity benefits when she realised that the international team I was in got less than anyone else in the company.
- Also see if you can spend time with people with kids and babies; not just a flying newborn cuddle to drop off a teddy bear and a blankie, but hanging out for a day or even a few days at a time. But, if you do – this from a dad – don't traumatise yourself about their poo and nappies. With your own kids, changing a nappy is more like going to the toilet yourself. Other people's kids are a different story.
- Learn to smile at children you meet. You'll be proud later that you weren't one of those snotty pre-kids people who sigh

dramatically when a two-year-old on a scooter delays them five seconds on their way to work.

- Do spend hours and hours reviewing everyone else's shit parenting and deciding how much better you are going to do it. This is a critical phase of figuring out between you what approach you'll take. Plus you'll be able to reflect later on what idiotic, smug gits you were when you were disgusted because Isaac's mum somehow let him roll in dog poo. She'll remember too and will be laughing her arse off in a few years' time.

What happened next?

NAVNEET HAS STOPPED TAKING the pill. She is holding onto pre-kids life by her fingernails but is coming to terms with the idea that if she waits too long for 'a good time' it may never come.

CHAPTER THREE

Wow, I feel like I've totally lost control and don't know who I am any more

WE TRIED FOR YEARS to get pregnant and Nick and I were ridiculously happy when it happened. We made our spare room into a nursery and had a 'bump' photoshoot and a 4D scan, did hypnobirthing and my mum bought us a great buggy. But then the morning sickness came and it was like being permanently hungover but without the good night out. People pushed past me on the bus because I was too slow, I felt edged out of things at work. I cried on the sofa for the two weeks of maternity leave because I just wanted to be at the office. The actual birth was.... traumatising, for me and him and the baby... everything went wrong and I totally lost it but the midwives were amazing – at least they knew what they were doing... I couldn't understand how I could be going into this and not having a clue?

The health visitor says I have to keep trying at breastfeeding because it's best, but how can it be best if it hurts so much? I've had no sleep, the baby is crying all day, I'm all alone. I went to a breastfeeding support group and thought how much easier it was to be running a meeting than listening to other women talking about their feeding problems, and her baby's reflux and tongue tie... I really did not even listen, just sat there watching her lips move wanting to cry. I told her a bit about my job but she wasn't interested.

Now Nick's just gone back to work after two weeks at home and all I want is to leave with him each morning, just like before. He doesn't understand and I feel isolated and trapped with a small thing that cries all day. I really need his help but I find myself in a sleep deprived hump by the time he gets home from work about how his life is somehow still normal, shoving a crying baby into his hands so I can go and hide under my duvet and howl. Even how he breathes is irritating me.

I'm going to be a shit mum… what was I thinking? I shouldn't have done this. I used to travel, meet interesting people, people wanted to hear about who I met and the gossip I knew. Now I feel lost, alone, isolated and completely incompetent without a clue of what to do next. It's like I'm waiting for something to happen, but I don't know what or when.

Alice, 37, Producer

****

Some women have a baby and realise it is what they are on this planet for. The rest of us don't quite get it, especially at first. Alice is the rest of us, suddenly crushed between what Dr Sue Gerhardt, author of *Why Love Matters – how affection shapes a baby's brain,* calls the 'twin stresses of inexperience and isolation'. In the last year, her sense of who she is, what she is good at and her ability to cope has been shattered into crappy little pieces. She hadn't clocked how strongly her sense of self was linked to her professional achievements. Given that psychologists say our mental welfare depends on us having a clear picture of who we are, it's no surprise that Alice feels low.

Dr Rebecca Moore, Consultant Perinatal Psychiatrist at the Royal London Hospital puts it in context:

'I often see women who are part of a professional couple who have lived an ordered, controlled life. They're used to making decisions and largely doing what they want. Sometimes our hopes and expectations of birth are unrealistic – we imagine that birth can be planned along with the way we have ordered our lives up to this point. The decline in antenatal classes offered and a lack of continuity in midwifery care in many places often means we don't get a chance to help discuss hopes and expectations around birth. For example, at our local hospital parents get limited sessions around birth and with many other women in the room. We don't then have space to have an in-depth talk about what we expect during labour and what we would feel/do if birth didn't go as planned. So when a difficult birth happens, it can blow women's minds and they can start their parenting life traumatised and isolated, having lost the structure and security of their working life. Women can find it enormously difficult: long days and loneliness, it's so hard and tiring with a newborn.'

Obsession

The beginning of pregnancy can be thrilling. A sense of achievement. A secret. A feeling that life is about to start. Alice devoured every piece of information she could about what she should do and celebrated the different stages: 'my baby is the size of a Kalamata olive', posting scans, having a baby shower and her dream-like pictures. She became, in her own words, 'a total fucking princess' about the whole thing. Which is all well and good to some extent – it might be the last time you get to be totally selfish – but there's a risk that the fall on the other side may be greater.

Take, Sarah, 39, a bookkeeper who also became obsessive about reading up on the potential risks of her first pregnancy. She meticulously managed her diet, avoiding everything from large fish that might contain too much mercury to a shop-bought trifle that might have had a snifter of sherry lurking at the bottom. She refused to go through the automatic barriers at train stations for fear of them crushing her belly.

She wore an elastic-type wrap around her bump to shield the baby from scary noises, such as ambulance sirens. She didn't dye her hair or wear deodorant, though she said she did something to her pits involving lemon juice. Her husband joined her crusade by refusing to let her weed the garden and put the rubbish out, to avoid 'hurting the baby'. She described her husband physically pushing her up a modest hill on a warm day so she didn't overdo it. She is also embarrassed to admit that she requested seat cushions in restaurants and generally behaved 'like a dictator with gold taps in the shape of swans'.

But by the time Sarah-Swan-Taps was heavily pregnant with her third child, she had no time for herself at all as she was too busy hoisting two toddlers in and out of baths and child carseats and insisting on a daily glass of wine to keep her going. Her husband retreated to his office and admitted later that he invented breakfast meetings and added an extra night to work trips to avoid the Weetabix carnage, and to allow him to catch up on sleep. When all the kids fell asleep in the car she would sometimes pull over and weep for the 'her' that came before. The one who was in focus, the one the world spun around. Before she became lost in the chaos.

This first-pregnancy obsession is the reason that second/third/fourth pregnancy mums can barely sit through a pregnancy yoga class. The first-timers use up half of the hour responding to the teacher's 'how is everyone feeling today?' by recounting the minutiae of their backache and pelvic pains and bad night's sleep. Those with a toddler or two at home gawp open-mouthed, aghast that anyone childless has anything to complain about, ever. Before remembering that, not so long ago, they too were just as self-absorbed and felt some inner need to take back control by studying themselves.

The obsession – of course – drives everyone else completely mad. Even my mother was bored by me, quietly observing: 'they do say women have been doing this for years, you know'. Listening to a first-time pregnancy obsessive is as bad as sitting next to bridezilla for 18 months as she plans her dream wedding. If you have to endure the wedding and then the 40 weeks of pregnancy with the same person, it would surely make you crack.

Perhaps it helps to know that we mostly do this stuff to try to reclaim a semblance of order. I'm not sure it works: it may just distract us from the very real need to adjust to the news that we're no longer in control of anything much. The worrying about every movement or non-movement of the baby, medical questions and bigger problems, if they emerge, is enormously draining, but as one mum who is currently pregnant says: 'All the things they are worried about, my placenta being in the wrong place, whether its abdomen is the right size ... when I ask what they can do about it, the answer is "nothing". I wonder if we'd be better off knowing less.'

The hormones

In *Lean In*, Sheryl Sandberg is disappointed by women who 'lean out' before they even have a baby – those women who stop going for promotions or working at full pelt. Which seems to perhaps overlook all those women who struggle so hard to get pregnant and who suffer in silence when they do.

Over the years, I've been told so many heart-wrenching stories of repeated miscarriages, fertility battles and other challenges that I wonder anyone gets through these things without their colleagues knowing. One woman who worked for a defence company set up her own infertility blog and became something of a leader in that world. She felt the growing disconnect between work and her social media 'minor celebrity' life pressing on her and eventually 'came out' at work about the problems they were having conceiving. Her employer was massively supportive but, after she had the baby, she felt she had to leave as she had become 'Mrs Fertility', which was not a good way to be branded professionally.

Even if you don't experience these challenges, pregnancy is a world changer. Says one mum: 'You quickly find out that actually being pregnant is totally shit. There's nothing glamorous about it whatsoever. You feel totally unattractive, like you don't recognise yourself. You don't know what's going on inside your body. It feels like a parasite is inside you. Your hormones go crazy and your husband begins to understand you even less than before. Crying – all the crying. I've never been a crier. Oh, how I cried, for no reason – still haven't stopped!' It's worth noting here that, of course, lots of women absolutely love being pregnant.

My husband's key recollection of all three pregnancies is that at some point around 11 weeks I'd crash through the door from work, lie on the kitchen floor weeping and say 'pass me a knife and I'll cut the bugger out myself'. As anyone who has had it knows, morning sickness isn't 'just' a feeling of nausea: prolonged and intense sickness can lead to feelings of isolation and low mood, and it's important to note the link between sickness and perinatal anxiety and depression. There are resources in the References section (see page 305) for more information about maternal mental health support and guidance. I was relatively lucky, my sickness would diminish after 13 or 14 weeks. Others are not.

A mum who is a baker describes it like this:

'Try morning, noon and night sickness. It was so bad I feel sick even thinking about it eight years later. My husband is banned from wearing a certain aftershave because the smell brings it all back. I can't use Persil non-bio for the same reason. I used to sit and rock backwards and forwards like a crazy person because I literally didn't know what to do with myself. I threw up at least 10 times a day. I used to say to my husband: "What have we done? I can't do this; I just want this thing out of me". It was so early, I didn't even know it was twins at that point. It affected everything. I couldn't go out. I didn't read baby mags and books, or do anything that reminded me of a baby. I even let him choose the buggy because I wanted no part in it. As time wore on (which seemed like a fffffffin eternity) the sickness came between 4 and 6pm, so at lunch I only ate what I knew wouldn't taste too bad coming up; Sprite was a killer because of the acid burns.'

For a woman who worked at a freight company, the sickness led to more problems:

'When I got pregnant I felt I had to hide it and didn't talk about it anyway. Even when it became very obvious, I avoided talking about it. I felt very, very sick and hid it. When the sickness went, in came the depression. I was crying all the time and I couldn't sleep. I went to the doctor for help. I think my boss saying he was leaving triggered it. But also my sister lost two children and I was scared of everything going wrong. Even now, a year after the birth, my doctor still thinks it's best for me to see a counsellor every week. I keep this as a lunchtime appointment and say it is a gym class. I would hate anyone at work to know the truth.'

Most women I interview try for as long as possible to just keep going. After 12 weeks they will usually talk about it, a bit anyway, but mostly don't take time off or change hours unless they have been signed off by a doctor. My view is that if men suffered morning sickness then the medical profession might take it seriously and maybe we would have found a way to manage the symptoms. Since there isn't a magic wand, it might generally be best for people to be honest and adjust their working patterns to suit their needs. Perhaps a more positive take is to accept that sickness and depressive feelings can help us slowly adjust to a different pace of life, if we let them. But if anyone had said that to me at the time, I'd have gone for them.

Medical teams

Another shock of your first pregnancy is the relentless interaction with our medical system. Healthcare goes from a concept you see debated by politicians on the news to part of your daily life. The sheer volume of appointments and amount of blood, piss and energy it takes from you is draining.

After having three babies at the same hospital I'm sometimes invited back to talk at conferences for midwives and doctors about my 'patient experience'. I start by describing how dealing with them is like walking from work into a wall of jelly. I would have a hospital appointment at 2pm and would be busy at the office up to the very last minute, quickly agreeing things, signing stuff off, delegating stuff that needed to be done that day. Inevitably, I would then leave work late and tear through the hospital's revolving doors at two minutes to two. I'd waddle up to the desk panting and collide into a queue of 12 heavily pregnant women and wait for 20 minutes. I'd then be registered as late, handed a pot in which to collect wee and would sit for the next 45 minutes sweating stress. Eventually, more than an hour after the stated time, I'd see a well-meaning but harassed midwife who would ask me to repeat every detail I'd gone through in the last three appointments. She would send me off to get blood taken but the person who did that would then be on a break so I'd sit holding a ticket, like the ones you get at the butcher's counter, fuming some more. Before I could leave they would insist on printing off a two-page letter about my next appointment via another queue and invariably run out of ink or paper. I'd stagger out hours later, feeling like I'd wasted the whole afternoon and mentally writing letters to the secretary of state for health about administrative chaos.

This common experience is a big part of why those who can afford it say they go private: to be seen and heard as an individual. To be visible as a person going through the most important event of their life so far. Since the invention of the NHS only two secretaries of state for health – out of almost 30 – have actually had a baby. Which is perhaps why we treat pregnant women as if they were going through an industrial process: check in here, scan over there, weigh-in third on the left, delivery on the top floor, 'no you can't visit in advance, risk of infection, love'. It is also why stories abound about being talked down to at scans, by midwives and by consultants, and the indignation and frustration that follows. A former colleague advised me to 'use every professional skill you have to ensure you are heard'. It's good advice but it doesn't always work, as everyone with a birth or pregnancy trauma story will tell you. If you can, connect yourself to a small, local midwife team rather than a big hospital. Many women say they found that much more personal and supportive but some only realised it was possible the second or third time around.

'A declining asset'

While fending off the impersonal and sometimes patronising help of the medical profession, many are also realising that they are being viewed as diminishing assets at work. The BBC drama *The Replacement* darkly illustrated how unnerving it is, as your pregnancy progresses, when others move in to take over your work, your team, your desk and your projects.

Producer mum Alice, who opened this chapter, battled with the realisation that many of the important decisions were not hers to make: others decided who would take over from her, how her projects would move forwards and who would manage people in her team. It felt, she said, like they were taking away part of her identity.

She also disliked the way pregnancy seems to give colleagues permission to talk to her in different, and more personal ways.

'I found people's responses to my pregnancy bewildering. Either they said it'll be the best thing that ever happened to you or they said it'll be awful and you'll never sleep again. Both answers completely stressed me out. I worried that the baby would unpick everything I valued in my life, my relationship with my husband, my sleep, our regular trips away. I like to be in control, I am very organised and also anxious. This pushed me over. Only one other pregnant woman I met admitted she felt the same.'

Alice particularly remembers the door closing on a meeting about a programme that would be made after her due date. It was like everything she had worked so hard to move towards was slipping away. Having staked her self-worth on her professional standing, she found this loss excruciatingly painful.

Birth

I was told the story of a pregnant woman who was giving a PowerPoint presentation to a group of men in a corporate boardroom. Without warning, her waters broke and, because her baby was distressed, meconium (baby poo) ran down her legs. It looked like she had a serious case of diarrhoea. In some panic, her colleagues decided that the best thing to do was to sit her on an Aeron office chair and wheel her down the pavement and over the road to a nearby hospital, where she proceeded to give birth in a different place, with different people and much sooner than she had planned. This for me sums up the contrast between calm, ordered work and the physical unpredictability of birth.

Yet somehow this isn't what we expect. Imagine, for a moment, writing a 'period plan' for your next period. 'Well, it'll arrive on a Monday, so as not to disrupt the weekend, in the morning, of course, don't want any mess after I just changed the beds. It'll be very light – much lighter than average – and over by Thursday so I can wear my white jeans to the drinks party. My partner is going to be sooooo supportive, I am going to talk to him a lot about it and I think he'll really understand how it feels.' Ridiculous. Yet this is basically what we do with birth plans – which, to be fair, finally do seem to be in decline since someone finally spotted that writing wholly unrealistic expectations of birth is, at best, unhelpful.

It may also be that we as a generation are having a worse time of this than our grandmothers did. French doctor and birthing guru Michel Odent – currently in his late 80s – spoke at a meeting in London recently. He's a controversial character, with a French accent someone once described as being 'as thick as Brie', who has been upsetting the medical profession for years with his calls for water births and less medical intervention. He believes that the reason modern women find birth so difficult isn't physiological – apparently gorillas give birth in approximately the same-size proportions as humans without the same problems – the issue, as he sees it, is that we have lost our ability to stop using our sophisticated analytical brains and just to let our bodies take over. We try to *think* about birth rather than letting our bodies *do* birth. And, if he is even only partly right, it stands to reason that high-control professionals are going to suffer.

The story of Annabel's first birth is an inelegant illustration of this transition from being thoughtful to being physical. She is a PA, one of the most efficient and in-control women I've ever met. She had studied natural water births and was committed to a positive, natural experience. This is how she remembers the reality:

'I came out of the house mid-contraction to go to hospital, and met the postman on the path. I was semi-dressed, in knickers and shirt, red in the face and howling. The postman backed down the path saying "it's OK, it's OK, I'm going!" I think he thought I was about to attack him with a machete. I later learnt that the neighbours were going to call the police as they thought someone was being murdered in our house. The birth took 24 hours, because I was traumatised at the thought of pushing in case I pooed in front of my husband. Poor baby, desperate to come out, and me just not going there, as the prospect of a public poo rather than meeting my new child overwhelmed me. In the end, I went to the bathroom, telling husband and midwives I needed to be alone, and got on the loo. I managed to jump off in time for her to be born on the floor next to the loo. My mental image is of me, naked on all fours, bellowing, with my head in the loo and my bum in the birthing suite. Pictures of me holding my child for the first time are of me sitting on the toilet.'

The unpredictability of birth is a problem for many. Some say that part of the reason they pushed for a C-section was that knowing the date of the birth was reassuring, and calmed their anxiety about everything being uncertain. Which doesn't always work: ask anyone who has experienced the stress of being booked in for a C-section and sitting around waiting for it all day before being rescheduled for a day or two later.

A midwife says:

'The timing of the baby's birth can be a big issue for some women, from trying to finalise business deals, delivering while their own mother is over from America, or before their partner goes away on a business trip. And, I notice that more and more women seemingly have not heard of maternity leave, the numbers who are still working at 38 or 39 weeks are increasing. They worry that they are indispensable, that they still have so much to do and to prove to their colleagues (men as well as women) that being pregnant doesn't make them incapable of work – even if labour does, albeit it temporarily. These are the women I most worry about when I think how they will adjust their lives to a baby. I sometimes think they see the pregnancy as a nine-month project before things return to whatever normal is for them.'

This scenario was the case with one IT project manager who was hospitalised for two weeks before the birth. 'I worked the whole time I was there in bed, I took calls and did emails and most people had no idea I wasn't at my office. Doctors would come in and I'd say "I'll have to call you back in 20 minutes" without explaining why. No one even tried to stop me and I figured I'd get more time at home after the baby was born.' It's not a decision that she's particularly proud of in retrospect.

When things go wrong

There are, of course, some births that go wrong; babies who are born very unwell and some who die. I can't do justice to all of these stories, but have interviewed women who have experienced all of these things. For them, the loss of self and sense of control is extreme. One describes the heartbreak of having to leave her very unwell one-week-old son at hospital, when she was discharged, because there wasn't a bed that would enable her to stay with him. She was in a wheelchair after an emergency C-section and remembers crying and crying in total desolation on the pavement as her mum went to get the car to take her home.

Another mum had a normal birth but started to notice problems with feeding. Five weeks in the midwife sent her to A&E because the baby was constipated. She recalls:

'That was the day I realised something wasn't right. The comments were blurring…. They said she had "low tone". I started to get very anxious….

That visit, it unlocked a series of events, and MRI, tests for everything. They were eliminating things – reflux, you take comfort from words "that's classic reflux, we can give you medicine". But it wasn't that and they started to look at genetics. By then I'd lost all of my baby weight and more. I was on the internet all day. I'm a project manager and I fix things, I make things right. It was my way of getting some control. Finally, blood tests came back when she was four months old at 6pm and they were abnormal. They said she had a degenerative disease and wouldn't make it to her fourth birthday. I couldn't look at her, I didn't want to face it. The good thing about having a toddler already was that he needed to be fed and put to bed and to go to nursery. You have to keep going and functioning. My professional background kicked in. They needed to do a lot of tests and planned four sets of procedures. I was having none of it. For her sake, I wanted all four sets of tests done under the same anaesthetic on the same day and, through sheer determination, I got my way. That early experience taught me that precedents are there to be broken. No one has all the answers – the specialists don't know the answers. To me, things before then had either been right or wrong, but I had to learn with this that it doesn't work that way. I carried so much anger, like "why did you tell me it might be degenerative disease if you weren't sure?" But I had to get away from expecting anyone to know everything – and focus on her. She is unique, there is no reference point, there is no syndrome, there is no support group. I found one similar case but I've not looked at the outcomes…. I don't want to know…. It's not statistically relevant and she is five now and at school. I've learned to work with what she presents each day. She's brought us heartache, trauma and joy all in the same hour. Compared to that, work – which was the cornerstone of my life before – seems mostly meaningless.'

Parents who have children with special needs sometimes have to adjust to the realisation that their lives have changed forever. A special educational needs teacher says: 'One thing I do see with parents with children with serious special needs is that some can't and won't ever go back to work. The needs are too great. It's hard to see those parents. In my experience, it's always been the mothers and you see them in so much pain: mourning for the child they imagined they would have and the career that they did have and can't go back to.' Others have to get back into work after a long absence. Either way, for families with a female breadwinner who has to then step out of work, this can be catastrophic.

Inevitably it also puts huge pressure on relationships.

'You're on edge and near to crisis a lot of the time and you have to hold on to yourself all the time, because of the very heightened emotions involved. It creates constant opportunities for a bad relationship by exposing the differences between us. I always think of my husband "Why aren't you fighting, why am I doing all the lifting, why is it me always driving everything?" It makes me angry, but those differences are important. My husband knows he has to let me get on and he is more present. I am constantly looking for the next project – and my child's needs create many projects – at a point you realise that you're not living in the now and you have to stop.'

Money doesn't necessarily help: very unwell children are, says a mother, a great leveller. At the severe end, the NHS is often the right place for very complex needs, in spite of its glacial pace and bureaucratic frustrations. At the less severe end, private schools may not be an option, even if you think it would help. One teacher told me: 'I think one of the things that's surprising is that having money often doesn't really help with special needs. In fact, some of the kids we see are the ones who got kicked out of private school because they don't have to accept them and often will only do so if the parents pay for all the extra help they need, on top of the standard school fees.'

In practical terms, one mum says she was given some great advice, which was to never ask any of these three questions: 'How long have they got?', 'Who will look after them when we're gone?' and 'How do they compare to the mainstream kids?' She credits this with keeping her sane. Her other thought is that: 'these Herculean problems needed my professional skills – negotiating, persistence, finding ways round when people say "no" all the time, just managing so many stakeholders, holding all of the technical information you need to remember because no one ever reads the notes properly…. Those things make normal work look like a piece of piss.' Another was told, after a two-year career break to look after her sick child, that she couldn't expect to go back as head of department but would have to work up again. Hearing this, she laughed bitterly. 'If only they knew what I had gone through and done in that time, they would have seen that there isn't a CEO job in the world that could scare me now.'

Sophie Walker, leader of the Women's Equality Party, relates to that. She says that it was having a child with special needs that energised her to lead a movement that hopes to change society:

'And then I had children. And I suddenly realised the lie of what of what I had been told, that I could have it all. And then my child was diagnosed with autism and I had to care for a child with disability and I sank deeper and deeper and deeper into the unseen, the unvalued, the unpaid…. The women who do care. And that was the point when I became an advocate for disability rights, an ambassador for the National Autistic Society, I ran marathons to raise money and stay well. All those people running marathons to raise money and all those lonely women who are lost – I was so lost – I saw them and I realised that the way out was to build an army. Because I could balance and balance and balance and make individual choices, including marrying a feminist, but, even with that, it was just us two trying to make our way. The only way for both of us to have real choices is to build a movement that opens up choice for everyone.'

Maternity leave

Our case-study Alice found that maternity leave made her depressed. After the baby came, Nick was around for two weeks before heading back to work and they seemed to share the baby care very equally – 50/50 parenting she called it. It was also a time of lots of activity, which she quite enjoyed; people sent presents and cards and she got an explosive gush of love on social media.

But, when it was time for Nick to return to work, she was devastated. She wanted to put on her work clothes and leave with him. She felt like a prisoner at home with a teeny baby she barely understood and struggled to feed.

Even when Nick got home from work, they never got back to the 50/50 teamwork they started with. It seemed she was suddenly the expert even though she had little idea herself. If the baby cried, he looked at her. If she did nothing, he took the baby to her. The breastfeeding slowly got better and she and Nick settled into rather different roles. She did almost everything for the baby and he organised dinner when he got in. He quickly learned never to admit to having stayed for even one drink at the office as she was overtaken with jealous rage when he was late. Even though she hated herself for feeling so dependent on someone else.

It was loneliness that she couldn't bear: it felt like it was just her and the baby surviving in a community she barely seemed to know, after years of working during the day. This isn't unusual: a mum who works for a consultancy firm, and commutes to work, used to take her crying baby to the corner shop when she got so exasperated she didn't know what else to do. The grandmother of the family who ran it didn't speak a word of English, but would take the baby and rock it, calming both mother and child. The mother had barely noticed the family in years of living there until she was on maternity leave. Action for Children did some research in 2017 that reports that 68 per cent of parents said they felt isolated amid the pressures of raising their sons and daughters, with parents of children under one the most likely to be affected.

A mum talks about a cringing post on Facebook: 'It said something along the lines of "You shouldn't criticise the mum on her phone at the swings because she'd already done crafts, singing, puzzles and a baby yoga class." Sodding nonsense. More likely she'd been up since five, put on two washes, made porridge and chucked it in the bin, scraped food out of her and the children's hair, changed a couple of outfits, dropped a potty full of piss down the stairs and left two cups of tea to go cold on the side. At the park she's texting her friends and saying "BEST DAYS OF YOUR FUCKING LIFE?? If someone so much as THINKS IT near me today I am going to beat them to a pulp with my Tripp Trapp".'

Dr Rebecca Moore, Consultant Perinatal Psychiatrist at the Royal London Hospital again:

'The more honest the conversations about the realities of parenting, what you need and what you expect to happen, the better. I advise women to map out a bespoke plan to build a support network – and do it before you have the baby. This might include sleep, exercise, friends and family support or finding other local mums with apps like Peanut or Mush. One woman I worked with did this brilliantly. She had a history of depression so thought very carefully about a way to build support networks that would work well for her. She joined pregnancy yoga and invited women out for a drink afterwards and that worked really well. She joined NCT and other local groups that she had researched. She also planned time for herself with yoga and swimming, because you need to carve out time for yourself, don't feel guilty about this! The thing was she worked at it – like a job – and she did it before the birth.'

If you're too tired and wired to read the above

- Having a baby is a massive and abrupt shift from being able to make choices about everything to ceding control over a lot of what happens. 'Not being in control' is one of the most common themes of my interviews – spanning getting pregnant to staying pregnant, giving birth, the baby and more.

- In 'babyworld' no one cares what you do for a living. You could be head of the UN and they'd ask you if your baby has slept through the night yet. At some point a midwife or doctor will call you 'mummy' instead of your name and call your child 'baby' without even the 'the' in front ('and how is baby today?'). Accept that it's a question of time before you give in to the change you are going through and become someone different – someone not wholly defined by your professional title.

- Immerse yourself in the world of pregnancy and babies: read, watch programmes, spend time with friends and family and others doing it. If you're with other pregnant women it seems totally normal, if you're the only one in a vast workplace you can feel like a freak.

- It's great if you can find someone else at a similar stage of pregnancy, who will be as fascinated as you by it all.

- Deciding that there are definitive right and wrong ways to be pregnant and to look after a little baby can add to the stress of the experience. Try to avoid making it harder for yourself by creating complex rules. You may reflect later that it wasn't worth the trouble. A dad laughs ruefully that his first daughter only ate organic vegetables, trimmed to avoid any possible contamination from fertiliser. He says his second kid has turned out remarkably robust, despite eating whatever was available.

- Try to avoid assumptions about how it will work: a woman told me 'us Indians are very fertile you know' and then really struggled when she didn't get pregnant with one click on Amazon Prime. It can all take a lot of time and effort but loads of other people have gone through it and will be happy to talk about it if you ask.

- Take your feelings seriously and get help and support if you need it. Medics and mental health experts know this is a brutal time and that professional women are at extra risk of depression. A neo-natal consultant I spoke to told me that suicides in the first month after birth are most likely among professional, middle-class women. A mental health charity worker told me that they see most of their work coming from two ends of the spectrum: the deprived at one end and socially disconnected professional women at the other. Hence going along to a breastfeeding clinic for help and support.

- Child psychotherapist Sarah Clarke says that the problem with postnatal depression is that many women don't even know they have it and are ashamed of the fact. A partner or savvy friends who are 'on it' are, she says, lifesavers if they can say 'it's OK not to be OK' and get you the help you need. She thinks that protecting the fragile well-being of mothers in that first year is critical for the well-being of both parents and the children, and should be the responsibility of us all.

- Plan as if it were an important project. Invest more time in talking about how it may actually turn out and thinking about what your personality is like. Take steps before the baby comes to ensure you get the right kind of local support and engagement from others. Also plan the balance of your relationship: who do you think will do what? Even if it changes, you will have set up a framework you can talk about and adjust.

- Watch your role models. Most of us know a successful woman with kids whose identity is utterly clear. You'll get there too.
- All that said, feel free to take a leaf from Sarah-Swan-Taps and exploit the privileges of your first pregnancy outrageously: it's the last time it'll ever be all about you again and you may as well go out in style.
- Try to enjoy what you can of it. Later, parents often say they wished they'd realised that, for all the challenges, this time is very precious and wish they'd given themselves to it more.
- Your fertility journey, pregnancy and the way you birth your baby can frame your mental health into motherhood. Perinatal anxiety and depression can leave a long-term mark if left unchecked. Have a look at the References (page 305) where you can find information and support for postnatal depression and related mental health issues.

What happened next?

ALICE MADE FRIENDS WITH one mum at the breastfeeding group. They started to hang out most days and over time attracted a little bunch of friends who got each other through the early days and to a place when they started to actually enjoy maternity leave. By the time she was ready to go back to work, Nick was jealous of her at-home social life.

As Alice settled into a routine and her baby slept a bit more, she gave herself time to think about Nick seemingly backing off from the childcare. She reflected that his going back to work after a short time was no more his fault than hers – it's just one of the ways that our society organises childcare that creates the sense that it is something women lead in and are expert at. She and he talked about this a lot. He wanted to be more involved and so, in addition to him being more hands-on in the evenings and mornings, they've set aside time for him to be on his own with their daughter on Saturdays while she goes for a swim and sauna at the local pool.

Alice treated her second pregnancy very differently to her first. She told her colleagues much earlier – before 12 weeks – and took time off when she was very sick. She worked part time from early on and started maternity leave weeks before the end. While she was sick, Nick took some time off work to look after their oldest daughter, which added to their connection. That said, it didn't do much for her career and she eventually decided to move to a less demanding role. She doesn't have the status that she did, but she's OK with how Nick breathes.

CHAPTER FOUR

Right, I need to get back to work

I MANAGE A SMALL group of privately owned shoe shops for the family that owns them. I've been there ten years. I love my job and have been happy doing it, but always felt like I was passing time until I could do what I've wanted for as long as I can remember - being a mother.

I know it's old fashioned but imagining spending all day being a mummy gave me such a thrill. I couldn't wait to dress my child, teach it to crawl, walk, talk, bake. So, the joy I felt when I gave birth was tinged with a sorrow that I would soon have to leave her with somebody other than me. I can't bear the thought of someone else looking after my child or even worse, my child turning to someone else for comfort before me. My maternity leave was an utter joy and I cherished every moment but it was bittersweet. The more time I spent with her the more I loved it and the prospect of it ending filled me with dread. As the time for me to return to work grew closer the knot in my stomach grew and I wasn't sure if I could actually go through with it.

The problem is that my partner earns less than I do, his job isn't the most secure and he has debts from before we met. It scares me that we might be left with nothing coming in. We simply can't afford for me not to work.

The first time I left her, I thought my heart would break. I felt like I had been kicked in the stomach. I didn't even make it out of the nursery before I embarrassed myself by collapsing in a heap of messy tears in the manager's office. I felt like I had let her down and abandoned her.

I cried every single time I left her. I looked at other mums with their children and a lump formed in my throat and on really bad days tears filled my eyes. It was so unfair, they got to spend time with their children whereas I couldn't. It wasn't fair. It was even worse when I saw them on their phones ignoring their children. Didn't they realise I would have cut off my right arm to be able to spend time with my child??

I cut back my hours and am managing a bit better but have just found out I am pregnant again. I know going back after the second will break me. What am I going to do?

Emily, 28, Retail Manager

****

The reality is that, whatever their emotions about their baby and returning to work, most people feel they have very limited choices for practical reasons. Some have to go back at a certain point to keep the household solvent and others, who want to go back, find that the cost of childcare (especially for multiple children) means it makes absolutely no sense to do so.

Broadly, there are three approaches I see:

1) There are women who run back, thrilled to escape this strange new world and revel in wearing proper clothes and spending time with adults.

2) There are those who walk back, torn between work and home, but ultimately feeling they need the stimulation and income of work enough that it's the right thing for them and their families.

3) And then there are those, like Emily, who are pushed or dragged back and never feel the same way about work again.

For the first two groups, returning to work comes with risks. A 2016 Equality and Human Rights Commission (EHRC) report found that three out of four mothers in the UK had negative or possibly discriminatory experiences during pregnancy, maternity or upon return. It also found that one in nine mothers reported they were let go in some way (dismissed, made redundant or treated so badly they had to leave). EHRC research in 2018 has shown that six in 10 businesses believe a woman should disclose whether she is pregnant during her recruitment process, while almost half think women should work for an organisation for at least a year before deciding to have children. In the same study, more than a third of private sector employers surveyed said it was reasonable to ask women about their future plans to have children during the recruitment process, while 41 per cent said pregnant employees put an 'unnecessary cost burden' on the workplace, findings that Rebecca Hilsenrath, EHRC chief executive, described as a 'depressing reality'. Similarly depressing is the need for the organisation Pregnant Then Screwed (pregnantthenscrewed.com), which documents cases of maternity or pregnancy discrimination and offers legal help and practical support to women who have been discriminated against.

Even if active discrimination is avoided, the process and return can be very difficult. A hairdresser explained how she was only allowed two hours' paid time off for each medical appointment throughout a complicated pregnancy but, because she drives 45 minutes to her salon, had to take unpaid half and full days every time she went to the doctor or hospital, despite having worked there for 10 years and having desperately tried to save up for the baby and maternity leave. Another mum told me that, as her second maternity leave ended, both of her children got chicken pox in succession. Her boss made her take this time as holiday, leaving her with almost no holiday days the first year she was back.

The report also found that slightly over half of the women who had flexible working requests approved after returning to work said it had negative consequences. The financial sector is, they report, the least tolerant, being the most likely to make pregnant women redundant and the most likely to turn down a flexible working request. What's more, if you earn £40,000 or above, you are more likely to experience financial loss or negative experience due to a flexible working request. Despite these experiences, the report found that only one in four raised the issue with their employer, only 3 per cent went through a grievance procedure and less that 1 per cent went to an employment tribunal.

Gemma has one daughter, a post-graduate degree and a hunger to work. She reflects on her transition to motherhood and the damage it did to her career:

'I worked at a Swiss bank before the financial crash and it suited me. But the crash and my daughter arrived at the same time. Initially they said they really wanted me back and put me forward for a promotion, saying I had to interview for the role. In the end, they gave the role to a man, I don't know why, they didn't give reasons, and they sidelined me into a back-office job. It became very stressful. I wasn't that well suited to the role and worked all the hours I could. On a Friday night with friends having dinner I was reading my emails and crying and they said I had to stop. I resigned and spent a lovely three months with my daughter. I then took a contract role at an American bank.... It started out OK but they wanted me to move to permanent and then it nearly destroyed me. The pressure and the hours were devastating. I didn't ever take lunch, I felt too busy to go to the toilet. I was happy to work long days and be on email but I just wanted to pick my daughter up twice a week and leave at 5.15pm to do it – however late I then had to work into the night to keep up. My female manager said no. She wouldn't even consider it, yet one

Friday she brought her baby to the office at lunchtime with the nanny. It was like she was taunting me with what I was missing. After that a friend offered me a job in a tech company with fully flexible hours. It was great. But after three years the company relocated abroad so I went to a hedge fund. It's a lovely company but not my ideal role – it's too focused on regulations. The truth is that I feel like all I've done since I became a mum is look for a job. I want to work, I want to work full time but I only want to be in an office 9am–5pm. It's not about money, I've taken huge pay cuts since becoming a mum and the search guys have gone from seeing me as A-list to very B-list. My career feels like it's falling down the other side of the mountain and I'm only just 40.'

Some evidence suggests that about six months is the longest you can take off without starting to risk losing status and future earning power at work. For example, Sylvia Ann Hewlett, who wrote *Off-Ramps and On-Ramps*, showed that a woman who took more than two years off lost 18 per cent of her earning power forever. If she took three years off, this soared to 38 per cent. But two maternity leaves of about six months had little or no effect on future earnings. Hewlett believes that the greater number of women at senior levels in American companies is an upside of their poor maternity policies (a paltry six weeks for many women): that by having and taking our long leaves in the UK we are setting women back in the workforce. Anyone ambitious might take note: although a degree of scepticism may be advised given that some American companies were among the worst pay gap offenders in the UK.

Part of the value of maternity leave (alongside bonding with your newborn, obviously) is that it is often the only protracted period during your career when you can see the world from a different place and perhaps make different decisions. It's a clear juncture in life when you can take time to think about what is really important and what you want for yourself, your kids and your family in the future. I recently heard a CEO at a conference saying she thought women should do leadership courses during their maternity leave. I understand her goal but would strongly argue that this is the one period of your life when you can think about something other than work.

Sarah Jaggers, MD of Managing Change, an organisation that coaches people through career transitions, says:

'Returning to work after a baby can be a very stressful time. From handing over your baby to someone else, to being judged by your mother-in-law, to worrying about your time and expressing milk. We suggest women consider three things before they return to work after maternity: their work needs, their personal needs and their family needs. They need to decide what is important to them. But we also caution against making big assumptions too early in the process. Some women assume they will go back to work and hate it. Others are unsure until they have their baby but then feel it's right to return. We find that women who have reasonable expectations and good support systems tend to do better: those who don't expect the house to be immaculately clean, and can live with the fact they've put on a stone and are often running late.'

She is certainly right that many women are surprised by their own decisions. I interviewed mothers who thought they would love being at home with their baby and then couldn't wait to get back, and those who thought their career was their pre-eminent motivator and never put a foot in an office again. The key is not to assume how you will feel until the time comes. Part of what changes the desire to go back to work or not is the experience of motherhood. Those who have a good birth, bond well and really enjoy mothering are unsurprisingly more likely to want to keep at it than those who might have started off in a bad place, and through no fault of their own, find it harder to adjust. A few working mums have imagined maternity leave would be so boring they would turn it into an extended holiday and explore Europe by train or get fit for a triathlon or convert the loft (this doesn't usually seem to work out too well!). And sometimes women who really enjoy their first maternity leave, perhaps thinking that motherhood comes pretty naturally to them, hate their second maternity leave if it follows within a few years. Unlike the first, which enables full attention on one baby, the second makes them feel ripped apart by the different demands of a baby and a toddler. This can trigger a personal crisis along the lines of 'I thought I was a career person but had a baby and realised I should be an at-home mum but now I find that I'm not good at that either.'

The following is a reflection on how people who've made those decisions reviewed them later.

Running back

Some mothers really, really want to go back to work and, aside from the actual birth, hardly seem to change pace. Describing this they will say: 'I had to go back to feel myself again' or 'I felt I had to go back to work to feel emotionally better, I felt that life would go back to normal'.

There are two ways to do this. One is to slink back in, without anyone really noticing, taking calls, a few meetings, picking up a few projects here and there and drifting back. Entrepreneurs and freelancers often say they did this and, without much external comment, returned to working very, very soon. People in very senior roles can often slide back into work mode this way too. Those who can work flexibly and mostly from home, taking breaks for feeding or bonding, while still keeping themselves solvent and engaged with adults, often feel pretty positive about their early return, even years later.

The second approach is to stride back in, and this can be harder practically and socially. For one thing, it tends to come with a huge amount of judgement from colleagues, family and new mum friends. 'I hopped and skipped back to work. Ran at 100 miles an hour. I don't regret not staying at home longer. I could not wait. I was going mad. I go to work feeling like I've climbed a mountain, run a marathon and wrestled with wild animals before 8am but, for me, it's so much better than being at home all day and my kids (aged one and two) do really well at nursery. But don't get my mother started on it, she makes me feel so guilty about working.'

Others share this experience. 'My NCT friends didn't understand me going back to work so soon. They were shocked, even though they are all working mums now. I felt very unsupported, they greeted the news that I was going back at six weeks with total silence.' Another said: 'I knew I was out of the group when even the woman who worked for McKinsey said "FUCK" when I told them I was going back at eight weeks.' Both of these women were motivated by their desire to work as well as their responsibility as the primary household earner. Some are unbothered by the judgement, others are devastated by it. One thing I note is that those whose own mothers encouraged work and themselves worked long hours – the children of first-generation immigrants for example ('My mum came here, barely spoke the language but worked all day and still had dinner for us on the table after school') – seem far better emotionally protected from this judgement.

Logistically there are of course some big hurdles. Babies usually sleep intermittently in these early weeks and being exhausted is a huge problem unless you have good overnight support. Lack of sleep is both a cause and symptom of postnatal depression so you need to keep an eye on how you're feeling and get help if you think you need it. If you're breastfeeding you have to deal with pumping and persuading your baby to take a bottle. There is also the rushing of the perennial problem of finding the right childcare for you – something affordable and accessible. A freelancer who wanted and needed to return at three months said, 'I would love nursery to be more affordable. In our area, the nurseries are massively oversubscribed – all have a one-and-half year waiting list – and cost upwards of £60 a day. That sort of money, £300 per week, makes it borderline cost neutral for us to go to work. The fact that we are both freelancers and spend a significant amount of time bidding for new projects makes that kind of expense very hard to justify and puts a lot of (impossible) pressure on making that work financially successful.' If you can find and afford the childcare you need though, the truth is that, *if you choose to do it*, returning early can feel fine. Women reclaim their identity, the baby can be very well cared for and life can return to 'normal'.

Women doing this, when interviewed, will sometimes say something pretty structured, such as: 'I get up at 6am, check my emails. Then I go to work. I leave the office at 5.30pm and spend an hour fully with my son and put him to bed. Then I sometimes go to a work event and get home at 10.30pm or 11pm and go to bed. It works really well for us and when I go on trips I always bring him a great present and when he's older he is going to be so proud of all the places his mum went to.'

Sometimes it works out that way. But some later come to reflect that their early return to full-on work created a force field shielding them from 'giving in' to parenthood. A way of not letting the baby take over your life. Over time, this doesn't always keep working so well. As they become more aware and more verbal, our children seem to have the ability to get to us and change how we see the world. Just ask a mother whose toddler only wants daddy, or whose baby doesn't crawl to her when she returns from that work trip with the toy, or who realises that her baby smells like their childminder or cries for her nursery carer when she bangs her head in the bath. Or the mum who found her daughter had written a letter to her boss saying that, as he always made her mum work long hours, she would like him to send her a pink computer by way of compensation. Therein lies heartbreak and, for some, a change in tack. If not, then much later still, these can be the children who say they felt ignored by their parents when they were children and plan to raise their own families very differently.

But for the consciously ambitious, running back has rewards, as described by a very experienced city-based headhunter:

'There are the women who are going to the very top, in largely male environments. To get those jobs there are rules, codes and prizes. You don't get them without following these: to be part of this group of people you have to be more driven than anyone else. The deal includes 16-hour days and absolute focus. You can't be the secondary breadwinner with kids and do that kind of a job because it's all-consuming: you can't not answer your phone on the Friday when *The Sunday Times* is planning an exposé, you can't be off on the day a scandal hits, things are time critical and you are paid to deal with them.

'To make it work at that level with kids you must have a partner who takes domestic responsibility. These are the kind of women who are often the first senior woman that the company has ever had, so often they find they end up writing their own maternity policies because the company has never done one for that level before. My advice to these women is not to be hidebound by the legal frameworks about the conversations you can and can't have but to take control and be very up front about how you manage your maternity leave – tell the CEO "this is how we're going to make it work" and explain the plan you've got, for you and for how the company will cover your responsibilities. Afterwards, you have to model behaviour because everyone is looking at you. Which might mean going to the nativity play and saying you're doing it and, if you do, the men may start to go too.

'You can make it work with a very supportive partner and a clear sense of team, when you both agree why you're doing this. I see women at very senior levels who are happy and working very hard – if they have a partnership at home and they feel that running the "team" of their family is a proper joint effort with their partner.

'That said, we shouldn't be dewy eyed about it. There will always be people with something eating at them who are super-, super-driven, who want the rewards and status of the very top of the tree. The prizes at the top remain high: we all know the increasing gap between the CEO salary and the shop floor. You justify those superhero salaries with superhero commitment. More often than not, those people are not particularly balanced. They will always work harder and be more driven than the rest of us – sometimes it's verging on the sociopathic. I'm not convinced it's something we all need to aspire to. It has a lot of personal cost and that won't suit most of us.'

An HR director who has watched many women return from maternity leave over the years reflects that some of those who run back become very tired of it all later: 'I watched a really driven women, who returned a few months after the birth, sitting in a meeting at 6pm, that would clearly go later, as a man said they'd all have to meet again the following morning at 8am. She was one of those women who just keeps going, but she looked utterly exhausted and drained. Afterwards I asked her about it and she said she was fed up with everyone else's inefficiency getting in the way of her seeing her child.'

That is the final aspect of returning to work (especially if early) that we just don't talk about enough: sleep deprivation. Says one mum: 'If your child's been feeding all night, or up vomiting, or has woken you three times with anxiety attacks, the next day is likely to be a write-off. But I think mostly working mothers are too stoical to mention these things. They just soldier on. But crikey, now the kids are older I think about the days I've sleep-walked through – luckily I've never operated heavy machinery for a living.'

I take two things from my own experience. One is that it's remarkable how well you can function on very, very little sleep even if, before kids, you were an eight-hours sort of person. The other is that this phase passes in such a daze that you don't remember it very well afterwards. Factually I know that our second daughter refused a bottle when I returned to work at six months and chose instead to feed all night, since I was there and she had no problem sleeping all day. If anyone can remember what happened in those months, do please let me know, because, for me, this whole period is like an old joke about not remembering the 60s. Minus the acid and casual sex.

Walking back

Then there are those in the middle, who come to appreciate their time at home but, as it approaches the end, feel the tug to return to the world of work. One said:

'I started to really enjoy the decadence of the 2pm coffee and cake and realised that I'd stopped admitting what I was doing to my husband because I felt slightly guilty about it. It feels so liberating to be pottering around in the day with your kids and your new friends rather than being in back-to-back meetings stressing about the business. But one day we were talking and this mum was wondering whether her husband would "allow" her to have a new cooker, when another mum says in this slightly too practical tone, "just buy it on the Visa card and give him a blowie when the bill comes." Everyone laughed but I knew at that moment that I had to go back to work. I mean we do need the money I earn but, more than that, I have to have financial independence.'

Many women who get to relish this time then also plan their transitions in a calm and ordered way. Trying out nurseries in the weeks before the actual return, doing their 'keeping in touch' days and generally being on top of the process. If the childcare works out and the feeding is sorted, this can work well. But there are no guarantees. Even in a short period a restructuring or change of leadership can upset the stability of the world you assumed would be constant. It's a strange feeling going back after maternity leave to find the layout has changed, the focus of work has moved on and someone new suddenly seems the centre of the world. Many a mother who felt they had planned well and stayed in touch and done everything right was gutted to get back and find that they still couldn't stay.

Back to the HR director, who observes that the pain point here is often struck as the agreement they have made about their hours becomes a reality:

> 'There is that moment at 4pm or 5pm when they stand up, having agreed they would do this, but you can see on their faces that they are torn to leave their work and their colleagues yet also know their child is waiting elsewhere. The conflict is palpable. Some screw up their faces and race out. Others try and sneak out unnoticed. I say, keep within what you've agreed and just leave. Walk. Just go.'

Dragged or pushed back

Then there are those like Emily who wanted to stay at home longer, perhaps forever, but feel they have no choice. Even if the law is on their side, many feel the psychological pressure bearing down on them:

> 'I felt huge pressure to get back at three months. People told me I had the right to have a year, I said "I might have the right but I'll make myself

redundant". So I went back. I asked to come back three days a week. I was told "no, it's a full-time job". I was surprised there was no flexibility. So I've come back and booked one or two days' holiday a week, just to show them it can be done. I hope that when my holiday runs out I'll have proved my point. I realised then that the working world is not designed for mothers. We talk about equal pay because we can measure that but we can't measure equal treatment and that is the problem.'

Some, like this mother, grit their teeth and do it because otherwise the household finances just don't work and are enraged by the people around them judging them for it: 'We had a new mortgage and my husband had been made redundant, I didn't do it because I'm a shit mother, I did it because we needed to be able to eat and not default. I'd say to anyone who has a view on it, shut your mouth, let people choose what is right for their family, you have no need to comment.'

Others feel later that they were too focused on the financial short term, and that money issues that seemed overwhelming in the moment look rather different within the context of two decades of active parenting. 'We couldn't afford for me not to return full time so I went back even though I didn't want to. The thing is our second child has special needs and I have taken almost a year off with him and now work part time but, by cutting back pretty significantly, we've managed to make it work. I guess that everyone thinks they can't afford it but if I did it again I would do it differently.'

Some admit their pain to their colleagues and others lock themselves in the toilets, work as part time and close to home as possible. Some will choose to roll one pregnancy into the next and go straight out on another maternity leave.

There are plenty of web chats exploring the pros and cons of having two children very close together. Burnt in my memory though is a woman I used to see locally who had a non-walking 18-month-old and a six-month-old. She was a delicate woman and to see her lugging these two chunky kids around playgroups was enough to put me off. A friend who did have kids very close together says that the upside is that the baby years seem to go very fast.

Some, of course, suck it up and return, albeit shaking with sadness. Sarah Jaggers, MD of Managing Change, adds: 'If someone is going back and they really don't want to work but must because of financial pressure, we would be concerned about the impact it could have on their mental health. We'd want to explore with them what they are trying to do: do they want to adjust and live with the situation or explore other ways of working that might suit them better? Ultimately if they really don't want to be at work their performance will suffer and it may become unsustainable anyway.'

How do you change it if it's not right?

Jaggers says:

'If people are struggling with choices, or feel trapped in the arrangement they have, we encourage them to consider what fulfilment looks like to them in broad terms. If they are driven by status and external approval that leads in one direction, if they are driven by wanting to provide wholesome meals and helping their children build dens at the end of the garden, that leads another way. Whatever their ideal is, we explore what choices they will make in order to make that possible for them.

'One conversation we encourage couples to have is about how their partnership works. At its most stark it is about whose work takes precedence in a crisis. If it always falls to the working mum to make sacrifices, and she has not signed up to that, then it can get very stressful. And – this is a generalisation – in our work we see that in many cases it is the mums who are the ones who step in when needed. It can seem like it's always the mum whose job it is to pop out at lunch for the red tights needed at school the next day. But ultimately, agreeing a pattern that works for you as a unit is what is important.'

She's quite right: take it from one full-time working mother who is married to an equally full-time dad: 'We never had a conversation where he said, "you have to put yourself on hold, it's all going to be about me and the kids". We never discussed that. We never agreed. It was a given. I feel stupid thinking it but I feel fucked off about that. I don't want to be a stay-at-home mum, I love my kids and I'd die for them but I don't want to be with them all the time and I don't want to sacrifice networking and nights out. But he assumes it will ALWAYS be me that compromises. It will always be me that finds a babysitter. It kills me. I am ambitious too.'

Setting boundaries with work

As before, doing this before you get pregnant can be massively helpful. But if afterwards, establish boundaries about what working from home means: will you go in if it's an important meeting, will you swap it for another day, will you not go? And then stick to those boundaries. The good news is that a book called *Great at Work* by American management professor Morten T. Hansen, which is based on a large business research project, says that we can be more successful in shorter times if we obsess over a smaller number of priorities. He argues that doing this – as well as some other changes – will ensure success over rivals who work longer hours.

All of that said, both parents and non-parents underline that working mums have a big responsibility to be fair to their employer and colleagues, too. New rules ensuring flexibility are resented by some managers and employers, including those who have children themselves, because they perceive people to be misusing them. Taking the piss and leaving work to others, not delivering what you said you will, being uncontactable on your 'working from home' days, playing fast and loose with sick days – these give working mums a bad reputation. Now I've never met a mum who has even implied she has done this, yet everyone seems to have worked with someone who has. A team manager underlines it: 'Don't fiddle and duck in and out, pretend to work from home and confuse everyone. Say what you will do and get on with it.'

If you're too tired and wired to read the above

- Before you do it, you don't really know how maternity leave will work or when you'll want to return. Try to leave your options open. Saving as much money as you can during your pregnancy (and before) helps to increase the range of options.
- It's possible, with a bit of money and determination, to shield yourself from some of the ravages and vulnerabilities of motherhood: you can ask for a C-section on a specific date (you may or may not get it of course), choose to bottle feed, recruit a support squad (paid or family) and return to work within the week. Initially this can seem to work really well but, down the line, some of the people who have done it talk about weak connections with their kids, a lack of support networks for themselves and emotional distance from their partners.
- You may find that gradual rather than sudden moves work better: taking a few calls, doing some emails, popping into some meetings rather than marching back into the office and sitting down as if nothing happened.

- If you haven't had kids yet you won't believe it but I'll say it anyway: small babies are more transportable and flexible than toddlers. You can put your baby into a sling and walk or bus into town and meet a colleague for lunch or coffee. You won't be able to do this with a rampaging two-year-old in tow if you have a second one, so make the most of it the first time round.

- Some talk with absolute glee about the first day they put their work clothes on and drove back to their 'safe, happy place'. I note that those who can work flexibly – almost irrespective of total hours – seem much more content with their lives. Recent research suggests these women are no less ambitious that those working full time.

- Whichever path you choose, you need to reassess and make active choices, adjusting as you go. The most frustrated parents are those who get locked into one working pattern that they feel powerless to change. Advice on how to do this effectively varies, but one critical thing to keep in mind for any conversation is to focus on what you will do and deliver ('I will run all of my projects and oversee the development plan to completion') *before* you talk about how you will do it ('I will do this with two full days of meetings in the office and three days of remote working, during which time I will be fully available in working hours.'). If you state these things the other way around, it's possible that, instead of focusing on the fact that you will be achieving what is asked of you, all they will hear is 'I'm dropping to a two-day week but you're still going to pay me for the full five.'

- Use your relationships and networks at work to stay in touch. Call a friend regularly and pop in now and again so you are not forgotten. Keep interested in what they are doing. Some prefer to keep an eye on key emails throughout maternity leave, some find it stressful and prefer to detach.

- Seek to bridge rather than extend the disconnect between non-parents and parents. They may not understand but you may not be helping them either. Using humour, honesty and clarity to explain the pressure you are under may help. If, for example, your boss knows the nursery charges you £10 for every minute you are late they may well be the one spotting you are cutting your leaving time very fine. Obviously this won't work for everyone.

- Be honest about the financial pressure but don't wang on boringly about it to your colleagues. Those without kids may find it irritating and mystifying, especially if you earn more than they do.

What happened next?

EMILY HAD HER SECOND baby and decided she couldn't go back to work whatever it cost. Her partner reluctantly agreed and they rearranged their lives to make it work. They moved to a smaller flat, cut out socialising and haven't taken a holiday since the baby was born. Emily walks round the supermarket looking for offers and mentally totting it up as she goes so she doesn't lose track of what she spends.

Watching working mothers drop their children off at school in their smart clothes, new cars and talking about where they are going for the half term holiday Emily sometimes feels a pang of jealousy. She wonders if her girls are missing out on the experiences their friends are having – they've never been on a plane or to a theme park.

But then she sees the bored childminders chatting, not taking any notice of the children they are supposed to be looking after; she remembers the tears of one of her daughter's classmates when her mother wasn't at the show and she remembers how proud her oldest one was when she showed her round the classroom and pointed out her work on the walls and knows that, despite everything, she wouldn't have it any other way. She's happy with her decision.

CHAPTER FIVE

I've always been able to cope with everything, so why do my kids make me so crazy?

MY BOYS ARE SIX, four and two. Before I had them I was a PA to the CEO of a local housebuilder. George travels a lot for work and is often away for the whole week so I'm on my own a lot for things like bath-and bedtime which I know should be idyllic times of the day but are mostly awful and involve sooooo much screaming.

When we had our first baby, I stopped working full time and now work three days a week helping out with events, board meetings, training and other projects that don't fit neatly into other buckets. My boss and I get on pretty well but he's famous for shouting when things go wrong. I cope by being really calm with him. The problem is that he doesn't like my replacement because she cries when he goes for her. So he involves me in everything he is worried about. I know it's a compliment but it takes more than the three days and I get pulled into really stressful things. Recently, I helped with some lay-offs and was online all weekend with it. But I still only get paid for three days.

I find the boys really hard to control. I call them 'the beasts' which I realise must sound awful but that's what they are. I nag them all the time and find myself screaming at them definitely at one point every day. And then I feel so guilty once they've gone to sleep and so annoyed with myself for losing it with them. Sometimes they rampage around the house long after bedtime simply because I'm too knackered to stop them and get them into bed. The house is always a mess, overrun with their toys and general junk. My oldest boy is struggling at school but I can't find time to read with him without being mobbed by the other two. And that's even more frustrating because I know I need to help him more at home but it's just so difficult with two other kids. The middle one has minor special needs so he needs to have quite a few appointments with hearing specialists which takes a lot of time. The youngest likes to have all of my attention which is exhausting and means I often have only one hand to do things because I'm holding him the whole time.

The breaking point was a visit to the park when the boys played hide-and-seek. The oldest deliberately wedged himself high up a tree while the youngest, who is recently potty trained, demanded to do a poo immediately. I had to let him do a shit in a bush. The middle one then had a tantrum about being hungry and refused to walk home. I really tried to stay calm but ended up shrieking, then crying and chasing the boys home, raging at them the whole way and then as soon as we made it home I locked myself in the toilet to cry. It was awful. People were staring but I honestly didn't care.

I can't understand why it's so damned hard when I see myself as a sensible, well-organised person who can cope with a lot of stress. My lack of control even seems to stretch beyond the boys. When George was away last week the TV broke and I called the call centre for help, desperate to settle the kids with their usual pre-bedtime programme. The man wasn't listening to me and I totally lost it on the phone as the boys fought and wailed in the background.

Most of the time I'm embarrassed at myself, embarrassed at the way I behave with my kids and of my life generally.

Monique, 42, PA

****

It is an easy conversational turn to remark lightly that working life prepares you well for small children. Long hours, conflict management, multitasking, impossible demands, difficult bosses, etc. We get the point. It's a nice line but it's bull. Our workplaces are far more civilised than we let on – even when your chief exec is prone to an emotional outburst. And our children, by definition, are much less so.

I was eavesdropping one morning in a coffee shop while a team of Kiwis and South Africans talked about their work. A woman said: 'I just want people who are efficient. Who do what they say when they say they'll do it. I just love that. That guy, Bill in Nairobi, you know him, he's so efficient he doesn't even sign off his emails. Fuck, I love that guy.'

Children are never like Bill in Nairobi.

Years of running to schedule, thinking through ideas, delivering practicalities, planning budgets, being listened to and massaging the ego of a big-cheese-boss doesn't prepare you for the nihilism of life with small children.

Why our children stress us out

As explored elsewhere, part of the problem is that many of us are not hugely experienced with kids.

'I never thought about how I would find having a baby. My mum had my sister when I was 17 so I thought I knew all about babies but I didn't know anything. I took six weeks' maternity leave before the birth and I should have relished that time but I didn't get it. I read Holly Willoughby's book, *Truly Happy Baby* and it seemed to come naturally to her, I thought it would for me.'

Historically, when extended family social groups lived together and spent evenings around fires they demonstrated experienced parenting and balanced each other's approaches. It didn't come naturally – it was observed, copied and improved through generations. As the Australian author and child psychologist Steve Biddulph frequently notes, children in less-industrial societies tend to be a lot happier than our Western children, as do their parents. But Monique is often alone with her boys and lacks good advice or much personal support. As she is finding, this is a hard way to parent and not one humans are designed for.

Single-generational modern living provides us with precious little observed experience to learn from. Not only that, but we are also so involved in getting through the working week that we're barely even aware of our high stress levels until we see them played out. A mum who works for the local authority watched her four-year-old daughter pushing their one-year-old son in his buggy, while she walked behind on a call from work. When her young son started to fuss and cry, her daughter imitated her mother, dramatically waving her arms and 'shhhhhhh shhhhhhing' aggressively before running her finger across her neck in her mother's own 'cut it out' gesture. The mother was mortified to see herself played out so accurately. A woman who works for a fashion brand was startled one day when a woman she'd never met asked her how her son Miles was. 'Sorry do I know you, do you know Miles?' she asked in some confusion. 'Well no,' said the woman cheerily, 'but I always hear you screaming "MILES, MILES!! COME BACK HERE RIGHT THIS SECOND!!" across the park.'

But it's not just the 'shushing' and suppressing of our children when they don't fit into our working life that's the problem. It can also be the explosive rage Monique is experiencing. In my house we call it 'doing the full Billingsgate Fish Wife'. The emotional place that you didn't think you'd ever get to. When stoical and unflappable adults find themselves screaming, shouting and slamming in ways that they find appalling. A first-time dad recalls his first sight of that rage in his usually serene wife. He was helpfully doing the first wash after the baby came home from the hospital but accidentally mixed the whites and colours. His wife wanted to do things perfectly. Which didn't include having her firstborn dressed in mucky greige. She was so upset that she picked up a discoloured babygro and yelled 'I am going to smash your fucking face in with this' to her stunned husband. He says they laughed about it later. But many, *many* months later. Monique's partner George would appreciate this story as he too has watched his previously calm wife turn into a person who can go from normal to postal in seconds. The Monday school run, fraught with missing shoes and reading books and yelling loud enough to disturb their long-dead dog buried in the garden, is a time he has learned it's best to keep his profile as low as possible.

There is something special about the speed, ferocity and frequency of professional parent rage. Which isn't to even hint that at-home parents don't lose their shit now and again. They surely do and, in some ways, it isn't so different. Yet it's certainly true that the workplace 'task' mindset is incompatible with happy childcare and this, combined with very limited skills to manage children, is a recipe for disaster. At its simplest it's rooted in a fundamental disconnection from the way children think and behave. It comes from being poor at predicting their next actions and motivators – you think 'I'm so damned late and he is trying to waste my time'; an experienced parent or childminder, in tune with their child, thinks 'he loves to pick up small rocks and talk to them as if they were his pets, I'll join in the chat.'

The contrast between our parenting style and the techniques of a childcare professional can be a stark reminder of that skills gap. When our second child was three, her nursery briefly lost its Ofsted approval on account of some missing paperwork. For her to attend, we had to be there and sit on teeny plastic chairs and watch. I became transfixed by Maureen, who'd run the place for 30 years. Maureen sailed through the children with effortless ease and grace. Nothing that any of the children did surprised her or stressed her. She seemed to see cups falling before they tipped, wees needed just before trousers were wet and to divert tantrums before they took hold. It was majestic, like an enchanted dance you could set to music in an Attenborough documentary. She absorbed warmth and joy from the children and reflected it right back to them. The only thing that remotely bothered her was us mums trying to intervene occasionally. This she would have none of, once sternly telling me I didn't need to follow my daughter round the room when I thought I was just watching her paint.

Executive Parenting Coach Lisa Reeves explains:

'As parents, we can get home from our workplaces and find ourselves "on task" again and may slip into the same "push" behaviours we use at work to get things done at home. We can be so focused on the "task" of parenting and everything that "needs to be achieved" that we may push our children away, drive our agenda over and above connecting with theirs, fail to connect and we may end up feeling the "guilt, frustration, sense of failure" emotions reported frequently. AND, our children don't do what we want!

'Emotions and stress can drive negative behaviours. The impact of this is that we may risk seriously damaging our relationships with our children, particularly in the "little people" period. If we do nothing, our legacy may very likely be that of the "busy, angry, distracted, impatient" parent our children see on a regular basis. If we want to have connected, positive, long-term relationships with our children, we may need to examine our own behaviour and make choices about what we can change … and then do it.'

Which is sound advice, albeit hard to act on when your mind is awhirl just dealing with everyday life. Let alone pissy emails from your boss while you are trying to manage three rambunctious boys.

The sources of professional parent stress

In contrast to magical Maureen, professional parent stress is reactive, scary and – as Lisa rightly says – unproductive. Our stress response is often triggered by our professional approach to five factors: time, tasks, relationships, behaviours and multitasking.

The first factor is our stress around time. This comes from our precise, professional reading of the importance of timeliness. The working parent thinks: 'I am two minutes late for baby swimming and I must resolve this by rushing Felix and stripping him off with ruthless efficiency even if he screams the roof off.' This ratchets up a notch if it's a real deadline, like the school bell. A market-researcher dad of two girls says: 'That's when the touchpaper really gets lit. When your child, through sheer stubbornness, makes others late and that lateness, from a personal perspective, is unacceptable. If you have all the time in the world, then you cajole, chivvy, distract or incentivise – on a deadline, you simply force shoes on unwilling feet and drag the – sometimes kicking, but always screaming – child.'

The second factor is our approach to task management. The parent views timeslots as precious and tries to get 'the best' use from each segment. The parent thinks: 'We have come to this museum and we have two hours here, and so Felix should use that opportunity to explore the stimulating exhibits.' Only to find that Felix would rather just run up and down the curved wheelchair ramp. Our professional eyes see a 'right way' to do things and a 'wrong way'. Our children don't distinguish and simply pursue what they fancy. Experienced childminders understand that little kids will explore naturally if given enough time; harassed parents try to fight this, to the detriment of happy children and their own sense of calm.

The third factor is that we think about our relationships in a rather transactional way. In an appraisal, for example, as a manager we may fully engage our concentration in building an understanding between ourselves and the person we are reviewing. We assume that the other adult in this scenario will respond positively to that intention and together we will use the time well. In life with children, it works very differently. The parent thinks: 'I don't see Felix enough in the week but I have taken off this afternoon to come to the museum with him. Now we need to get together and build the polystyrene bridge and have a good chat about the importance of keystones.' In our eyes, we are generously bringing the useful skill of knowing how to build a bridge to our child and they are benefiting from our total attention. Less promisingly, we'll probably do this loudly so that the other toddlers, whose parents may not be so architecturally well informed, will also benefit. To convey that we're a good parent, doing a good job of educating our child and this is important to us and ... because I am used to quite a bit of external validation. But none of this works out very well when Felix decides to kick the shit out of the keystone and we look like a pompous arse.

The fourth challenge is that many working parents have unrealistic behavioural expectations of small kids and lack the skills to moderate those behaviours. We think something like: 'Felix is now two and should not do things that are monumentally irritating *all the time*'. Like repeatedly asking to touch mummy's boobies. Very loudly. Or to sing the same inane song again and again and again. On a bad day, this can feel like a relentless personal attack. We apply adult thinking and wonder why our child is being so mean. Then we also lack the skills to distract them towards something more positive without them even noticing it has happened. A content manager described how her three young sons go round and round constantly on their squeaky swivel chairs in the kitchen. It drives her crazy and she ends up yelling 'STOP STOP STOP!!! GET OFF!!!! GO TO BED'. Anything to make it end. Naturally this makes the swivelling even more exciting. She recently asked her four-year-old son how she could be a better mummy. He said, 'Please shout less'. She cried and then he cried because she was sad. A Montessori teacher who listened to this story being told was bemused. 'If you don't want them to swing, don't have the chairs' she said reasonably, and we laughed at the simplicity of the answer. While knowing that the chairs look great, she spent time and money on them, and there's no way she's chucking them out.

The fifth factor is that we are unable to resist applying our usual multitasking approach to work to child management. Something Monique is really finding with those emails she can't help but read. We are thinking (but not even saying): 'Felix, just sit quietly and enjoy your sandwich while I try and crush a work stressball that's just exploded in my email'. Felix feels your attention slip away from him. Distracted, he squeezes his smoothie carton down his front, drops the carrot crisps into the puddle on the filthy floor, eats them anyway and snatches some other kid's scooter for a spin round the cafe, chased by the scooter owner and their granny, who wants you to know that she knows you are a dismal parent.

When this happens, the professional parent feels judged and gets very cross. Thinking 'Oh FFS, not only is it kicking off with work but the damned child is running riot in a restaurant when I only needed, like, FIVE MINUTES to sort this out'. Poor Felix gets a right bollocking and starts to cry for his nanny/gran or other more sympathetic carer, compounding the chaotic failure of the special afternoon at the museum.

Partnership

But it isn't just the children who are fuelling this anger. Monique and George had been together for years before they had kids and he was always a big supporter of hers. He helped with her career, talked through problems and generally gave her a lot of encouragement. Their friends saw them as a great team.

However, since the kids arrived, he's had less capacity to do that. The boys are all-consuming. They seem to take up all the space and air in the house and garden. By the time they are in bed there seems to be nothing left for the adults aside from cleaning up mess and sorting the boring admin. George gets overwhelmed with it all and often slinks off to the sofa with a beer to watch mindless TV. Which Monique understands and wishes she could copy but never does because she washes, irons, packs lunch boxes, tidies away train sets and sorts out 'endless fucking pants and socks'. It's not that George isn't helpful – he does stuff in the house – it's just that he doesn't seem to 'see' a lot of the monotonous boring stuff. She once heard him explaining to one of the boys that the washing basket was magic. 'You put your clothes in dirty and they appear back in your drawers clean and folded.' He says he was joking and was just encouraging him to use it. Monique couldn't look at him for three days.

At night, the boys often shift beds through the house and, as George is often away, are used to snuggling with mum when they fancy a cuddle. Monique knows she should return them to their own beds but she is often too tired to get up and loves those warm, peaceful moments. George doesn't though and, when they do it when he is home, he gives up and moves to the spare room. He has often packed up and gone for a few days by the time everyone rises. Some weeks she feels she may as well be a single mum. When he returns it takes a few days for him to settle back into family life and then, of course, off he goes again.

Another mum whose partner is often away has similar challenges:

'It really disturbs me how much conflict the kids can create between us. We have the same general style and agree on the big themes but disagree on so many little details. He will go away for a fortnight with work and not understand that in that space of time I might have negotiated a 10-minute increase in bedtime with the oldest, for example, and then he comes back and expects everything to be the same and enforces the old rules when quite a lot of to-ing and fro-ing might have gone on between me and the kids to agree what we have. And he expects me to agree with him for the sake of solidarity, but sometimes I have to be on the kids' side because it would totally betray them to change all the rules again because dad is back. I am also driven insane by his obsession with table manners – he thinks there is a correct way to eat a chocolate croissant for God's sake – so many meals have been ruined by his constant nit-picking at the kids. I really notice that, on those rare occasions when the two of us are away on our own without the kids, all that stress seems to just fall away and things seem much easier. When it's just me and the kids it's hard work – but at least I'm not constantly having to run every bloody tiny decision by someone else. Which gets exhausting.'

This disconnection from the day-to-day is a problem that limits how much George can help even if he wants to. Monique doesn't think George has a clue what reading level the oldest is on: he doesn't engage with spellings or times tables at all. He doesn't know any of their shoe sizes or think about haircuts or the dentist. Monique thinks this is pretty normal. Her friends say their partners are just the same. But it still drives her crazy and, when he heads to the airport, she often feels a stab of raging jealousy that it's never her who gets to escape for a few days. The very thought of being on an aeroplane without kids is a fantasy.

They both know they need to reconnect and talk about doing things together. But it rarely works. Even when they make plans they are often too tired to follow through. Sometimes his mum stays and they plan to go out, but then they feel guilty because she wants to catch up with them so they stay at home with her. They have a teenage babysitter who lives a few doors away but she struggles to manage the boys at the best of times. Monique doesn't like to risk leaving her in charge for fear of coming home at 11pm and finding the kids wrestling and the kitchen ransacked.

Release

Because George is away, Monique doesn't get to carve out time to regularly do what she wants to do. She has been putting on weight and would very much like to join a park running club, as she used to run when she was younger, but needs a group to get going again. Because of his erratic travel schedule, though, she hasn't managed to attend a regular group. She knows she could and should go alone when George is home and feels guilty that she doesn't have the motivation to get up before the kids and just do it.

Somehow this cycle of wanting to exercise and failing has become a sticky issue between them. She blames him for not helping her sort it out. He thinks if running is important to her she should 'stop talking about it and bloody well get on with it'. He means this supportively but Monique doesn't hear it that way.

George doesn't say much about it but she also suspects – knows – that he resents that the boys have destroyed their sex life. They can't remember the last time they so much as spent a whole night alone in the same bed, let alone had sex. They've ignored this for years while the kids were feeding, but now they are bigger it's not getting better. He tries to make a move now and again but she's too pissed off about the magic washing basket to agree. He also, rather unsubtly, tried buying her sexy underwear for her birthday but she won't wear it because she feels too fat. It's ironic that, after three glasses of wine, she'll happily admit to her friends that sex is exactly what they both need to feel better.

How the world treating us differently adds to that anger

Parental rage can also be triggered by discovering that the wider world treats us differently as adults when we are with young children. When Monique thinks about the TV call centre she knows that what set her off was the implication that fixing the TV to please her kids was indulgent and trivial. When, at that moment, it felt very important to her.

I have only twice engaged with the C-word in public and it can't be a coincidence that both involved being attached to very small babies. The first time was when I tapped my Oyster card to check into the local DLR station (part of the London underground network). If you are lucky enough not to need to understand the oddities of London's transport system, it's like this: when you check in and don't then check out again at the other end, your card is charged the maximum possible fare for any journey. Approximately the price of a penthouse in Mayfair. So, after checking in I went to the lift to take the buggy down to the train and found a biro-ed A4 note taped to it saying the lift was broken. I asked the man at the station to help me downstairs with my buggy, which on another occasion had happened without incident. But this guy said – in these exact words, but in the fabulously patronising tone beloved of authority when speaking to a very stupid child – 'We do not help mummies with their buggies down the stairs because of health and safety'. As you might imagine, my reasonable tone whipped to incandescent rage and he simply repeated this mantra many times and told me to walk my buggy to the next station, while also refusing to concede that there was no external signage about the broken lift and the fact that I'd already paid for the journey. I resorted to yelling obscenities at him – see above – and then dramatically hoiked up my giant newborn buggy and stormed down four flights of stairs while he hollered health and safety warnings after me including my favourite line: 'I just don't understand why you are so angry'. I was so angry because he was treating me as a less-than-person. Not fully adult. Not significant. Just another mum.

When I called an old friend about the DLR incident she was reassuring: 'Oh it's because you're really tired – people get to you more. When my daughter was that age I got so cross with my sister that I punched her, with my fist, in the face. Over Christmas dinner. With all of our kids watching. Yeah, it was bloody awful but we get on OK now.'

If you're too tired and wired to read the above

- Try to give in to life with small children being demented, exhausting, boring and filthy: it's not you. Remember that we weren't supposed to bring up kids in small household units separated from the rest of the world.
- Forgive yourself: the working world is terrible preparation for looking after children – however much we joke that it sets us up well. You are used to getting stuff done, meeting deadlines and being listened to. You now have to learn a whole new set of skills – akin to herding mutinous cats – slow down.
- Ignore all the media mum stories in glossies and on Instagram: they have different challenges to you. Most of them are entrepreneurs who run their own businesses, or freelancers who can control the hours they work and have loads of help – if you have time to set up baby pictures with your child dressed as a furry animal, then you don't have a real job. I work flexibly now but I didn't before and know there is a big, big difference between a fixed job and freelancing.

- Accept that you don't get any thanks or praise or recognition for any of it. A manager with three kids said: 'If I deliver three kids to their schools on time and with the right kit I feel a monumental sense of achievement, but no one else notices. If I say one reasonably smart thing in a work meeting, someone is quite likely to come up to me afterwards and comment on it being helpful. Yet the former is soooooo much harder than the latter.'

- Learn stuff. Read parenting books, do a parenting course, try out what they suggest, watch and copy from the Maureens of this world: the childminders, au pairs, nannies, grannies and teachers. Child psychotherapist Sarah Clarke has two specific pointers on the kind of techniques you need. First, the golden rule is to 'follow the child'. If they want to take all the pans out of the cupboard and drum them with wooden spoons, go with it. It'll save you a fortune in softplay. Second, as they get older, offer them a choice of two things that are acceptable and manageable to you: 'We can go to the park or make biscuits, which would you prefer?' The point is that you can learn the skills you need to manage small children just as much as you can learn to dodge the thrown lunches of shouty bosses.

- Seek to get the best out of your partnership, if you have one. Yes, easier said than done. But sulking along in parallel is no good for anyone. Get therapy if you need it. There are a hundred different techniques to think about but the often-cited ones are to turn off the TV and chat over dinner. Ideally not just about the kids or your peanut-brained new boss.

- Sort out the household jobs. Be brutal about what jobs you can drop: a mum of seven kids once told me to never sort sibling pants and socks. Just put them in a drawer and let them choose their own. They know exactly what size is theirs. Advice I have followed since. The world is also divided into mums that iron and those who do not. My headline take is that having any aspirations to 'domestic goddess' status is a big risk after kids as the more perfectionist you are the harder it is. I will simply observe that others who are similarly slovenly seem to get more sleep. Mum-of-seven also said to only cook one dinner a night, even if parents and kids eat at different times. And ensure that the kids help around the house (see parenting advice books for help on how to do that, but withholding the stuff they want until they do what you need them to is a fair start). And if you have multiple kids' clothes to sort and spend half your life squinting at faded age labels, try the dot labelling system I read about once on Mumsnet. Quoting RainWildsGirl: 'I use the "label dot" method: DC1's [this means the "oldest darling child" for anyone who is not a user] clothes get one Sharpie pen dot on the label. DC2's [child two] get two dots, DC3's [third child] get three dots. This means when it's time to hand something down you add a dot so it becomes the next DC's item.' It also helps pre-readers spot their own clothes.

- Exercise is very often the difference between a happy and a broken parent. Don't treat it lightly. Make it a priority.
- Don't ignore sex. As one woman who is often furious with her partner for not doing enough at home says, 'you know, we did it last week and I actually liked him for 24 hours'. Relationship therapists tend to agree, reporting that lots of people use kids as an excuse to avoid sex and that this is really damaging to relationships. Relationship therapist and coach, Karen Doherty,

says, 'Sex can be a great "connecter" throughout the years of a relationship because it can put you back in touch with the self you were and the partner you fell in love with. But it doesn't just happen. Sex needs to be remembered and the effort needs to be made to have it. Whether it's a merger, the kids or just life taking its toll… you have to *choose* to take the time and make the effort to connect sexually. A divorced woman in her 50s said wistfully to me recently, "It's funny, we used to laugh at Saf when she moaned about always having to have Sunday morning sex but she's the only one of us still married". The irony is that loads of Sundays, one or the other of them didn't want sex, but the routine maintained the intimacy and a kind of communication. More and more relationships are breaking down and people are seeking solace and sex outside of the marriage. If a couple can at least talk about sex, or the lack of it, or how they miss it or how they want it and maintain a sense of humour about it (because, let's face it, sex can be very funny) then they have a chance of navigating the minefield called a relationship.'

What happened next?

MONIQUE AND GEORGE HAD a big rethink after she described events at the park. He realised that working and managing the boys was too much and so has accepted an in-house consultancy job two days a week, which allows him to be home more. They also looked at all of the household jobs that needed doing each week and rebalanced them between them. George said he had been giving up helping because whatever he did seemed to be wrong. Monique gets that she can't be critical of how he does things if she wants his help and that the happiness she feels at sharing the responsibility means it is well worth accepting that he'll never hang the washing neatly.

Monique also decided that her habit of following work emails and trying to manage the kids at the same time was a disaster and stopped checking her email when not at work. This dramatically changed the behaviour of the kids – somehow they know when she is watching and when she is mentally in another world – and she recommends it to everyone. Her mother gave them a tatty copy of *Positive Discipline* by Dr Jane Nelsen and they're trying out some techniques with mixed success. On advice from friends, they also signed the older boys up for tae kwon-do, which they hope may help manage their energy levels. Things are definitely calmer but Monique still fantasises about using a flame-thrower on the mess.

CHAPTER SIX

How come I feel lonely even though I'm surrounded by people all the time?

WORK IS SHOCKING. ABSOLUTELY brutal. After two rounds of cuts I'm exhausted from doing a job that used to be done by three people and annoyed about it too. At home, our toddler has been up every night this week teething and only wants me not his dad, who pretends not to hear him anyway. As I go into work in the morning my eyelids flicker with exhaustion and I only get through it with too much coffee and chocolate brownies.

As I left yesterday the team was going out to a comedy night. I knew they'd end up totally pissed, smoking in some dodgy nightclub. Even though I am on my knees, I sort of wanted to go and have some irresponsible fun, but I knew I had to go home. I'll have to work at some point over the weekend anyway so can't miss out on the kids and catching up with Dan whom I've barely seen since Sunday. And I have no brake pedal, so would have ended up an additional world of pain – it would have been a bad idea for so many reasons.

But as I left the train station, I went past the local wine bar and, glancing in, saw a big table of women in the window, drinking and laughing. I stared as I realised most of the mums in my daughter Betty's class were there. Even that bitch Rachel who's had way too much Botox. I longed to walk in but I obviously wasn't invited, I didn't even know they all went out together like that. I needed to get home so tore myself away from staring, terrified they would see me gawping at them from the street. In my head I was furious, jealous, angry with those yummy mummies who sit around all fucking day drinking flat whites, planning park runs and talking about diets.

I got home upset, only to find Dan watching sodding re-runs of Top Gear in his boxer shorts drinking a large glass of red wine. Milo was wearing his nappy and what he ate for dinner and Betty was upstairs with an iPad. The kitchen was piled high with everything used since breakfast. No one even said hello.

I wonder how it can be that I am so lonely when I am never, ever alone.
Jackie, 37, Computer Programmer

****

When she first had Betty, making friends was pretty low down Jackie's list of priorities. Her focus was surviving the first few months. Which she coped with by visiting her mum a lot and seeing a few old school friends who came to stay. Then she went back to work.

For a long time, she didn't see herself as lonely. Quite the reverse, she saw herself as overwhelmed with people needing her time, her attention and, in the case of her kids and husband, her body. She used to actively fantasise about days of just being alone.

But staring through the window of the bar she realised that part of the reason her life doesn't work is that she has so few friends. Oh, she has 400 on Facebook and a few dozen at work and a gang of mates from university but no one she sees week in and week out. The ones who are hyper-local and tackling the same challenges, who share the same highs and lows. The ones she can slag off Dan to before tottering home tipsy to fall asleep in his arms.

Part of the reason is that work eats so much of her time. One mum who has since resigned to take a much lower-paid but less demanding job put it like this:

'In recent years, when I was very busy, I felt all I was doing was work and said goodbye to exercise, seeing friends – I just ended up with a very unhealthy, unbalanced life. You also have nothing to talk about except work and work issues, which is incredibly boring for everyone around you but you genuinely have nothing else to say. This was one of the reasons why I left – I just felt I needed to get my life rebalanced. I remember being excited about lunch from the office canteen – seriously – because it was a part of a day when you'd be away from your desk, experiencing new things, tasting new foods, I kid you not. When you are working very long hours, the world retreats from you – you live your life in your small radius of work and home and you never go out so the canteen "taste of Persia" or "Korean fried chicken" was a highlight for me. When I say this now, I sound mad but it is like extreme cabin fever.' Jackie would completely relate to this description.

Why she doesn't have friends

Jackie comes across as rather intense in a work setting, but is shy among people she doesn't know. She found the early days of mothering hard and found what she calls 'mummy-land' alienating. There were no men in any groups and she's never socialised in all-female groups at work or college. She found it hard to connect with the other women who all seemed much more maternal than she felt. It seemed that all they wanted to talk about was wee, poo, boobs and sleep all the time and she wasn't sure how to contribute.

She reminds me of a (not remotely shy) chef I interviewed who said she'd never met 'such a bunch of boring, precious, obsessive, rabbits in headlights' than after she'd had her first daughter. 'I spent most of the time that I spent with those women just wishing I was back at work. It was the waiting, the endless waiting for something to happen, monotony, endless hours of killing time, chatting about nothing, getting nothing done. I remember this one conversation that went on for ages…. "Her poo was green this morning, do you think that's normal, I mean I'd changed her twice and then she did another poo and it soaked right through her body suit and all up her back, but have you tried Vanish Gold, it's the best for poo stains you know, but you do have to get the liquid and not the powder, I think I saw it on offer in Sainsbury's but maybe it'll be in ASDA's baby week, listen let me check and get back to you". I had to leave their WhatsApp chat because it was too stupid.' Both she and Jackie drifted away from these groups quickly, confident that their existing group of friends would be more than enough. They also both returned to work pretty promptly after relatively short maternity leaves.

When Betty started school, Jackie was invited to Reception birthday parties almost every weekend, but declined most of them because she was drained after crazy long weeks and wanted to spend the time with her own family. On the occasions when she did go, she felt excluded by the 'in' group of mums who were running the food and drinks tables and knew all the kids by name. At one, in a church hall, it occurred to her that they had a supply of wine in the kitchen that they were sharing like schoolgirls behind the bike sheds but she wasn't offered any. At a school fund-raiser she went to, she found herself drawn into a debate about cybercrime that the dads were having. Afterwards she thought it perhaps hadn't endeared her to the other mums but she wasn't too troubled by the thought.

Yet since then, even before the bar, she's started to wonder if she's made a mistake.

Her old social life has declined

Her social life in town has dwindled to nothing other than work events she cannot miss and most of these are too work-orientated to be fun.

She sometimes stops for one quick drink at the end of the day but then charges home to see her children, feeling guilty about it. On the rare occasions when she and Dan do go out – for their birthdays or anniversary – they seem to get drunk and end up squabbling about why he doesn't ever clean up and why she is always working.

An exception to this was when they were invited to an ex-colleague's 40th a few weeks ago when they impulsively and nostalgically took ecstasy. They enjoyed a night of wild dancing and mutual adoration before being shocked to see the sun coming up and realising it was the day of their daughter's ninth birthday. They panic-called Uber, tore across town and crept into bed in their sweaty party clothes and 'zoned out'. They heard their kids and a cousin they'd drafted in to babysit pottering about for a while but were left cringing with shame as the home phone rang: 'Thanks Nan, no I've not had any presents because mum and dad are still in bed – I know it's 9.30am – but they weren't there at 5am when I went to find them….'

She isn't 25 any more, her old friends have moved on, her family is far away and Dan is driving her nuts.

The risks of lacking a local social group

A notable difference between many happy and unhappy working mums is their access to a strong network of local friends. These may well be very different to the women they would have socialised with before kids. This can be a problem from the earliest days.

One mum, who is a civil servant, commutes into London every day but lives in Kent, by the sea. She was depressed after her daughter was born and couldn't seem to connect with anyone. Her husband often travels for work and she would find herself home alone for endless days and restless nights going mad with loneliness. She'd never really been alone before. She remembers pushing her pram up and down the prom just to see other people and watch other women with babies and feel less isolated. She wanted to reach out and touch them, such was her need for a connection with another adult.

Another who works for a charity says:

'I hadn't expected the loneliness that came with becoming a mum. I worked right up until the end of my pregnancy, so I didn't have much down time beforehand, and then once the adrenaline had worn off and my husband went back to work after two measly weeks of paternity leave, I was on my own with a precious little thing that only communicates by crying. It was such a contrast to daily back-to-back meetings, decision making and problem solving. I was off during the winter, so I'd force myself out of the house every day for a walk in usually the wind and rain, and when I did meet up with other mums, they just didn't get how much I missed working – they were all delighted to be off for a whole year. Being in the house with no one to talk to all day – after a night of hardly any sleep – made me feel so low, and after the first six weeks my head was literally hurting. I ended up using up all my keep in touch days within the first three months because I was so desperate for human contact and intellectual stimulation. Even now, four years on, seeing mums walking round our local park on their own with a pram makes me shudder.'

Sarah Hesz, founder of mum-networking app Mush, also experienced the isolation of motherhood to the extent that it drove her to change careers and set up a networking business.

'Being a mum is an amazing leveller and a time when your social network can widen. It's a time when female friendship can become incredibly important – to stay sane, remind yourself you are more than a machine to keep a baby alive and also to figure out how your life is going to change. This is true whether you choose to stay at home or go to work; but there is something particularly bonding about meeting another mum who is also working. Instantly you can share the "hanging on by your fingernails" approach to life; not only the abject fear that accompanies it, but also the pride that you are surviving, maybe if you're kind on yourself, thriving.'

Jackie has fallen into the trap of assuming that her friends locally need to be like her other friends. She's also mistaken difference for dislike and turned 'the yummy mummies' into an enemy in her own mind. Another woman to express this view in an interview I did with her in *Management Today* was, perhaps unsurprisingly, Katie Hopkins: 'Oh I've seen it all at the school gates – though not at our current school [she adds hastily]. You see the stay-at-home mummies in dreary clothes doing the school run and then drinking coffee and going back and they can't abide the working mums. And then there is the eco-mum with 18 kids and then the mother running the PTA wanting you to make a cake…' In her view, they all just need to go back to work.

It's not an unusual theme, if usually expressed rather more diplomatically. Sometimes the take, like Katie's, is that mums need to contribute to society more actively than they do by 'just raising kids'. Sometimes it's presented as being poor role models. Sometimes it's no more than thinly veiled jealousy that these women get to do what they want all day, especially once their kids have started school.

Whatever the reasons, the challenges of not having a strong local support network are multiple:

It can be hard on your relationship (if you have one)

I recently picked up a very old-fashioned book on marriage advice. It primly recommended that wives never moan to their husbands about raising their kids because it's a boring and draining conversation that's bad for your marriage. It made me laugh but I also wondered if there was a kernel of truth in it. Having only one ally (your partner) puts enormous pressure on them to cover every base all the time: lover, co-parent, best friend. However great your partner is, that is a big ask and can create spirals of dispiriting conversations. Someone described it as 'coming through the door on a Friday night to find their partner hiding behind the remote control, scanning Netflix, while you swallow 20,000 unsaid words.'

The release of having people who fully get your life experience cannot be underestimated. Finding people who are radiators – not drains – who increase your energy, make you belly laugh and leave smiling are the answer to pretty much everything. They will also be good for your relationship if you arrive home happier, calmer and furnished with stories of people having a worse time than you. When I get depressed or frustrated, my husband has learned to say 'please just book a night out with the gang': he sees it as being in all our interests.

Leadership expert and executive coach Noomi Natan says:

'When it seems selfish or indulgent to get a massage or spend a night with great girlfriends, or even just 15 minutes alone hidden in a room to get some silence, remember this: when us mums don't look after our emotional well-being, our children are impacted. They soak up everything and, if we were short-tempered, they might respond by having a tantrum because they feed off of our energy. Long term though, if children realise that their mum doesn't have much to give, they will stop asking to have their needs met. Instead they will try to take care of their mum by being more adult than is good for them, by trying to make things better for their mother. That's not their job. Similarly, it's not that our spouses can't nourish us – it's just that we can't expect them to meet *all* our needs. The point to remember is that we are so much happier and better functioning, both at work and at home, when we have what we need. Quiet time, connecting conversations, exercise or body treatments. Whatever works for you. Pay for it, schedule it, ask for it, make it happen – whatever it takes. Give yourself permission. It's a massive gift to your family. An hour alone can do wonders for your patience levels with your family. My absolute minimum is 10 minutes of meditation each day. Families work better when the mum is at her best, and in most families, that means that mum needs to (at least partially) be resourced from outside the family.'

You lack people who just 'get it'

Among a group of connected mums, when one shares that 'my four-year-old took off his swimming trunks, grabbed his willy and pissed down my leg in the open area of the pool showers', she is met with appreciative howling laughter and a dozen other wee horror stories. Likewise, when someone shares with mortification how she scratched her head during a major presentation to clients and then realised she had a live, wriggling nit under her fingernail, everyone has a nit tale to ease her pain (she crushed it and carried on like it hadn't happened, but her colleague said later that she went a bit pale as she did it). Many women acknowledge this shift and say their female friendships become more and more important as they get older. A mum with a child with special needs puts it like this:

'There is big stuff going on and I'm gravitating to more female friends, in similar situations. You just need to share your shit. They make you feel better in a way men can't. I don't have time for a lot of new people either because I only have so much time. I also feel that if spending time with them means I never get promoted, that's OK. I just want to be surrounded by nice people – I am tired of posturing. I am much bolder in what I say and don't say. Partly because whether I work or not has become almost meaningless as all my money goes on childcare anyway.'

Some start going on holidays with female friends as well as separate family trips, which can be a good way to get the benefit of non-term-time holidays without babysitting costs. Listening to this kind of group of women talking, you can't help but be struck by the detail and emotional intimacy of the information shared.

Your children are invited to less stuff

The lack of this network also has an impact on the children. Especially when kids are young, mothers essentially invite other mothers to play dates. Partly because a toddler doesn't much care who it hangs out with and its parent really, really does. Which is why antenatal groups often shake out into sub-groups of people who genuinely get on and then collect other local mums around them. Those groups will do loads of activities together and invite all the children along. Being a part of one gives you great access to social events for you and your kids locally that don't depend on babysitting.

Some mums, like Jackie, don't even realise that there is another world they are not part of. An accountant who attended her three-year-old daughter's ballet lesson for the first time, when the nanny was on holiday, realised that all the mums and daughters at the class were heading en masse to a regular coffee shop and that her daughter wasn't invited too because they didn't think to include the nannies. She was gutted that her daughter was excluded from this social group and felt a little pained for herself as well. She thought the mums were obnoxious for not inviting the nannies but then wondered if she might have done the same had she been them and if, if the group already knew each other a little, it would seem to have happened naturally. On the same theme, and this will be covered elsewhere in the book, dads are often not invited either.

It's worth noting here that when I ask older kids of working mums, some say they were totally unbothered by their parents being socially disconnected. But others did care very much. The daughter of a retired corporate HR manager says she felt the loss of her mum very keenly. She sometimes fantasised about swapping her mum for her best friend's, who was the vicar's wife and always at the gate. In reality, she said that what she wanted was her mum to be there 'just once a week', something regular she could depend on. Something that consultant Dr Rebecca Moore relates to: 'The school gate is a very important place for kids to see their parents socially connected and socially functioning well. They love seeing their parents involved and it makes them feel really supported.' Her brother, meanwhile, was perfectly happy with the way things worked out.

The 'mummy wars' emerge (in your head, even if nowhere else)

A feeling of having been excluded is what fuels some of the 'mummy war' banter whereby women assume some conscious exclusion when the more likely reality is that the other mums just don't know the mum well enough or see her often enough to ask her. As the penny drops that their family has missed out on an annual Easter egg hunt, regular Sunday-morning park meets and other rituals, it's easy to imagine that it was a decision rather than an omission.

A mum of four teens said: 'I see the mums who never talk to anyone at the school gate and they are the very people who like to know what's what and get annoyed if they don't but somehow haven't spotted that, by not talking to anyone, they are missing out on loads of invitations. Some get it later and try and throw themselves into it. But it doesn't work like that – not immediately anyway – you have to put in the hours to make friends.'

You lack access to useful information

The loss isn't just a social problem. It can also lead to a lack of access to useful information. How to get into the best gymnastics class, which school you have to apply for early, the news that everyone else is tutoring kids for secondary school and so on. Not knowing this kind of information is often exactly the kind of pitfall professional mums would avoid at work. Thinking back, Jackie admits that she didn't send Betty to pre-school because she didn't know she had to apply in a certain month. It wasn't a crisis as she was happy at nursery but they did notice she was a little behind the other kids in Reception and had to catch up. It isn't a mistake Jackie will make with Milo. A start-up entrepreneur I spoke to who did get her son into pre-school was mortified to be called in after day two and told it was unacceptable for him to come to school in nappies and that he had to be potty trained immediately. She had no idea that this was a requirement and hadn't given much thought to when kids should be using the toilet because she spent no time with people who talk about these things. She laughs about it now but admits she was very embarrassed and it wasn't the best start to school for him.

It can be harder to solve problems

Not being connected can also make it more difficult when your kids have social problems. I was recently with a mum a few days after her son had told her he was being bullied at school. Because she knew the other parents in the class well, she was able to call them and talk openly and frankly about the problems. The mums banded together and, between them and the school, the matter was sorted out in a matter of days with remarkably little acrimony. A more isolated parent would have no choice but to go only through official school channels, which may or may not work effectively and, without stable friendships in place, might result in them falling out with the parents of the other child.

Being quite sensitive to social issues can be a bigger risk for parents embedded in their work, especially if they have only one child. Discussing things at the gate daily, or a few times a week, creates maps of how things tend to get handled and worked out and what strategies seem to help and those that don't. This knowledge can be invaluable if you have a problem and help you see the issue from the different perspectives involved. A working parent who is told in isolation that their child is a bully or being bullied – for example – may instinctively react in response to their child's needs rather than, perhaps, taking a wider perspective on the players involved.

How not to make those connections

Some mums I talked to described ways that they tried to engage that hadn't worked for them.

One told me that she is connected at the school gate because she does pick-up every other Thursday. Nothing else she said suggested she really was remotely connected or supported locally. Going to the school gate to network every other week would be like popping into your work canteen for coffee every other week and assuming you knew the hot gossip.

Another approach is to compensate by throwing 'the best' birthday party annually and inviting all the class along. The risks of this are multiple: first you look like a show-off. Sensing this, you may feel highly vulnerable and insecure about it. A construction manager who is in charge of hundreds of men on site told me she vomited with nerves before her five-year-old's bubble disco party because she knew no one coming but they all knew each other and that scared her. There is also a risk that fewer parents will sign up if they don't know the hosts well, which can be awkward. Finally, it can go wrong on the day if you don't know who the kids are, which parents are which and get mistaken for the photographer.

The process of finding mum friends can be fraught and give you the same sense you had when starting at a new school or surviving Fresher's week at university. It takes both resolve and calm. A mum who'd done a few rounds of IVF told me that because the conception had come hard, she was so determined to make friends at her NCT group that she almost failed. 'I was so keen to find the group I'd go on Tuscan villa holidays with I could barely get my words out and acted like a bit of a nutter. For some reason, I thought I needed them far more than they needed me. Once I calmed down it was fine, but it took a while.'

What does work?

Ultimately, as with any relationship, it does take time and attention, ideally when your kids are as young as possible. Most key parent friendships are born with their first child. The others fit in with the siblings who come behind, if and when they do. So, it makes sense to use your maternity leave to find a group of local friends to see you through the journey. Go to pregnancy yoga and musical monkeys and baby swimming. Not for what any of them teach (God forbid), but to find the one or two people who make you laugh every time they roll their eyes at the teacher for calling everyone 'mummy'.

It's wise to be open-minded about how different they may be from you. Whether you think the people in your area are too posh for you or too parochial, you'll be surprised how much you might have in common when you're all weaning or choosing nurseries or researching schools. Having a mixed group is ultimately helpful to everyone as you can balance your skills and knowledge. One ends up being good at research into SATs, one is great at getting early tickets to local events and one is always bloody late to pick up but at least buys a couple of rounds.

If you miss the maternity leave slot, the next access points are the toddler groups – events that strike fear into many a parent's heart: stay and plays, library mornings, baby ballet, football and the like. They mostly happen midweek but you can go if you work flexibly, and some are on weekend mornings if you can bear it. Just turning up may not be enough at this point as groups may be well established, so you might have to help out at them to meet more people and get to know them a bit. A mum who does a four-day week jokes that she used to hoover up after a toddler group on a Friday morning in a shitty local-authority Portacabin® while paying her cleaner £10 an hour to hoover her house around the corner.

The next social meet is the primary school gate, arguably the most powerful local network group there is. The place where every piece of valuable information is shared within the school community. Some people hate it, others get overinvolved and then spend years cat-fighting in the PTA. Two signs you have it right: when your friends have a sub-group on the class WhatsApp and when you forget a packed lunch for the school trip and everyone takes apart their kids' lunches to create a semblance of a meal for yours.

As your children grow up, they of course start choosing their own friends and you have to make decisions about whether their parents are people you also want to connect with.

'With some of their mates' parents I smile politely and make nice, others have turned out to be great friends and some others … well you just have to suck it up and tolerate them. There was one girl my daughter was really into and was bugging me to have over but I kept missing her mum so at one drop-off, in a rush to get to work, I ran up to what I thought was the child's dad and beamed, saying "Hi, I'm Rachel, here's my phone number", only to gather from his stunned face that he had no idea who I was or why I was thrusting my phone number at him!'

Moving house

Moving house and changing schools can be really hard if you have to start building these groups again – or indeed if you didn't build them the first time – though if you move to an area where there are more like-minded people in a similar situation then it can provide access to loads of new friends. Some women, for example, who started in more central, city locations say they found it easier to connect with other parents in more 'down-to-earth' areas outside of town. But others have really struggled with moves. Happiness guru Nic Marks says to bear in mind thick and thin relationships. Thick relationships are the people you know very well and are close to. Thin relationships are the people you say hi to or nod to, the neighbours, the people you see in the park. Over time, thin relationships thicken so, when you move, you need to work hard at the thin relationships that may flourish in the future.

Those who move from cities into areas where people have grown up together can find it particularly hard. 'The mums here all went to school together themselves, their own mums are friends, they drive everywhere and it feels impossible to break in' said one. Some advise moving to an area where you know a few people to begin with, as they may give you access to existing groups. It's not without risks but it can help. As can specific hobbies or religious groups: choirs, tennis, Italian lessons. It hardly matters as long as you meet people you want to know.

All that said, no friendship group is perfect. So, find one, engage with it as suits you and know when to go home.

If you're too tired and wired to read the above

- By having a baby and being on maternity leave/going back full or part time but legging it out of the office on cue, you've probably lost access to an important social group in the work networks you have spent years building: work friends, ex-colleagues, contacts. You can't be out boozing at networking events every night and, initially at least, that might hurt like hell.
- If you only take one thing from this book, make it that you need a new group of super-local friends in the form of local mums with kids the same age. Turn up at antenatal classes/NCT and stay for the coffee afterwards and find ways to keep in with the group.
- I know you're thinking 'Oh I tried but they're not my kind of people' because they are either stuck-up snobs or dozy cows. Everyone thinks this: get over yourself. Sure, they probably aren't very interested in what you do for work and there will always be one who talks far too much about her perineum. But children are a lifelong endeavour and you'll be surprised whom you end up connecting with. Relationship therapist and coach, Karen Doherty urges: 'Don't be scared, accept that people are different and take pleasure in that variety. Take all the opportunities that kids provide to chat, linger and get to

know people. The sooner we start laying down real friendships, the happier we are.'

- Even if you really like them, don't believe everything your new friends say. First-timers are especially guilty of the 'oh mine slept through from six weeks' bullshit. It's rarely true and even if it is they will have other problems. Be wary of anyone who makes it look perfect. A dad told me the story of the locally known 'perfect mum' who he bumped into at the cafe. She went to the loo for 45 minutes while she shouted at the kids, not realising that everyone drinking coffee could hear her.

- If you really can't find stuff that suits your schedule, create your own group. An American mum I interviewed built her own local network of working mums to meet at parks on Saturday morning. She saw this as both a practical solution as well as a good way to network with other businesswomen – an intention some Brits would be squeamish about, but it worked for her.

- Even if you have the 'perfect partner', expecting them to meet all of your tumultuous emotional needs through this journey puts a lot of pressure on your partnership. Some chats are best saved for people you'll never have sex with. And, if you're a couple, there are many more opportunities to socialise individually while the other is home with the kids.

- On which theme, don't idealise other people's partners who seem to do more than yours. Ten years – and many cocktails – into a friendship and a more complex truth about their relationship will be well known.

- Overlook this if it's too late, but many do recommend timing babies for spring and early summer to get the best out of your maternity leave.

What happened next?

JACKIE JOINED THE PTA. We'll talk about this in the school chapter.

But the real breakthrough came from putting limits on her working hours and doing less in the evenings. She thought it would damage her career but says she feels strangely calmer and more efficient as a result. Partly because she sleeps better.

CHAPTER SEVEN

Help, I think I've done a crap job of raising my child

MY HUSBAND AND I have a lovely wee one, Orla, who's five. My husband Den also has a son from a previous relationship, he is 16, but they don't see each other much and my husband really wants to make sure the same doesn't happen this time around.

I'm a Pilates teacher and he is a builder, so we're both self-employed. He is such a hard worker and really wants to build his business to support our family, but it's a competitive industry and he's still trying to build a network of people to recommend him. My hours are quite long and irregular, including early mornings and many evenings and the income is unpredictable. Being self-employed meant that getting maternity pay was a nightmare [side note, others haven't found this: it seems to depend on your tolerance of government forms and how 'standard' and well-established your freelance working structure is]. I eventually got a government contribution when Orla was three months old but I felt huge financial pressure to get back to work quickly, because my husband had just lost money on a job that overran.

We both love Orla so much and try to make up for our crazy hours. We do let her stay up late with us and one of us usually ends up sleeping in her room. Good childcare is really important to us but a nursery wouldn't work because of our schedules. I wanted a nanny but we don't have that kind of money so we hired a young local girl who was very sweet and kind. But then after a year, we decided it wasn't quite right as she was just giving Orla whatever she asked for. Since then we've had a few one-on-one childminders along with au pairs and support from my mother-in-law, who is a lovely granny but does totally indulge her. It does seem noticeable to me now that Orla definitely prefers the company of other adults to kids her own age.

Recently, Orla started school and we were hoping she'd do well, as she loves reading. But her teachers are talking about some 'challenges', saying she often has tantrums, doesn't like to be told what to do and isn't making friends in class. Her teacher says that when Orla finishes her banana at lunch, she dangles the skin in the air, waiting for someone else to put it in the bin! Also, during one of her tantrums, she told her teacher that she needed to be nice to her because otherwise her mummy would be very cross and the teacher wouldn't work here anymore. I am so ashamed of her behaviour and desperate for her to have friends… but don't know how to change things. I'm starting to really, really worry that we've messed this up. It's causing arguments and friction at home and I'm wishing I could start over again and do everything differently.

Anya, 35, Pilates Teacher

****

My great-grandmother is credited with a piece of childcare advice: 'You will love your children. Your job is to make sure other people love them too.' Anya and Den haven't managed this yet. Orla isn't treating others in a way that leads to positive feelings and good relationships. In fact, Orla is treating the adults around her as personal service providers and other kids as competition to her needs being met. Anya is troubled by a feeling that other parents and kids seem a bit wary of Orla right now. If she is really honest, she knows that they haven't said 'no' often or consistently set clear boundaries: psychotherapists tell us that children without boundaries are frightened. Some would urge us to see tantrums as an expression of that fear.

Anya and Den aren't alone in this. A dad shares a similar story about the risk you run if your children get so much one-to-one care that they grow up to view adults as people who exist *just* to meet their needs. He described his daughter throwing a massive fit on the driveway after Sunday lunch with friends, when the screen she watched TV on in the back of the car didn't work. He found himself in the street begging her to calm down. 'Shhhhh, darling, shuuuuush, don't worry darling, daddy is going to fix it for you right now, I'm doing it right now, you calm down, shhhhhhhh.' He winces at the memory of himself – a well-respected partner at an accountancy firm – being belittled in front of friends by a seven-year-old. 'By the time you realise you've lost control of your kid's expectations of adults, it feels like it's way too late to take it back', he says regretfully.

A piece in the *New Yorker* magazine, by Carolina Izquierdo and Elinor Ochs, on this subject went as far as to write: 'With the exception of the imperial offspring of the Ming dynasty and the dauphins of pre-Revolutionary France, contemporary American kids may represent the most indulged young people in the history of the world.' It goes on to say that they've been given so much stuff (clothes, toys, electronics, etc) as well as so much authority, with middle-class parents so desiring their kids' approval that they end up at the beck and call of the children, that two-thirds of American parents think their children are spoiled.

Good quality early years care could help to mitigate this and it's no secret that public subsidies of high-quality early years childcare both make parents happier and deliver better outcomes for kids. In fact, a research project by the *American Journal of Sociology* shows that the parents who are most miserable – Americans, since you're wondering – are those with the least access to family friendly policies. The happiest are those with access to a package of policies but it is notable that subsidised early years care is one of the most important.

Informal childcare

Where we lack good-quality and affordable childcare we end up with parents making do as best they can – as Den and Anya have done. In their case the better-qualified options – nurseries and nannies – didn't work. So, they managed their own childcare, mostly based in their house, provided by carers who were paid in cash, which, while still feeling extremely expensive to them, was cheaper than the taxed, official options.

Which on one level shouldn't matter because parents are untrained, too. But it can matter if those carers see the world in the short-term rather than the long-term good. 'I just need to get to 7pm without a massive meltdown' thinks an au pair who is in the UK to experience life and pass her English exams. Families and professionally trained childcarers are more likely to see challenges in the long term. Which makes dealing with issues much harder work: it is harder to get kids to do their homework, clean up and eat sensibly than it is to let them do as they please and pick up after them. If you have to live with them for the next 15 years, though, you may well decide that the battle to put shoes in the same place and stack the dishwasher after dinner is one that's worth fighting.

Like many others, Anya and Den also found managing childcare in their own home awkward and difficult. 'There are people in your house, looking at you to know what to do and it's all quite weird and uncomfortable' says Anya. With one child, they were adjusting as they went and tended to let the people they hired get on with the job if Orla seemed happy. Their stated priorities were that she was cherished, stimulated and outside a lot. They achieved those goals but unintentionally lost out on the finer points of emotional regulation and reasonable expectations of the world.

To understand why, take the hypothetical example of an au pair called Maria who arrives from Portugal, keen to work. Her experience of childcare is limited to looking after various cousins and two younger siblings. In truth, she wants to be a clothes designer but, to get a good job, she first needs to improve her English.

On Maria's first full day, having been given little guidance, Orla lets it be known that she fancies some sweets immediately after breakfast and works herself towards a spectacular tantrum. Maria, still short on English and keen to curry favour, can refuse and let her go postal. But if they are out – say at story time at the library – there's a good chance that Anya would be informed by one her friends that the new au pair had lost control of her darling girl. How much easier would it be for her to discreetly concede to the sweets? Learning a lesson about avoiding stressful confrontations, Maria might start carrying treats with her and dishing them out at every tricky moment. Orla now has her own personal sugar dispenser following her around her various clubs and hobbies: as well as her walking banana-skin bin. And she's re-established that the threat of a tantrum gets her exactly what she wants. What Anya hears is that they had a lovely morning at story time and her friend Nas says how great it is that Orla seems to really like the new au pair.

This instinct to appeasement isn't of course just a problem for external help – lots of parents also struggle with managing expectations. Even over the last 10 years there has been a shift towards greater child-centricity. An administrator whose kids are now in their teens says, 'I see these women, strapped to their giant slug babies, still feeding, still at home, doting on them and wonder how they don't go mad. It's different now even from when we had our kids when sleep and eat routines were still fashionable and you got on with your life too.'

A dentist said that she sees this trend increasingly played out when mums come in for family appointments. Middle-class, professional mothers will race in on a 'working at home day' with a toddler and an iPad and packaged snacks. Checking the kids' teeth is one thing (cue a bit of power play and bribing with stickers) but then she moves to the mother. At which point some children seem confused that they are not in charge of this situation and demand constant interaction. As she's checking and then trying to clean, the mother starts mumbling apologies to their child, chomping on the saliva suction ejector in her mouth. 'Darling I am so sorry, mummy promises she won't be long and then we'll go straight to your play date, you just hang on in there a moment.'

In contrast, less-stressy mums will rock up with a two-year-old in tow who is happy to sit on the floor and play with a few toys, not expecting any intervention at all. The mother feels no need to apologise and, instead, heads out saying they'll be doing the family food shop on the way home. The dentist says: 'The kids brought up in extended families of grandparents, aunts and cousins, even if they are more financially deprived, tend to be better managed and the mothers I see also seem to cope with having their kids better than a lot of the middle-class career mums. They don't seem to stress each other out in the same way.'

But Den and Anya don't have that big extended network of parental expertise: Den was an only child, he barely knows his older son who lives abroad with his ex, and Anya's family live in Aberdeen. They are so grateful for help from his mum and keen not to upset her that they let her do things her way when she is childminding. This includes letting Orla demand whatever she wants for dinner, even if that means an extra trip to the shops, as well as a lot of time playing the games in which Orla is always the queen or king. Granny doesn't mind being the frog but, as Orla is starting to find, other kids are less accommodating.

Her pre-school years also included a lot of time in which Orla was attached to electronic devices. A teacher who deals with kids with behavioural problems says he really worries about the impact of all this screen time: 'The child on an iPad or phone all the time is not expressing themselves and not having their needs met. I worry that we don't hear enough babies crying anymore, you see kids being pushed around the supermarket with a phone in their little hands. And then the parents complain that they can't get them to sleep at night and you have to wonder how much exercise they get and how much the screen affects their brains.'

Looking back now, Anya also sees their various childcarers rather differently. She recalls that she did once get rid of an older lady who was a local childminder, when she found Orla very upset at the end of the day after an incident over cleaning up her toys. Anya assumed that the childminder was a cow. Looking back, she wonders whether she was actually trying to change some behaviours.

Formal/trained childcare

Good, trained childcarers consciously work to create positive patterns and reward the behaviour they want while ignoring or dealing with anything undesirable. But they too struggle if parents won't let them take charge.

Amy, the wife of John the tax accountant whose daughter went berserk over the broken car screen, went the other way to Anya and Den. In the early days, she hired a series of nannies and then micromanaged them until she drove them away. She recalls:

'I felt I had to bring my project management skills into my house. I learned slowly to trust the people I left my kids with to do what they knew best. That having everything done exactly the way I would do it was less important than having the right person for my child and letting them get on with it. But I remember with our first nanny being really cross with her because she wouldn't rock my baby to sleep on her arm in the way I told her to. I just knew it worked and wanted her to sleep. Looking back, I know she knew a lot more about sleep training than I did. But, somehow, I missed the point that I'd hired her for those skills. Initially we went through a lot of nannies as I learned how to build more positive relationships: supportive without being overfriendly or overmanagerial.'

An experienced nanny says she often sees an inverse correlation between mothers who are very high-control about external factors – creating detailed spreadsheets of meals involving kale and quinoa and the timing of sunscreen and colour-coordinated outfits – and engaging in the emotional development of their children. 'These are women who are working so hard to appear like they are the perfect mothers yet actually their one-to-one interaction with their own children is minimal,' she says. 'It's sometimes like they are scared of being on their own with their kids. I watch them coming through the door stressed and glued to their phones just when the kids really want their attention. Then later they compensate by being overly adoring of the child in a way that's not very helpful either.'

Another nanny told me about getting a new job caring for a seven-year-old boy who, so used to having attentive staff, refused to eat unless he was quite literally spoon-fed at the table. When she started working with him she was appalled and firmly said he could go to his room if he was too tired to feed himself. Unfortunately, his mother was listening on the baby monitor from her home office and swiftly intervened. To keep her job the nanny complied but stayed with the family only two months.

The nannies also report that busy parents have a tendency to impose rules on them that they don't enforce themselves: 'They say to me "they must always make their own beds, use proper cutlery for all meals, eat no refined sugar and be in bed by 7pm." I'm happy to enforce all of that as long as it is consistent with what happens when they are in charge too. If it isn't, and it often isn't, then I end up with an almighty battle and children who are pushing every rule. It's exhausting and counter-productive, especially when dad comes through the door at 6.45pm, throws the kids in the air, cancels bath time, dishes out a tray of doughnuts and keeps them up watching telly 'til 9.00pm.'

If parents act this way, then even trained nannies can – against their better judgement – pragmatically accept working with the wrong messages about who is in charge. At least in the short term. But anyone worth their salt will move on, and leave a revolving door of carers and, potentially, escalating mistrust between the parents and their replacements.

Teachers

Many teachers and nursery staff recognise the problem of children, like Orla, who see adults as their service providers and talk behind staffroom doors about it.

One head of a nursery I spoke to reports that she is used to seeing children drop their coat on the floor and run off assuming that an adult will dash forwards to pick it up. Or children who think nothing of getting to the highest level of the tree or climbing frame, deciding they can't or don't want to get down, and kicking off to demand some adult climbs up to get them. She tells of a boy who, in his first week of school, informed her he didn't do tidy-up time because he had a cleaning lady.

Similarly, a music teacher says he is used to kids telling him that their mum won't pay for their class if they don't like it so he should ease off about their lack of practice. For £30 an hour, it's a not a battle he cares to fight, so those entitled kids are failing to learn the piano at considerable expense to their parents, who then, of course, conclude that the teacher is useless and move on to someone else.

A pre-school teacher, overrun with 30 children – including those with real problems and some heart-winning charmers – guiltily admits (after two glasses of wine) that these demanding children are the ones they are most likely to overlook in class. 'I look at the child when they arrive and I think, "Will I spend the next year of my life trying to fix them or will I ignore them and let them go on to primary school and let them deal with it?" A big part of that decision will come down to whether I will get support from the family at home. If I can talk to a parent and say "Listen, Orla's finding this transition really quite challenging, let's talk about how we can help her together" and get a positive response, I'll definitely try. If the response is defensive, angry or critical – "she is never like this at home so, clearly, you're no good at your job, perhaps we should move her" – I'll give up and let Orla behave like a little shit until we post her off to school and she becomes someone else's problem.'

But this can be further complicated by the fact some teachers and nursery staff rarely actually see either of the parents because they are working full time. One manager with an hour-long commute said that she only does school pick-up on the last day of term and every time she does it she worries she'll go in through the wrong door. A regular face – be it grandparent or au pair or nanny – is a fine substitute, but many report kids with a conveyor belt of carers they can't keep track of.

A teacher explains: 'You get this young, shy woman at the gate smiling at you and asking for Fred: her English isn't great and you guess she's just off a flight. You've never seen her before in your life. The child doesn't recognise her. So, you call the mum or dad of Fred and they say breezily "Oh yes it's our new au pair – she is taking Fred home". It unsettles you, especially when the child is clinging on to your leg and crying because you are the person they know best in that moment. But what can you do? You send them off, knowing that in a few weeks' time the same thing may well happen again.'

If the problems continue into secondary school, they can escalate. Secondary school teachers report angry kids of 11 or 12 who, they say, resent the lack of parental engagement. 'Don't assume it just gets better and they grow out of it' is their caution on this. A managing director who is proud to be known professionally as someone who has 'never knowingly suffered a fool' told me her two teenage daughters regularly text her 'Fuck Off' messages and threaten to self-harm if they don't get their own way. She is now working really hard to sort it out but wishes she'd done so a long, long time ago, when she was too busy setting up the business to be much engaged at home.

Other parents

One of the problems for these adult-dependent children is that their behaviour limits the very thing they need: positive interactions with people they are not in charge of. Other adults tend to turn away from difficult kids and other parents avoid inviting tricky children to play dates and parties. 'They might come once but never twice' says one working mother of four, darkly. Mothers who worry they may not able to handle the child will avoid it: 'We had an eight-year-old boy over and every two minutes he was demanding that I do things for him: get a snack, do a puzzle, get out another toy, let him into the garden, find more food because he doesn't like pasta... There were six other kids here who just went with the flow. Let me be clear, he is never coming back.' Another mum said she lives in fear of her daughter inviting over the child who shouted that their toys were boring and their food was 'dis-GUST-ing' (she 'accidentally' dropped it on the floor and broke the plate) and then was found in their bedroom trying on all the mother's expensive make-up and face crèmes. Also 'Never Coming Back'.

Some parents mistake their child having good relationships with adults as a universally positive sign. They might say, with pride, 'Oh Riley is so confident about talking to adults, it's fantastic, he's so mature.' Of course it can be fantastic to have that confidence but it can also be that the child finds adult interaction easier because they are used to getting what they want and most adults will tend towards being polite to other people's kids. The parent may not give much thought to what other adults get out of their talk to Riley, given they likely have a few kids the same age who also have plenty of chat. A teacher adds that kids like Riley often have pretty good verbal skills and may be able to read and count early because of the sheer volume of one-to-one interaction they've had. What they lack are the skills to negotiate with their peers in a productive way*.

The behavioural challenges above can all sound quite scary and depressing, but none of it is inevitable. Setting up good childcare, even informally, is possible if you are clear about the boundaries and behaviours you are after. Which isn't about micromanaging the household but is about flagging what you expect to see in terms of standards and making it very clear to your child and their carer that the carer is in charge at all times.

*There is of course a caveat here: some children have special needs that make it harder for them to 'read' other kids. As one mum describes it "my eldest is autistic, and struggles with peer relationships and prefers adults as she finds them a bit easier to read. Many parents don't know this, as we recently moved to a new school, and I was noticing a lack of invitations to people's houses. Now I openly tell the mums in the playground that my child is autistic, and to instruct their own children to be very clear about what they want, rather than relying on body language as a means of communication. The play dates she has been on have, as a result, been fine, because the mums knew in advance."

If you do make mistakes, then there are opportunities to address them. Sarah Clarke says:

'One of the most reassuring things I can offer parents who feel they may have made a mess of things is that it's never too late. Wonderful psychologists, psychiatrists and psychotherapists, such as Professor Dan Siegel and Louis Cozolino, have given us "neuroplasticity". Whereas we used to think that attachment was something that happened (or didn't) in those crucial early years of infancy we now know that the brains continues to change into adulthood and loving, well-attuned relationships can bring about a "re-wiring" that overrides any early fragilities.'

A Montessori teacher is also positive about the capacity of kids to adjust: 'It's astonishing how quickly these kids can change in a short period. A few sessions in the reading corner and some focused attention on manners can make a big difference in the early years.' She says she wishes she could tell more parents to give the right kind of attention themselves, as even small doses can have a big impact. When she meets parents who are finding their kids really hard work and challenging, she often wants to say: 'He's just fighting for your attention, give it to him – without trying to control or indulge him – and things will be easier.' Unless of course there is a special need, in which case she would recommend getting the earliest possible intervention to help move forwards and manage it appropriately.

In the early years, if you can afford it, appointing a qualified and experienced nanny who will not be bullied is a good start. Some working mums are proud of having found the right person and kept the same carer for all of their children over many years.

Shared nannies are also increasingly popular. Rachel Carrell, founder of nanny-share company Koru Kids explains they are: 'More flexible than a nursery, more sociable than a sole nanny, and excellent value for money. The nanny looks after the children from both families at once, so the children grow up with a friend to play with. With a nanny share they get the social benefits of being around other kids while still being in a home setting. For many parents it's a way to access far more convenient and high-quality care that they otherwise couldn't afford, since each family in a share saves roughly a third on the cost of their nanny. Meanwhile the nanny gets a pay rise, typically of about 25 per cent.'

She warns, though, that: 'Nanny share doesn't work for everyone. Parents who want to specify in detail what their nanny does with their children (for example, sleeping/eating schedules) are probably best off getting their own sole nanny. It's also not the cheapest option – depending on where you live, that's probably a childminder. But it's perfect for families who have one baby and want care that is personal but also social, or who need longer hours than a nursery can provide, and who are relatively flexible and willing to compromise.'

Others swear by working really hard to find great local childminders, who are good value compared to a nanny. They caution that the selection on offer may be a mixed bag but, if you keep at it and follow recommendations, you may find someone brilliant. Bear in mind that, because there are tight limits on ratios, especially for little kids, you may also have to wait for spaces to become available.

Au pairs also come laden with risk as you rarely meet them before they land in the UK. However, they are totally worth a try if you have space for them to live with you, and only need a few hours' help a day – especially if you are willing to commit time and attention to a proper search. If you imagine you are hiring for a full-time member of your team who also lives in your house, you will have an idea of the importance of the decision you are making. Even when you try really hard, though – and we have drawn up many an Excel database of point-scored candidates that a board-level job search would be impressed by – there is always risk. We've had an au pair who came into our house one awful February when we were besieged by chickenpox and our oldest had just had her adenoids out. Yet somehow, despite her basic English, she just fitted in, cheered everyone up and made life so much easier. She tells a story now about our then four-year-old demanding what sounded like 'sosiges' and her carrying her two year-old sister to the fridge so she could point to the sausages, to find out what she wanted. She stayed for a year and seemed to light up the house: the children adored her and so did we. She now teaches Spanish at our local school and still feels like part of our extended family. But we also had one glamourpuss who, while dressed for the cover of *Vogue* herself, took our three-year-old out without a coat, two days running, in February and was, I only half joke, fired by our lovely local vicar's wife, who on the second day crossed the road to make her views so abundantly clear that the au pair resigned that evening! It was one of the moments when you truly get what people mean when they say 'it takes a village'.

What those who have experience with au pairs advise is that you get on one of the big search websites, do a very positive – but real – profile of your family, with pictures that make your kids look beguiling rather than bloodthirsty, and offer over-the-average pay if you can afford it to get the best candidates. Decide what's important to you – being sporty, experience of young kids, specific languages you want, whatever – and then go at it, giving it a lot of attention for a relatively short period (a couple of weeks). Respond to everyone you like and work out how to keep yourself up the top of the listings so you maximise your chance of finding people. Draw up a list of those you like and Skype them. These can be awkward – the au pair candidates understandably have pretty serious willies about being interviewed in a foreign language, let alone moving country into a house of strangers and being left with their feral kids – so they usually have parents or siblings listening in to help them make the decision. If they are 'on the bounce' from another UK home that hasn't worked out, they may be whispering so their current host doesn't realise what they are doing. If they are local and you like them then invite them over to visit and see how they are with the kids. Limit your list and be enthusiastic, and never forget they are choosing as much as you are. Then go with your gut and hope for the best.

When they arrive, the first thing to do is give them the wifi code (their whole family is worrying right now about whether you are an axe murderer) and then be really specific and clear about what you want them to do and give it a bit of time – some are horribly homesick for a while. Don't fall into treating them like 'staff' and expecting them to pick up your knickers or scrub the patio. Accept some foibles: they will all have some stuff they are great at and some things they just can't get their head around. See if you can live with the upsides and ignore the down. If you're not sure how to handle something, imagine it's one of your kids who's in a foreign country, living with a family they don't know and think what you would like that family to do. If it cannot work out, be direct and move on fast: ideally help them find something better for them or to head home if they never want to step foot in the UK again. Try not to leave on bad terms, not only because that's the grown-up and classy thing to do, but also because they have highly active Facebook pages in which they revel in slagging off their hosts, which could mean you can never hire again....

Whatever option you choose, you have to do all the homework you possibly can to find the right person, accept that perfection doesn't exist and work with what you have. If it really doesn't work then move on swiftly. Whoever looks after your offspring, stay close to what they are doing and monitor how they are managing your kids. Because no one wants a monster child at five, let alone 15.

If you're too tired and wired to read the above

- People generally won't directly tell you your child is turning out to be a little shit. You need to listen very carefully to hear it. One childcare professional says:

  'As a teacher I steer clear of saying the children "lack coping skills" because it can get a very bad parental response. I talk about "struggling to engage with friends", or describe the child as "becoming frustrated quite quickly when things don't go their way". Given that in pre-school the issues tend to manifest themselves in tantrums, rage and tears, I generally describe a situation and how they respond. Ideally parents will nod and share something similar from home. But sometimes they lash out and say "well you're not stimulating him enough, he's very clever you know and obviously bored in your classroom." My heart sinks when I hear that.'

- Also watch yourself. If you find yourself constantly making excuses for your child, saying s/he's tired, unwell, not had lunch, had too much lunch, too hot, too cold etc in order to explain poor behaviour, start to think seriously about whether the problem is more about your child's ability to regulate feelings. If you feel you have an issue, don't be mollified by friends or family sweetly saying 'oh it's just a phase'. They may be being polite and they won't have to deal with that out-of-control teenager roaring down the track.

- If you think you have a problem then work with your partner (if you have one) and other carers on it. Psychologists will tell you that there is little more confusing or distressing to a child than inconsistent messages.

- Get advice from nursery, school, friends, family and professional support if you need it. Read books and blogs and find out more. Many schools and local community groups offer parenting classes of some sort and many parents have found them very helpful. Consider paying for help from a family psychologist if you think you need it and can afford it.
- Aim for consistent care. In the early years, appointing a qualified and experienced nanny who will not be bullied is great, if (big if!) you can afford it. Nanny shares and childminders are often overlooked by working parents as a way to cut bills. Trust the people you appoint to do a good job and let them get on with it – while keeping a watchful eye on the outcomes. Also look at both working more flexibly so you need less care. For example, if both parents work a four-day week you only need three days of cover.
- Have faith that you can tackle the problems if you choose to: relatively straightforward plans can work. Some parents of a football-mad boy told me they were worried their son seemed to have tantrums at the park after school almost every day if he didn't win. So, they told him that as soon as he started to blow up they would immediately leave. They stuck to this, a few times carrying home a raging child, but, as soon as he realised they were serious, the tantrums vanished.
- If you are worried your child may have a special need, talk to teachers and carers about it. Try not to jump to conclusions or panic, but do get an assessment if advised to. Karen Doherty says: 'There is no shame at all in seeking help and diagnoses are only ever helpful: knowledge increases our sense of empowerment.'

What happened next?

ANYA TOOK ADVICE FROM a friend who specialises in child development. Working with Orla and her teacher, they built a plan to help her engage differently with the world. It was really hard work for all of them. Initially they had more emotional outbursts as Orla settled into a regular earlier bedtime, eating what was on offer and not getting her way when she kicked off. Granny struggled as much as Orla did and fretted that they were being mean. There were moments when everyone wanted to give in, but, a year later, the household and Orla are much happier and calmer. Having never thought they could cope with another child, they are now seriously considering it.

CHAPTER EIGHT

Alpha/beta, the pros and cons of dads as lead parents

I'VE BEEN WORKING AT the same hotel since I graduated. For most of the last ten years I have worked nights but have recently started a new role with more normal daytime hours. Because of the nights, I used to catch up on sleep in the daytime and it made sense for my husband Matt to do the majority the childcare so he gave up work. This wasn't a hard decision for him as he's struggled to find the right role for himself and changed jobs quite a few times.

My job can be stressful, things sometimes go wrong, like recently a guest reported she'd been attacked during a function. It can be emotionally draining. And while it's great that he does the childcare, and he is a really good dad, the fact is that he doesn't do any of the other things… when I worked nights I would help out when I woke up in the day but now I come home and the house is a mess. He gives the kids tea before I get in – but not a great meal, more fishfingers and chips even though it's time they grew out of that – and he doesn't cook or shop for a decent evening meal for us. I usually just pick at leftovers or have eggs and toast or tinned soup. When I get home the kids are thrilled to see me and mob me, he often uses that moment to run out to the gym, letting me know that the kids need bathing and that their homework isn't started yet. Sometimes, in that moment it takes all my resolve not to burst into tears knowing that the homework still needs to be done, the kids need bathing, reading to… and I'm so exhausted.

I am so jealous of the time he gets to spend with them and, if I'm honest, I don't think he's delivering his side of the deal. Because I really do miss the children and don't think they get the care they need and deserve, let alone me getting any care. Which all might be fine if he was enjoying it. But he's not. He says he is depressed and I know he doesn't like telling people he's an at-home dad. Sometimes I get home late because something has gone wrong and he gets cross with me for delaying his gym trip. I find myself wondering if he has forgotten the real pressures of work and or how hard this job can be.

It sometimes feels like we've ended up with the worst of all worlds.

Joanna, 35, Hotel Manager

****

Do you believe?

I know you want to believe. Christ I *want* to believe in the super-cool papa, jogging his double buggy round the park, while his stunningly talented partner rocks her profession. For the sake of gender equality, for our kids' and for our own ambitions, we have to know that the at-home, lead-parent-dad model works, whether it's full time or alongside a part-time job or them running a business from home. As someone who has been able to thrive professionally because my husband works from home, I'm grateful and enthusiastic about our dash towards more dads as lead parents. But I also notice how often it doesn't work as well as we hope.

After I had my first baby I went to a lecture by the psychotherapist Dr Sue Gerhardt, author of *Why Love Matters – how affection shapes a baby's brain*. She explained that the problem with 1960s feminism was that it wanted to release women from caring roles but never explained who *would* do the caring in their place. Now, we have at least part of an answer: men. And all the trends show us men are far more engaged in family life than before and that many more fathers are compromising their own career progression while mothers rise in the workforce.

Many young women say they've never felt professionally hard done by based on their gender. This is recognised by former CEO and best-selling author Margaret Heffernan who, when women say they don't see the discrimination she talks about, smiles darkly and says simply, 'you will': meaning that some combination of having kids and increased power or authority will ensure you see it later. When you first date, being the female big earner is foxy and clever and irrelevant. It's later you find out the downsides. These challenges range from the basics, such as dealing with school, through to the financial structures that actively prevent gender equality. I can't count how many working mothers rage about the fact that school *still* calls her when their child is sick, even when the dad has been their listed primary carer since nursery and they have just woken her up at 3am in San Diego. In one school, parental letters were until very recently still being addressed 'Dear Mums'. Until one mother died of cancer and the letters started being addressed to 'Dear Mums and Richard.' Thankfully most schools finally seem to be fixing this one.

But it's the double blue line of their pregnancy test that is the first indication that you are at the boggy end of an unlevel playing field. Most women in the UK are eligible to statutory maternity pay of £145.18 a week, which is less than half minimum wage. Yes, nurturing a newborn is worth half an entry-level job. This would explain the results of a USwitch survey that found almost a third of new mothers in Britain end up in debt in the region of £2,500. This is at a time when, in a third of UK households, women are the main breadwinners. Yet this subject isn't even on the political agenda. When you did you last hear a debate about the rates of maternity pay? There have been recent efforts to even things up so dads can also get paternity benefits. Currently, if dads take two weeks' paternity leave they get the same amount – but of course 34 per cent don't, saying they can't afford to.

Now some companies have enlightened policies that ensure mums get most or all of their pay for up to a year after the birth. This is to be highly commended. But also observed with a hard head. Because there is often a correlation between jobs that demand lunatic hours and those offering the most generous maternity packages. So, management consultancies and big law firms are often the most, ahem, benevolent. They are also the places where I have found working parents of both genders to be most struggling over the years, oppressed by the insatiable demand for billable hours and new clients.

The problem for the dads – and part of the reason so few are taking up the change in the law that allows them to take paternity leave shared evenly with their partner in the form of Shared Parental Leave (currently its estimated that about 1–2 per cent of dads take what they are entitled to) – is that most companies don't offer equality in the enhanced packages if fathers take the leave. So, a man taking four months out from a professional job often isn't eligible for the top-up pay, even if women in his organisation are. Until this is addressed, lead parenting from dads is likely to remain a minority sport in the UK. There also remains some social stigma around men taking parental leave, the fast pace of change in the workplace meaning that some feel they will fall behind in their career just by taking a few months off. The good news is that younger men, born between the early 1980s and mid 1990s, are more keen to be involved. Culturally, though, paternity leave remains an easy target, with comedian Frankie Boyle recently joking that any party that wanted his vote should cut all parental leave to fathers.

It also means that one important intent of this policy – to reduce discrimination against women 'of child-bearing age' when employers see them as a risk and don't choose to hire them – is undone. It will clearly only work if men too take up the leave. It is also a problem if both parents are freelancers that dads cannot access the maternity allowance if they take over full-time caring. 'I was shocked that, as freelancers, while my wife could get a (very small) state maternity allowance, there was no equivalent for men – i.e. she was entitled to nine months' statutory maternity pay but she only took eight as she had to return to work. For the remaining time I was essentially looking after Molly full time but wasn't able to claim any paternity allowance. That seemed a bit unfair to me.'

This latter issue is irrelevant for many, as fewer than half (48 per cent) of employers offer anything more than the minimum stipulated by the government, and even those that do often tail-sting with precise expectations of the terms on which you return. The advertising agency I worked for very reluctantly agreed to pay me 90 per cent of my salary for 12 weeks on condition that I returned full time for at least a year. Failing to do so meant I'd have to repay the money. I sent the contract back to HR unsigned and they filed it that way so I never paid out. But I still felt the policy breathing down my neck.

The upshot of this inequality and complexity is that, aside from households like Joanna's, where the woman is so much the established earner that no other arrangement makes financial sense, woman remain the lead parents and at-home dads remain a minority. The problem is that being a minority is hard and comes with some big, and usually unspoken, risks.

On and off the record

Interviews with alpha mums (by which I mean those who are the main breadwinner rather than those who are assertive) are littered with the hero-words of dad funerals: 'my rock', 'my hero', 'my biggest supporter'. Similarly typical are the comments like: 'I must give credit to my husband who, for the past few years, has mostly worked from home. He's incredibly hands-on, does all the shopping and cooking and, irritatingly, makes it look easy'. Many object fiercely to 'moron' stereotype portrayals of stay-at-home dads.

'I am always astonished at how many working women seem to infantilise their husbands as if they can't cook or pick up their own pants. Women whose big jobs depend on their partners being based at home have to celebrate the husbands who make it possible.'

Which is incredibly heart-warming, until I tell you that the woman who said this point-blank refused to have her name attached to it. I'm not sure I can fully explain why but my sense was that talking publicly about how her family lives made her feel more vulnerable than she expected. Whatever the reason, she is correct, though, that those who are making it work tend to actively appreciate and enthuse about the value of their partner's contribution. But I also realised that while some mums are publicly adamant that the dad as lead-parent model works brilliantly for their families, others flash snapshots of cosy family idylls, only to replace them later with something troublingly different.

It was an interview about the role of dads that first alerted me to the ginormous gulf between the on- and off-record accounts mums sometimes give. A particularly glossy mother, dressed as elegantly as Claire Underwood in *House of Cards*, talked about the fabulous and extraordinary contribution her husband made to their family life. So much so that she called afterwards and sheepishly asked me to tone down her quotes so he wasn't embarrassed. A few months later, she summoned me to a weekday afternoon glass of wine as large as her head and told me that, shortly after we spoke, he had left their house one day and not come back.

Clearly one break-up doesn't tell us that everyone who prides themselves on the lead-parent-dad arrangement is overlooking the pitfalls. But it did focus my mind on relationship challenges that are bigger than those that are publicly stated. His departure highlighted that things are not always as they are told.

After five years of interviews – hide behind the sofa if you need to – I can categorically tell you that dads, like this one, in the eyes of many mums, don't get it right. And this has consequences. It can also be very hard to talk about. A full-time working mum whose husband runs a business from home that makes, in her words, 'absolutely no money' described talking to a male colleague about an argument he'd had with his wife. He'd complained to her that he works a very long week but she is at home with school-aged kids and a cleaner and isn't doing as much heavy lifting as he is. They had a big row. But the full-time working mum's reaction to this tale was jealousy: 'If I so much as opened up that conversation with my partner…. Christ. It's the nuclear button. I couldn't even say to him how I feel.' The implication being that it would be a questioning of his masculinity and a conversation their relationship would struggle to cope with. Now you can say that your relationship would survive that kind of a conversation and very pragmatically decide such consequences are small change for a successful career, or you might not give a shit about them at all, but I am going to be frank about what they are. Because if we know more about what does and doesn't work for others, we have a much better chance of being able to do it ourselves.

Morons vs monsters

Matt doesn't like telling people what he does because he thinks people see stay-at-home dads as failures. This is common. Another dad said: 'It's difficult to say you're not working and do not have a business card. Your sense of worth goes. And then you are buoyed by someone calling you for urgent help and you remember you have skills and then it crashes down again when no one calls for the next three weeks.' This isn't just anecdotal: a Rutgers University team studied nearly 2,000 couples over 30 years, monitoring changes in earnings and status. They found much higher rates of stress-related illness as well as heart problems and diabetes in men financially overtaken by their wives. When he took voluntary redundancy, after our first child was born and before he started his business, my husband used to tell people socially that he'd retired. It helped other people respond positively to his news because the idea of a man in his early 40s retiring was funny, perhaps admirable: stepping out to take care of a household is something many still interpret as weird or a downgrade.

But it didn't prevent judgement from all around. When I was working full time and Chris was running a nascent business at home, his dad used to say to me: 'Why do you let him exploit you like this, why don't you send him out to work and let you enjoy the girls?' On some level, this amused us because I can't run a house for love nor money, and didn't want to be at home all day, every day with toddlers, but the underlying assumption wasn't very comfortable: your husband/ my son is letting you and the kids down and you're a fool for letting him. Neither of us was too bothered but others are more affected by views like this.

There is an unhelpful cultural norm around dads who are primary carers of their children. Dr Elwood Watson, a history professor at East Tennessee State University who wrote *Performing American Masculinities: The 21st-Century Man in Popular Culture*, says that most on-screen house husbands are presented as 'dysfunctional'. 'They tend to be people who lack motivation or they are emasculated or they're not the smartest men.' Even in the recent BBC comedy drama *Motherland*, the stay-at-home dad is depicted as a sweet but hopeless bloke who never gets to shag his wife because, when he books appointments for sex in their shared calendar, she deletes them. As with all good comedy, this taps into a wider social perception. One dad who very reluctantly agreed to move to a four-day week when his wife got a new job that wouldn't allow any flexibility was stunned to be welcomed at the school gate by the administrator with the enthusiastic 'Oh I forgot today is your Mrs Doubtfire day!'

This social perception isn't helped by the lack of strong male role models based at home. Interviewing Swedish and Finnish mums, they say that they have been working on parenting equality since the 1970s and very senior, A-type men can be seen taking chunks of time out for their kids. Finland is the only country where dads spend, on average, slightly more time with children than mums: *The Global Gender Gap Report* rated Finland the second most-equal country in the world in 2016, and the *Economist* recently rated it the third-best country in which to be a working mum. Yet parents living in Finland and Sweden say they still feel they have a long way to go and that this level of dad involvement isn't universal. There are still companies and sectors where, despite the strong policy support for parental leave, it is culturally unusual for men to take it. Finance and consultancy are the usual culprits: someone I spoke to who was working in Sweden met the head of a consultancy who was proud that its staff's *average* working week was hitting 80 hours per person (although they were taking steps to reduce this figure). This, for them, demonstrates that, whatever the policy or legal framework, it is the living reality that leads to change.

This imbalance is so uncomfortable that there is some anecdotal evidence it may even threaten the security of our relationships: women who earn less than their partners are more likely to be faithful, the opposite is said to be true of men. According to Cornell sociology doctoral candidate Christin Munsch, cheating is not about money but about men's sexual identity. The idea of studying the effects of income on infidelity came to Munsch after hearing from a friend who had cheated on his partner. He told Munsch: 'She made all the money, she had all the friends....' He 'felt completely powerless'.

Yet despite some men saying they feel powerless, the women in this scenario often feel vulnerable too. Many say that, even when they are many miles away from their kids, they still feel their own status is innately attached to their children's successes and failures. For example, whatever her job, she often still perceives sharp social judgement for her children's appearance and behaviour. If they are dressed as street urchins and pissing against a wall, she feels it reflects negatively on her status and competence. The dads I interview rarely feel so judged. One says: 'I clean them up before we go out but only so my wife doesn't have a go at me if she hears about it later'. He doesn't much care and attaches little personal status to the elegance or delinquency of his kids; but he does feel the status loss of not having 'a proper job'.

Years ago, my husband sent me a proud picture of our oldest daughter's first school disco while I was at work. Of 200 Key Stage One kids bopping in a hall she was the only one in her school uniform, the other girls having gone home to swathe themselves in Frozen-themed nylon and the boys to change into tracksuits (gender-neutral clothing hasn't reached our neck of the woods yet). At the time, I was furious with him for 'shaming' our daughter with her parents' lack of interest in appropriate clothing. Something I felt sure she would be scarred by for years. He rightly – I'm now able to concede, but let's be honest it's taken a while to get here – told me I was being ridiculous given that she was perfectly happy and they'd used the time to play on the slides instead of watching YouTube videos on how to do Elsa hair. Reflecting on this, with as close to objectivity as I can muster, my anger came from feeling that the adults would be pitying our daughter's lack of a hands-on mum to get the dress code right. Our daughter has, of course, never given any indication of having noticed.

However much the mother sees herself as driven and career minded, in difficult moments, that social judgement can fuel darker thoughts about 'how it should be' in some idealised sunny-day picture of parenting. Things like, 'I not only trashed my core strength to produce this family, but I also finance the whole shebang and, while he frolics over picnics in the park with my beautiful babies, I milk myself alone in a stationery cupboard.'

This brooding festers if the dad turns out not to be delivering the lifestyle of Boden ads, #blessedlife and so on. Coming home to find the lounge strewn like Glastonbury post-flood. Hearing on the grapevine that the children were hurled into holiday club late with crazy hair and the snots. Granny noticing an endless stream of orange dinners (beans, fish fingers, chips) and that none of her grandchildren are able to eat with cutlery. Him, compounding this shit-show of a performance by saying that, far from being grateful for all she is doing, he's bloody miserable and lonely.

The ticker-tape-of-mum

It may be this perceived risk to our status, or just conditioning, but one consequence of this extended feeling of responsibility is that few women – even those with partners who are at home full time – are able to switch off 'the ticker-tape-of-mum'. Otherwise known as the mental load of motherhood, or as a husband of one my friends puts it, 'her incredible domestic memory'. The interminable mental scroll of Things That Must Be Done: book dentist, book haircut, book jabs, buy more chicken nuggets; replace stamped-on recorder; RSVP Freddie robot party; buy Freddie talking robot; remove suspicious brown stains from hall carpet; invent names of sponsors for school walk form; attach own £20 to form; practise six times table; etc, etc. On and on, all through the day and night. There are few dads – at home or working elsewhere – who describe the anxious, rhino-stampede of parenting lists in quite the way that mums do.

The psychologist and writer Graham Music says: 'In our culture, females hold more worry/anxiety and males can protect themselves by being strong and "problem solving". Testosterone inures against worry and can act as an anti-depressant in its way'. Perhaps that's why I keep reading about taking testosterone as a way to counteract the impact of menopause: it's starting to make me wonder whether we should all start taking it sooner. A dad summed this up by talking about how both he and his wife work full time with three children. 'Thinking about what needs to be done for all the kids is a big job. Maybe that's the really big job and that's what Natalie does.... Natalie does all the planning for the family.' So one full-time job plus another big job on top for Natalie.

And it's not just the thinking. An Office for National Statistics report, based on 2017 data, shows that men spend six hours and nine minutes on leisure time each day, compared with five hours and 29 minutes for women — meaning an extra 243 hours with their feet up each year. This is compounded by the fact women breadwinners seem to be more likely to also take on responsibility for financial management, so worries about paying bills, budgeting, saving and pension planning can be added to the ticker tape. If you scale this up you can end up with her 'playing the full Victorian husband': moaning he spends all day drinking flat whites, doesn't fold the laundry the Marie Kondo way and that the avocadoes are hard while he sulks that she's drinking Chablis at another business dinner in a fancy restaurant.

There is a final nuance to this, which is that some dads can seek to reclaim the ticker tape by celebrating their own expertise and repainting the moron theme around the mother. 'The sparkle shoes don't fit her any more,' he sighs as she tries to buckle them on. 'Why did you take them out in the torrential rain?' he rolls his eyes and winks conspiratorially at the oldest child. 'Don't worry, I'll put him to bed,

I know just how to get him down' he says, as she feels the sting of failure. Often compounded by the child responding to the tension and its mother's absence by howling for daddy when he or she falls over, pushing mummy away or hiding when she arrives home at the end of the day. This can feed into a cycle of mums becoming less connected with their children and retreating further into work, where they often feel more competent. But also more judged.

Disconnecting

Couples disconnect when they stop relating to the other's situation. An actor, who put his career on hold to raise three kids, explains how the power imbalance he feels plays out on a day-to-day basis: 'The tension points with my wife were around my ego. I felt I was being treated as the person who did the chores. A day with a toddler is long and boring and mundane. You need your partner to come home and be present and take over the chores and the mundane stuff because your head is exploding by then. That first half an hour when they get home is really critical to how it works. Or doesn't.'

But hear a mother's take of the same scenario: 'When I am at the office I never stop, not for a second. I leave the house at 8.30 and get home at 6.30 and am never alone in that time – even travelling and commuting I am on the phone all the time. When I come through the door he hands me the baby because he's tired and needs space and I've not been with her. It feels totally, utterly overwhelming.'

One mum with a stay-at-home partner and three kids was exasperated to find him cooking elaborate family dinners every evening. She crashed through the door embattled after a 12-hour day and saw him as hiding in the kitchen while she climbed into the warzone of bedtime. He'd say, with a sulphurous edge, that he thought the children would like to see their mother given she'd been out all day.

She'd accuse him of hiding in his Madhur Jaffrey curry. It's not hard to picture a testy dinner and too much weekday wine in that house. To be fair to the dads in this scenario, a stay-at-home mum friend laughs at this description and says she does exactly the same to her banker husband. And then reflects that her own mother handed her dad a large whisky and soda as he walked through the door at the end of the day to help him transition into the home zone. Such an awareness of the need for that shift isn't something that had occurred to her before, just as it hasn't occurred to Matt.

Disconnection can start small and grow and then become destructive. 'I was afraid we were losing sight of our marriage,' said one mum who, off-the-record, slated her stay-at-home husband's pitiful attempts at housework. One said she and her husband 'saw things differently': she had a big job but still did everything possible in order to get to do school drop-off and pick-up when she could. He said she did that for her own reasons, to see her friends. Over drinks a month later she said she'd married the wrong man. Six months after that she'd left him for someone else.

One divorced mother who had previously had an at-home partner described the marriage downfall as caused by 'living in different worlds'. She realised much later that she'd been glossing over the pissing, punching and picking-up of his life at home with small children. Equally he wasn't interested in what the CFO said to the client about what went wrong in July's billings.

Online

If there is one recurring point of conflict between alpha and beta parents it is their online behaviour. The actor dad says it's his wife coming home and remaining totally connected to work that made him crazy.

A dad who runs a business at home and has four kids describes his wife's online engagement and its impact like this:

'My wife typically checks her phone the minute she wakes up. I'm up first in our house, so I get her and kids up in good time to get out of the house. If she's busy at work, in essence she's in work mode as soon as she is awake. Usually, I'm getting the kids ready and she's getting herself ready (she often drops our eldest at school on her way to work). During this time, the only conversation is about the pressing issue on email. That could be someone has done something stupid/ evil, or she has had some new and unexpected task dumped on her. We – me and the kids – carry on with our breakfast routine as best we can until they're out the door or the nanny arrives to take over the rest of the children. My eldest often complains that her mother talks more about the people at work than family members or indeed us. "She only cares what Harriet, Mark and John say," she complains. I say: "That's not the case. Your mother cares about what you have to say and is very interested in hearing your stories." I get a roll of the eyes. Once the nanny is ready to leave in the evening, everyone wants to know "Where's mummy?" Often she's late. Not by much, 20 minutes is quite frequent; rarely more. But the children want to see her and become agitated if she's not around. I'll be dealing with them in the crucial pre- bed phase, trying to calm things down. Once mum walks through the door, excitement levels go through the roof; the more so, the later she is. This leads to late bedtime, no grown-up evening/quality time, and sleepy kids in the morning. Often she'll work in the evenings, catching up on email or working on a presentation. Often, she'll ask me to review it, which I do. She doesn't always realise that I have worked a full day as well. The fact that I work from home sometimes translates into: "He'll be available for pick-up/drop-off/plumber/etc duties". To be fair, she won't commit me to things without asking. But she does expect me to handle anything that happens during the working day if it relates to the house or the children.'

Another says: 'I go to bed and she's on her phone, I fall asleep and she's on her phone, I wake at 6am and she's on her phone. We went on holiday recently and she was on her phone for two or three hours every morning, all the way through breakfast with the kids, and it annoyed me but I didn't say anything. I get she has to work but I also want to have some family time.'

Social capital

Dads being the lead parent can also hit a family's social capital: its access to useful networks that help it flourish locally. As discussed in previous chapters, some working mums don't establish good friendship networks in their local areas. Those who have partners who are more based at home often assume that they will also step into this breach. 'I left it to him. He knew all the mums and I didn't have a clue,' said a mum. The problem is that this largely doesn't seem to work in the way they hope it might.

An at-home dad puts it like this:

'School gossip drives me demented. It feels like a download of information that's not interesting or relevant, it is narcissistic at times. I actively select not to be part of it. It's not the information that's useful it's the relationship building…. As a dad you're not part of the coffee mornings and the park runs – or the ubiquitous leggings. If there is a playground hierarchy I reckon it goes: mums first, nannies second, au pairs third, at-home dads last. Dads in suits have a bubble of their own, they make sense to everyone. I think if you don't have a suit people wonder about your purpose although it's better now than it was 10 years ago'.

Another dad says: 'Socially you are in a different group to the mums. What I notice is that women get together *just* to talk. Men meet to *do something* – *watch* cricket or *play* football or *walk*. Even when I was invited over by the mums – which I often wasn't – I would get there and realise it wasn't where I wanted to be.'

To his point about exclusion, a lawyer I interviewed was invited to a 'mum dinner' and asked if her husband could go in her place because he was the one at the gate every day. The mums doing the inviting said no and she thought they were extremely rude – akin to the men at her work going to golf and not inviting female colleagues, which would be deemed unacceptable. But when I played this scenario out with my school mum friends they shrieked in horror and said that my husband Chris was *never* invited to a mum dinner. Even though they do really like him, yada, yada, yada.

I was told recently about a male headteacher making a light gag about mums gossiping at the school gate. The mum who told me was struck that he places a low value on the information exchanged daily right in front of his nose, which many mothers find valuable. At any drop-off or pick-up there are a hundred, two hundred, a thousand conversations going on around the school. 'A bloke's been picked up for taking pictures in the park, be careful.' 'The street dance moves for the show are on YouTube so you can practise at home.' 'There's a diving club opening, you have to sign up on Facebook or you won't get a place.' 'Tom's mum found a lump, we need to invite the boys on play dates.' 'She is the best maths tutor in the area but she only works Tuesdays.' 'Miss Beverly is pregnant, we're getting a supply teacher … wait, who do we think the father is…?'

The school gate is a true matriarchy. These conversations – to that head's point – are either terrifying tittle-tattle (one mum calls it the 'tyranny of the playground') or the very stuff life is made of. But even those who hate them tend to sign up to the WhatsApp groups and keep an eye on the chatter. A friend who moved 100 miles away months ago confesses she is still signed in with her old groups so she knows what's going on.

But when I ask my husband what he does when he drops our kids at school he is immediately on his guard, suspecting he has done something wrong: 'Wave them through the gate and get on with my day...', he is wondering what I might be gunning for. Who do you talk to, I ask? 'The kids.' Anyone else? 'No....' If he were part of any parental social media groups (which he would go to some trouble to avoid) he would never bother to read them anyway.

To this end, a dad recently told me about the setting up of a Reception WhatsApp group for his daughter's class. The group was called 'Reception Mums' and all were invited to join. There initially was very positive celebration of the group's creation until one mum asked if there was a reason why dads were not invited because her husband Graham was interested and had asked her what the group was for. 'Dads are absolutely welcome' came the hasty reply, and, as Graham was added, the mums in the group fell over themselves to welcome Graham and any other dads who wanted to join, to talk about the importance of dads in today's society and to explore the many benefits of the group. From invitations to events, reminders of book change day, help with homework, calls from the PTA for volunteers, finding lost cardigans and updating each other on the changing school lunch policies. Some 150 messages later – all within two hours of the group being formed – and a Blue Line appeared in the chat: 'Graham left.' They still laugh about it while I reflect on what it tells us about how men and women choose to communicate.

I often see a group of dads leave our school gate, put in their headphones and get on the train, standing in the same carriage in amiable silence all the way to work. Their partners, in the same scenario, talk all the way to town and are still talking on the platform of the station when the train behind ours pulls in and we dash off late for work (usually still having to send a few WhatsApps during the day too).

For lots of women, this is an exchange of social currency. Useful pieces of information that build supportive networks and help you make good decisions about everything. At a recent post-drop-off Friday brunch, a bunch of mums attached to various toddlers and babies covered a review of the best secondary schools, a PE teacher's managing of boys (and how he looks in shorts), special needs provision at the school, development stages, dyslexia and the Zara sale. Throw in some breastfeeding and our parental social groups can be as gender separate as they have been for hundreds of years, locked within their own networks of information.

David Willans, who set up the blog *Being Dads: for dads who want to be better*, agrees:

'My experience is that mums chat really easily at the gate and tend to have the main relationship with other parents where a lot of dads stand back. I wonder if it's because the mums make strong relationships on maternity leave and most dads still don't do it – maybe it'll change if more dads take up shared parental leave.

'My conversation with other mums and dads is more about hearing how their family's doing and having a bit of a laugh, rather than gossip about the school or the local area. As soon as the kids come out I'm focused on talking to them, more than the other parents because it's my kids I really want to connect with. That's not to say dads don't talk about issues to do with their kids, it just doesn't seem to come as naturally. I think it's changing though, very slowly. There's a group on Facebook called The Dad Network where dads do ask each other questions about being a parent and kids, but it's not something you see translated into the real world much.'

Another dad said: 'I'll think I've done really well: picked up the kids on time, checked they have their clobber and got everyone home only to realise I've screwed up because I can't answer my wife's question about why so-and-so got thrown out of choir. If it was up to me, I might talk to other dads about football or cars but nothing more.'

While some of these examples are trivial, not all are. A working mother told me that she found out too late that all the kids in her daughter's class were being privately tutored for the local grammar school's entrance exams. She asked a couple of mums she knew a little whether people were hiring extra help and they had denied it. She found out the truth much later when she bumped into a tutor leaving a house and was furious that her children were disadvantaged by her exclusion from this information.

Another mum I talked to runs her own small business. Her husband works part time so he can take primary care of their school-age daughter. To their surprise, their daughter did poorly in her SATs at age seven. They went to see her teacher to understand what was going wrong and said, slightly crossly, that they had no idea the test was happening. The teacher was taken aback, explaining that parents had been talking about pretty much nothing else for the last two months. They had been working through books and revising grammar to help their kids do well. Hence her child falling behind. The mother knew nothing of this because she never did the school run. Her husband did and he was defensive: his job was to get the child to school and collect her, not to chat up the bloody mothers.

'Chatting up' the mums is, of course, the below-the-water bit of this iceberg. Some men *are* happy to mingle at the gate yet still find they're not invited to the coffee morning at Kelly's house, the park run after drop-off or margarita night. Even more subtly, their kids may not be invited to as many social occasions. Because, especially when kids are small, women arrange play dates to meet their own social needs. They invite their friends out and the kids fit around what they want to do. A child most visibly connected to a dad may miss out on some of these occasions – unless the mum has tapped into social groups in other ways. This doesn't happen because the women are total bitches, but because they don't want to be seen to be hitting on anyone else's partner. This exclusion can make life harder for dads. One who stays at home with three kids told me about the anxiety he feels as eight weeks of summer holiday looms. He knows the mum networks organise days out to the beach and swap kids regularly. Not being part of that network, he has to plan things independently for all three kids every day.

One dad compared the exclusion he feels at the school gate to his late teens when he had a series of gay relationships and felt pushed out of groups of straight men talking about women. 'It's the same at a gate. I like talking to the mums but I know I'm on the outside of their world and will never be one of them.' The former editor of *Loaded*, Martin Daubney, summed all this up brilliantly in an article about his six months as a stay-at-home dad, which left him isolated, depressed and concerned about his status. It was very bad for his marriage and after the final snub of being asked to leave a toddler group so someone could breastfeed he went home and immediately booked their son a place in nursery. Anecdotally, lawyers also say that being a stay-at-home dad is a risk factor in divorces.

Now I get push-back on this point: people say it's old-fashioned stereotyping and we all ought to grow up. Quite right. But is it ever that simple?

So what does work?

At the heart of the challenge here is the crisis of masculinity explored so engagingly by artist Grayson Perry. The men who are happy at home are those who are at ease with not being 'the family provider'. Where that confidence or self-assurance comes from is hard to say, but Karen, the relationship therapist, says they need to have their own 'thing' that they own and are positive about.

A clear role

Which is why dads who run small business or freelance on an ad-hoc basis – even if they don't contribute a huge amount financially – often seem to do better than those who devote themselves to being at home full time over a long period. For example, one dad I interviewed teaches IT skills in the community locally while parking his youngest with a relative for a few hours. He likes contributing to their community and is well connected as a result. Another is making over the house and putting his DIY skills to good use around the kids' activities. He doesn't get as much done as he would like but says that, as he wasn't enjoying his job before, this way he can make a big contribution by making them a nice home that will, he hopes, also increase in value.

The key thing seems to be to have an answer to the 'what do you do' question that you are 100 per cent comfortable with, so that you are never socially diminished by a fear of being judged. One who didn't work when he was at home says he wishes he had found a part-time job when the kids went to school, to keep his brain engaged and himself out and about. Instead, he took up golf (mostly with retired men, but he gets on with them), bought a dog who makes him really happy and gives him a routine, and took up leading the local Scout group, enjoying teaching modern kids the stuff he did as a kid (cooking on fires, night hikes and building catapults).

A deal

To make it work well depends on her *wanting* to be at work and him *wanting* to be at home. She will appreciate what he does and he will appreciate what she does. But if he is staying a home not because he wants to but because there really isn't a good alternative, it may not work out as you hope. In this situation, even if the money is a car crash – i.e. you are losing money by him working and paying for childcare – it may make long-term financial sense to do that if you can because staying in work increases your chances of promotions and pay rises and contributions towards your pension that do, in the end, work out beneficial. In America a website has been built to help families make financial decisions about work over the long rather than short term. Michael Madowitz, an economist at the Center for American Progress (which calls itself a progressive research and advocacy organisation) says families often forget the long-term picture when making these calculations. So he developed a calculator that does just that. Although it's not based on the UK system, it stands to reason that the disadvantages would be comparable, even before you consider the impact of a parent being at home with a child who hates the experience and is clamouring to get out to work.

The main thing at the core of making being the lead-carer father a happy experience is for both of you to actively support what the other does. He needs to enable your job and success and not be pissed off that it includes working late or travel or evening socialising. A dad says: 'It works for us because I put no pressure on her during the week. If she's late or has to go away for work, to be honest, it doesn't make a huge amount of difference to me. I operate like we have a one-parent family and put no expectations on her while she's working. That's our deal and I don't mind.' Equally, his wife accepts that he makes most of the decisions without her involvement. She can't come in later and decide that actually the child can't give up the guitar or sign up for the French exchange. You also have to appreciate what he does at home even if it isn't the way you would like it to be done.

Within this there also has to be clarity about who does what. One working mum said that when her husband first took a career break to look after their kids she would still try to make the lunch boxes. He stopped her, saying 'This is my job now, you have to let me do it or I'll never be in control'. Mutual expectations also need be in line with what your partner can realistically do. Just as we know that the wildly creative colleague at work is bound to be rubbish at process, there's no point in expecting your partner to do French plaits, pack lip balm on freezing days or check the kids are drinking enough water if his brain doesn't work that way.

This agreement also has to include how the ticker tape of things that must be done is organised. In many cases the working mum still carries a lot of it: 'I'm at my office booking clubs, doing a supermarket order and signing a consent form for a camping trip.' As long as she is happy running that list then it can work well this way. Others split between them. A dad explains: 'I hold in my head all their clubs and parties and play dates and sport fixtures and consent forms but she – and we never talked about this – does healthcare. I think it's because she cares more than I do. I'm a bit ambivalent about teeth and see fewer visits to medical people as a good thing.' It is unusual for the dad to carry the whole ticker tape but some report that they do. The question is always whether the mum agrees with that: some do and others, even when he thinks he is doing everything, say that he missed a lot of things from it that she still thinks are important.

One mum who went away for work for a week was astonished to come home and find only one uniform per child in the washing. Their dad had told them to wear the same stuff every day, including socks. He made exceptions only for pants and vests. She can't decide if this is genius or madness but has come back to changing their outfits every day. Her ticker tape includes a lot of washing and ironing.... The question she now faces is whether she could reduce her own load by not changing their uniforms daily, even though that's what she prefers to do. She is undecided. But it seems one partner being away is a trigger for greater awareness. An at-home dad said he feels validated when the house tumbles into utter carnage when he goes away for a few days. He gets home to find school bags, coats, shoes, half-eaten lunches and scattered laundry leading through the house from the front door to the back. Suddenly his wife and kids notice how much he does by dint of the house falling apart without him being there.

Friends

The next important factor is for the family to build their own networks of friends and supporters. Some working mums focus on this during their maternity leave and it serves the whole family well after they return to work. When the mum has stable relationships with female friends, it seems dads (or at least the kids) are more likely to get included in activities. Especially if the whole family connect at weekends.

Dads also need their own crew, though.

'Raising kids as a dad can be a lonely job at times. At the school gate, some mums just don't interact with you at all. Even if their kid is playing with yours they won't say "hi" and will take their kid home without saying "goodbye", without any interaction. But there are some lovely mums who cross the line. The sports groups offer networks than can be easier to access as a dad – football for example. For me, having local friends from university has been a saviour. That's our social network although the kids are at different schools. That has saved me from accepting play dates to facilitate social interaction. I think our kids are happiest on the common with each other and me and no one else, rather than at a slightly anxious social encounter. I just think "does it fit with our schedule?" and make a decision based on that.'

Others have found networks through local sports, clubs or just by meeting other dads around and about, and have found the groups to be supportive.

Advantages

When you ask lead-parent dads about the benefits of doing it this way, they are enthusiastic. They say things are improving all the time as more dads do it. That it has helped them to grow up and enjoy their kids more, especially keeping them well connected to girls as they become teens. 'I walk my 14-year-old to the bus stop every day and it's the joy of my life. I don't really speak – she updates me on everything that's happening. She says: "You remember what happened on Monday, well this is what happened next...". You have to find those moments. They really matter.' This is different to what they see some other dads experiencing. It has also opened their kids up to different activities. I notice that when dads are at home more, parents often report that girls seem to do more sports and – often – develop more interests that we have traditionally thought of as masculine. A mum who agrees with this says: 'Before he took over I'd have told you my girls would, like me, have focused on history and languages. But seven years later, I have one applying for chemical engineering and one at university studying computer science. They both also played football competitively throughout secondary school.' A teacher says she notices this trend from early on: even from Reception, girls raised by dads tend to have better gross motor skills (catching, kicking, climbing, etc).

The good news is that if you both want it and can keep connected to each other – taking some time out to do things together, seeing each other's perspectives and enjoying your life with the kids – Scandi 'papaland' can work brilliantly. A dad who spent his time with the kids when they were small says it's the best thing he ever did. 'I attribute the really strong connection I've kept with my children to those hours. It wasn't "quality time", it was just being together, rubbing along, annoying each other and pottering through the mundane, which has served us really well.' Now they are grown up, he's completely positive about that time and says it's why they remain so close.

One cites an additional bonus: 'The mums expect you to be useless and are mildly surprised if you are competent. They are amazed, for example, if you bake a cake for the sale. But in 12 years as an at-home dad I've never been asked to join the PTA or be class rep….' There are a few mums who envy that achievement.

If you're too tired and wired to read the above

- If we want dads to stay home, we have to celebrate what they do and support their success. And we're more likely to do better if we're honest about the challenges of doing it this way round.
- It's best not to idealise spending your days in the filth and anarchy of small children. Equally, don't demonise being out at work. Both have considerable capacity to suck.
- Try not to walk in at the end of the day and say 'the house is a mess' (applies to both parents, whatever the roles).
- The father *needs to want to be at home* for it to work and feel he has useful skills for the role. Where it goes wrong is when he gets bounced into it and feels not very inclined or well suited to it. Keep in mind that this may not be an indefinite arrangement: it might last a few months or a few years; it doesn't have to be forever.
- The mother *needs to want to be the one working*. If she is happy at work the arrangement can work brilliantly. If she is battling

out of the house every day dreading her job it can breed real resentment.

- You have to value and boost each other to make it fly: actively appreciating what the other is providing to family life and accepting that it's a bit harder this way round because others still don't get it and role models are hard to find. Playing either 'moron wife' role or 'long-suffering Victorian husband moaning about the price of nappies' are both shit looks. Stop it. You have to be mutually appreciative.

- You have to take the time to connect. That transition time as you come through the door is really important. Turn off your phone and say hello. Agree that he won't throw the kids straight at you and run away. Have at least half an hour to overlap and catch up. And still take adult time out to do stuff together and separately. Just because you've been at work all day doesn't mean you shouldn't go to a class later or that he shouldn't go and see a film on his own or vice versa.

- If you're at work, don't even hope that the circus at home will be run to your specification. He'll do it his way and that has to be OK. Even if he does buy the most expensive bin bags in the world and lets the kids eat cheese on toast with ketchup every night of the week.

- Finding some kind of acceptance that the ticker tape in your head isn't going away, whatever he does, helps. Write the list, practise yoga breathing and try to sleep. Don't turn on your phone and don't hate him because your mind works that way.

- Men don't gossip in the same way as women and can't/don't usually replicate social networks for you. If you assume they will, you may end up lonely and out of the loop. But if both of you can use the time you do have to make friends and dads get engaged in local activities – running a club, providing some sort of training or doing some sort of volunteering – they may find it easier to build connections and feel more valued. A local part-time job may also help.

- Have a financial plan. Otherwise you may feel that your job is to constantly pump money in the tank and his job is to constantly spend it. Be fair about this: him paying for the weekly shop isn't him boozing on the town of a Friday night.
- If it doesn't work the way you have it, change it or risk trashing the stuff that really matters: your relationships with your partner and kids.

What happened next?

MATT NEEDED TO GO back to work. With a drive fuelled by three years at home, he drew up a business plan to get his personal training business off the ground. Starting small and working with a local childminder he was able to build up a stable client base and justify being out for chunks of the day.

As a result, he and Joanna renegotiated their household deal. With him now bringing in some money she is more relaxed about doing the shopping and cooking dinner. The childminder is great at getting the kids out and about and doing more activities. She has also helped Joanna to connect with some other families with kids of matching ages.

Matt and Joanna have agreed a goal for them to be able to afford for her to work four days a week for one year before their youngest starts school. Both are optimistic they can achieve it.

CHAPTER NINE

The alpha/alpha couples

I HAVE THREE KIDS aged five, 10 and 15, my husband Simon is on the board of an IT company and I work for a law firm. I'm not a partner and not client-facing, I do marketing and new business. My boss, the managing partner, is demanding, the grads call her 'the hatchet-faced bitch' because of her piercing stare. She never talks about her personal life and we assume she doesn't have one.

All our kids are in private school and we have a nanny, a cleaning lady, a gardener and a daily dog walker. I know that that is a lot of help and we're lucky to have it, but it's also a lot to deal with and Simon says he supports me but in truth he doesn't notice, much less sort out a broken dishwasher or an unreliable gardener.

I've always said that I'm a 'Type-A people pleaser'. I want to do exceptional work and be the go-to person on everything. I've never set boundaries – over email or travel or hours – and see maxing out my air miles as a mark of achievement. I've somehow turned working remotely on myself – doing a shortish day in the office, going home for the kids' dinner and working until 1 or 2am at home and drinking a glass or three of Sancerre to calm down. I'm always on – I sleep with my phone by my bed and answer emails late into the night and during holidays partly because, if I don't, my boss will usually call within 15 minutes after not getting a response. Pretty much all my validation comes through work, my life is always a crescendo, never a diminuendo.

But recently the wheels have been wobbling. I organised a worldwide strategy meeting in Chicago that meant I didn't see daylight all week as I was working in a huge hotel complex. Increasingly anxious and paranoid, I ran a bath during lunch and breaks and hid in it. I slept worse than usual, despite using a mindfulness app, which I've now given up on. A number of things didn't go to plan and I can't stop endlessly replaying what I should have done to get it right. I've started watching a more junior member of my team who seems more detached and wondering whether some of the partners prefer to deal with her.

I would say that my life focus is three-quarters dedicated to work and one quarter to my kids, husband and home. We're always multitasking – but I'm famous for it, emailing in supermarkets while shopping. I don't have time to return the trolley after the shop so abandon it with the money in. Recently, when I was waiting for a meeting to start, I got chatting to the caterer, who told me that she was taking the next day off because it was her daughter's birthday. I realised that such an idea had never occurred to me, even though two of our children have birthdays out of term time.

I've become more and more prone to flying off the handle with the kids and recently struggled to list all of our daughter's GCSE subjects. I also find it hard to control their behaviour: sometimes observing them like they are strangers in our house. Sometimes I admit that I don't even like the company of the older two very much, while somehow still craving them. This craving leads me to try intermittently to connect with them but it often ends badly. Last weekend I booked a day out with my son but ended up furious because he complained bitterly that he missed a clip-and-climb trip with his friends and I blew up at him for being ungrateful.

I'm wondering how to escape this cycle before I have a proper breakdown and before our youngest becomes detached from me too.

Jane, 47, Marketing

****

When thinking about this book, I asked my mother to convene a group of her friends, who are retired with grown-up children and grandchildren, for what I called a 'grandmothers' focus group'. I asked them what had changed since they had kids. They were enthusiastic: 'Your generation is so lucky, you have maternity pay, paternity pay, flexible working, job shares and your men do so much more than the ones in our generation ever did.' I asked if they thought we were any happier for these changes, at which point their enthusiasm deflated. They thought not. In fact, they reflected, their daughters and daughters-in-law are more stressed and under more financial pressure than they felt with their kids.

We explored why and much of it came down to expectations. They were brought up to expect to be the primary parent, mostly based at home. While that could be frustrating at times, they broadly accepted it was a logical way to organise life since their husbands earned more than they did. That said, they all did some work outside of the home, as teachers or bookkeepers or administrators. Between them they also took lodgers, did tutoring and made curtains to contribute to the household finances but always saw their main responsibility as being the home and kids.

One of my mother's friends said she once went for the headship at her school but, after the interview, on her drive home, reflected that it was a mistake. Of course she couldn't combine leading a school with raising her children and running their house, what had she been thinking? When they called to say she hadn't got it she was relieved and vowed never to go for a headship again – which she never did. It struck me that she'd have made a brilliant head – she's articulate, fun and deeply sensible – and had she been born 30 years later I doubt she would have made the same decision.

The grandmothers of my focus group lived in bigger houses than many similarly middle-class families do now because mortgages were still calculated on one salary and were – by modern standards – affordable. But they didn't renovate or heat them much, they largely holidayed in the UK, they didn't drink wine at home except on special occasions and certainly didn't chuck cash at pre-packaged lunch snacks made of squashed dried fruit. They also didn't spend much time on electronic devices. They had a TV and radio that were both expected to last a decade or more. This was in the era when using the phone before 6pm (when premium day rates ended), was worthy of discussion. My grandmother used to answer calls in the daytime with 'Why are you calling NOW?'

Jane and Simon live on another planet to the grandmothers' with their 'alpha/alpha' partnership in which they both have big, time-consuming and mentally draining jobs. The alpha description isn't to suggest that Jane has a domineering personality – she is quite gently spoken, if also singularly determined. Their dual career track gives them the benefit of a great income and social status but also very high levels of stress and low levels of connection with their children or each other.

Jane could hardly bear to tell me at first but later she confessed that her son was so badly bullied when he started secondary school that he didn't attend on some days. She didn't notice and was only alerted to the problem when the school got in touch and the problems all came out. She thought her husband was more engaged than she was. He thought she was on it. This really resonates with a child protection officer I spoke to (who trained as a social worker) who says that she worries about professional parents completely missing the cues their kids give them. She reflects on all the abuse and neglect she has seen and how often someone says 'I just didn't see it'. For her own children, it has given her a very heightened sense of how carefully you must listen to what they say, even when they don't have the words or emotional vocabulary to say anything very specific.

It's not surprising we miss these clues when you think about how people describe modern working patterns. A dad who works in media says:

'Fifteen, 20 years ago, I would probably have answered the question of how much I work with "around 50 hours a week plus at least three evenings out with clients". Today it is much harder to give any meaningful response since the boundaries between working and not are totally blurred by technology. I'm always "on" email at weekends and on holidays and any one of my team know they can get a response within an hour 24/7, 52 weeks of the year. I also travel a lot for work and in those weeks I'm with clients or our people from 8am breakfast through to dinner maybe for four days of a week. I'll then work from home on the Friday. So increasingly over the past 10 years I make less and less of a distinction between being "at work" and "at home".' For this man, who has always had an anchor parent based at home, this change in working pattern hasn't presented any great difficulties. Without another parent who is more 'on' at home though, it's crushing.

Both Jane and her husband are always, always on, day and night; home, office and holiday. Neither is ever really disconnected from a screen. This isn't unusual. Interviewing women in their 50s and 60s, I notice how they divide their working lives into two distinct phases. The first was when they worked long and hard and went home to be physically and mentally with their family. The second is now, when they work long and hard and go home and do a conference call, write a proposal or answer emails long into the night. Now there are jobs that remain protected from this kind of email intrusion, but in many, many professional jobs – from law to finance to marketing and for almost any form of consultancy – the rise of women in the workplace has coincided with a lengthening of the working day *and* an invasion of home life.

Of those people who check email out of the office, half say that it increases stress and overall 50 per cent of workers say they feel exhausted. It's not unusual to hear that the 'old' working day (from 9am until early evening) is dedicated to meetings and networking and conferences. The 'real' desk work gets done after 6pm and before 9am and at weekends. The kicker is that, in the grandmothers' era, when people assumed there would be a wife at home to run the household, the working day was so much shorter than it is now. If both parents are out working, there is *literally no time left* to do anything else. What makes it even worse for women is that they still tend to do the majority of tasks and carry the household ticker tape.

A full-time working mum whose partner works in the same sector says: 'Oh yes he is very supportive of my career and me working late but assumes I will organise EVERYTHING. So, if we're both at a work function I have to find and book and pay the babysitter. He doesn't get up in the night, he doesn't put the washing on and appears not to see the mess that he generates. So we both have big jobs but in reality I have two jobs, one of which he doesn't even seem to see.'

This way of working creates disadvantages for women: a mum who is head of sales at a cleaning company has one competitor who she is usually up against for new contracts. Let's call him Ben. They often meet at client sites. She says that Ben isn't that smart and doesn't listen closely enough to what clients need and that works for her because she often wins against him. But recently, three bids came up in the same week and he won the biggest. She got feedback from the client who chose him, which said: 'Look, he's just always available, I could really see how keen and committed he was'. She shrugs. 'Ben and I both have two kids about the same age. But the difference is that his wife is at home and, when there is a lot on, he can work from 6am until midnight without consequence. But I always – always – have to get home for the kids and take those hours out and it limits the amount of time I can work in the evening. However hard I try, I just can't keep up with that pace and trying to is killing me.'

It is this coincidence, of women establishing themselves as a powerful professional force at just the moment when the working day explodes into a black hole that preys on my mind when I think about workplace equality. Apparently, if a person falls into an actual black hole they get 'spaghettified', which would seem an appropriate description of how some of the women I spoke to feel. Because our way of working leaves no space to breathe or think or be present at home. And the competitive nature of workplaces means that if either parent chooses not to be engaged for these hours, they can lose status, through being perceived as less committed or shown to be less productive. A lawyer I spoke to, who achieved all of her annual targets in term of business wins and hours billed, was still failed by a new boss in her appraisal because she hadn't completed the marketing database showing her commitment to all the networking events and dinners that she was required to attend.

A mum of three who works at a tech company says that her enduring memory of her kids' early years is her on her Blackberry in the garden, negotiating a major round of redundancies while her three boys begged, banged and sobbed on the patio doors to get to her. She turned her back on them – walking towards the fence at the far end to ensure their increasing noise couldn't be heard in Seoul – and continued the call. The story might suggest that she's a cold-hearted bitch but, quite the reverse, she is someone who is very involved with her kids and tries to do the right thing. But, like Jane, at some point 'doing the right thing' became overly focused on work. So perhaps it's no great surprise that the 2014 report *Gender, Job Authority, and Depression* by T. Pudrovska and A. Karraker found that the more senior a woman is at work, the more likely she is to suffer from depression. The opposite is true of men: 'women with job authority [defined as control over others' work] exhibit more depressive symptoms than women without job authority, whereas men in authority positions are overall less depressed than men without job authority.' They attribute this difference partly to our expectations of gendered behaviour.

This picture also illustrates how the 'flexibility' promised by technology makes so many people prisoners to professional life. How often do you hear business leaders proudly claiming their support for flexibility because they 'let' women leave the office at 5pm to cook the family dinner and catch up the hours later. 'I don't mind when they do the work as long as they do it' they say, smiling at their generous spirit. As if the best solution that a modern society can come up with to support working families is to allow people to leave at a time that used to be the end of working day, take a 'break' as they corral children into meals, bath and bed, and then compensate for all that slacking off by working into the small hours.

It is not even a pattern that generates good results a work. An in-house lawyer who works for a drinks company confided that she despairs of the law firms she works with. She will call asking for their advice on a tricky subject at some point in the afternoon and they will promise to reflect on it and send her a memo, which she will use for a discussion with the board in the coming weeks. Even though the memo isn't urgent, she will frequently find it in her inbox at 9am the next day, which means someone, probably a junior, has worked late into the night putting it together. Someone senior has signed it off it first thing, perhaps on their commute to the office. She often reviews the document and is disappointed at the lack of real thought that seems to have gone into it, as it tells her what she mostly already knew. She wonders if the quality of the work she gets would be better if her request was processed over days rather than hours and given some clear-headed time for reflection and fresh thinking.

Meanwhile, a senior associate at a law firm rolls her eyes at being on the receiving end of this process. The partner she works for takes the request and delegates it just at the point she was hoping to leave to see her kids before bed. She either stays at the office and leaves her husband to take over from the nanny, or goes home and then resumes working late into the night. She has already been going for 12 hours and is tired and grumpy. The words and references come slowly. When she finally falls into bed with her brain fizzing, to sleep fitfully and anxiously, she finds her husband is irritated with her for leaving him to pick up all the kids' stuff after his own long day. She notes that in the same scenario in reverse, it wouldn't occur to her to be irritated or for him to imagine she would be. A few hours later a two-year-old wakes her and gets into her bed to wriggle about for a bit saying 'I didn't see you today mummy'. She is too exhausted to return him to his own bed and is in a dead sleep at 6am when her alarm goes off and she dispatches her son with an iPad laden with *Peppa Pig*. At which point her husband makes a doomed attempt to interest her in sex. She gets up feeling exhausted, drained and irritable, staggers past the overflowing washing basket and dishwasher that wasn't turned on the night before, and reads a stream of rushed amends from her partner before sending the memo to the client, who doesn't seem remotely grateful. And people ask why male partners at law firms outnumber women by more than four to one.

And this is before we delve into the real psychological impact of our addiction to our electronic devices. So much has been written about the impact of phones and iPads on our children – the iGeneration as some call them – who are so completely connected that they don't feel the need to go out. US data shows that they actually seem to grow up later than previous generations did as they date less, drink less, have sex later and are less motivated to learn to drive. Yet as parents we are also changed by our relationship with these devices, something that rather less is said about.

At a conference recently, there was a talk on the latest generation to enter the workforce and their technology habits. I was helping to run the event and asked the attendees – mostly in their 40s and 50s – if they were online 10 or more hours a day, whether they engaged with causes and people across countries and time zones, if they got most of their news from social media. The vast majority raised their hand for every question. By the definition we'd just heard, they were behaving in exactly the same way as their own children.

Just being with Jane you can see she is twitchily addicted to her phone. Hearing her, you get a strong impression that she and Simon largely live in their own worlds. Sure, they share a glass of wine sometimes and bitch about colleagues or things that go wrong, but they do little together, both lack hobbies or exercise, and they tend to spend time with the children alternately to be 'efficient'. Of an evening, they can be seen, sitting at home at different desks in different rooms, on their own devices, buzzing from their communications with people outside of their home and oblivious to each other. Partly what they do is work but both also check social media and intertwine chatting with friends and family with their tasks.

There is increasing commentary on how and why we're addicted to our phones – something we are all now more aware of. As expert on consumer psychology and behavioural design Nir Eyal explained in the *Guardian* recently: 'The technologies we use have turned into compulsions, if not fully fledged addictions, it's the impulse to check a message notification. It's the pull to visit YouTube, Facebook, or Twitter for just a few minutes, only to find yourself still tapping and scrolling an hour later.' None of this is an accident, he writes. It is all 'just as their designers intended'.

Technology-driven distracted-parenting is part of the reason Jane feels jealous of their nanny. She doesn't register that the nanny is fully present with the kids. She is not on her phone, she is with them; something neither of their parents regularly manage. Jane and Simon are not alone in this, and some schools have put up signs in playgrounds banning parents from using their phone at pick-up in the hope they might make eye contact and talk to their kids as they come out of school.

A mum of two who has since stepped down from a senior marketing role reflects how the buzz of work is all-important when you're in it: your colleagues, the politics, the product you are launching. Nothing said or done at home can compete with the rush of excitement and sense of priority. 'There is something quite sexy and glamorous about jetting off to different countries and being stimulated. But the kids don't connect with it. There is no one to share it with. You're like a child yourself, you want some acknowledgment. You lose perspective, it's a kind of hubris.'

She goes on:

'You know when you are ashamed of what you thought? I remember I flew in from India one morning and had to go straight to the school to see Poppy's teacher at 9am. In my head, I was thinking "aren't I great, getting off a plane and coming straight here". Like I was a hero! When actually I was a completely absent mother.

'The awful thing was that there was even an element of resentment within me for the time the kids demanded. I'd be doing a conference call on my mobile and would be really interested in the conversation – while dragging my eight-year-old round M&S and not having a conversation with her. Even though she was desperate for my attention.'

Another retired professional mother reflects on social problems her teenage son was having that escalated into exclusion from school and an incident with the police. He is back on track and at college but she deeply regrets not having given him the bandwidth he needed before things got really difficult.

Why do we do this?

It's obvious what has changed since the grandmothers' time: it is normal for both parents to work; paying the bills often depends on it; technology has enabled work to rampage through our home lives; and the ever-more competitive world of work demands better and better financial results. But, you still have to ask why we allow ourselves to live like this. I see three, perhaps four, reasons.

The first is that some of us are specifically hired for it. In *Leading Professionals: Power, Politics, and Prima Donnas* Professor Laura Empson explains that this dynamic is, for some firms at least, completely conscious and intentional. She has interviewed HR people at law firms, accounting firms and consultancies who say that they deliberately recruit 'insecure overachievers': people with stellar academic records who are motivated to prove themselves worthy but, in their hearts, will never be satisfied. Those hiring know these are the people who can be motivated to work extraordinarily hard through relatively simple psychological techniques.

They identify their targets though a review of their academic and social achievements and some psychological profiling, and then go to work to exploit these tendencies. First of all, they celebrate that being hired by their firm is a huge mark of achievement: they have joined an elite club. This is proved by salaries and benefits: starting salaries at top-end law firms are £60–70,000 a year or more. Health and social benefits will exceed what many of their peers dream of. They will be taken to fancy restaurants, specifically chosen because their parents will have heard of them: 'oh we had dinner at the Ivy last night mum' they say casually as they post a picture of themselves there on social media and resist the urge to steal a branded side plate. These signals will become the latest markers of their continued stream of successes (Grade 8 cello at 14, county-level hockey, starred As at A-levels, head girl or boy).

But these companies also operate highly competitive models where success is both measureable and public. How many hours you bill and how much business you are able to attract are your visible status symbols. Year after year your job is to keep these numbers high. At any point those who cannot compete are cast aside and those who remain live in a state of high anxiety about failing. If one in 14 (or even fewer, for some firms one in 20) entry-level lawyers will make partner, you have 13 colleagues you need to get ahead of before you start your battle in earnest to make it to retirement without being superseded by someone even more determined.

Insecure overachievers are particularly susceptible to this kind of social control, and many work to the point that it can become damaging to their own health and family lives. The city-based search expert sees this every day:

'The most difficult places for mothers I see are the professional service firms where performance is measured by time and billings (law firms, management consultancies, accountancy firms). Those organisations tend to have a partnership model, and that means the partners are co-owners of the firm and expect to make a lot of money. You get to partner level in your mid–late 30s or early 40s (the ideal window tends to be 35–40). In many firms if you reach 42 without having made partner, the chances are you won't make it at the firm you're at. Of course, this is the period when many women are having their kids and they often return wanting to work flexibly. The problem is that these are all-or-nothing jobs. Partners at the big law firms earn four times what a senior associate would earn (eg £1m to £250k) and if you're earning that kind of money you're doing the networking breakfasts, dinners and late-night deals. It isn't gender discrimination, it's the reality of commercial life at that level. It's a choice and if you're not up for those hours you might well be better off not going for partnership – lawyers can still have remunerative and interesting jobs going in-house for instance.'

What's intriguing – and what we'll come back to – is that Jane does have a sort of in-house job, albeit for a law firm. She doesn't have to win and retain clients. Yet she behaves as though she does.

The second reason is that we are trained to work that way. In workshops with professional women with children, I always explore their 'before kids' and 'after kids' life experience. Before kids, they (like their male peers) mostly worked insanely hard. They were competing to get ahead and, for many, that meant answering emails within minutes, taking calls at any hour, working nights and weekends if required (and even when, with better planning and less neurosis, it was completely avoidable). They were trained, as Pavlov's dog to the bell, to respond to the buzzes and beeps of their devices. Not only that but their social lives were based around work – Friday night out with the team was a regular feature. They often dated people at work and some ended up settling down with them. Outside interests, if they had them, tended to be focused: gym classes, weekly fixtures with a sports team or going to films. The point is that none of these activities are hugely time-consuming. They all fit neatly around work and tend to require going off grid for no more than an hour or two.

Yet some still refuse to do even that. A married 30-year-old management accountant told me she can't have a baby, even though her husband and in-laws are desperate for her to, because she works so hard that her back is killing her. When I asked why she didn't sort it out, she said she didn't have time for an exercise class or a chiropractor. She laughed it off like it was a perfectly normal thing to say, without leaving herself the space to consider she's living in unnecessary pain and putting off a family for the sake of working 70 hours a week.

This is a group of people who are firmly attached to their jobs. They – quite literally – rarely put them down in terms of not being on the end of an electronic device. Some do this for 10, 15, 20 years before they have a baby. I spoke to a woman of 46 planning to have her first baby last week: she will have worked for a quarter of a century – more than half of her life – in this wholly work-centric way.

So, when they have a baby, this is how both men and women are primed to work. Unless they consciously choose to change these patterns, this is how people keep working. Maternity leave can be a time of reflections and an adjustment but doesn't always alter anything; some barely take it and others return to exactly the ways of working they have always adopted. Jane remembers rocking a newborn on her knee as she typed. For her, having a baby wasn't allowed to be a distraction from work. Her self-worth depended on keeping going and that is what she did.

The third reason we work like this is that we are hardwired not to stop. As Michael Fishbein writes in his *Harvard Business Review* article 'If working less is so productive, why is it so hard?': 'Our brain's anxiety about survival and reproduction motivates us to work more even though it's not always in our best interest over the long-term.' He sees this as comparable to the way that our primitive brains unhelpfully still seek sugar even when food is not in short supply (and/or we are too fat to need it). In evolutionary terms, those who were anxious and worked hard to accumulate resources would have been more likely to survive a crisis than those who were more relaxed.

This rings true because Jane, like others, constantly reviews the options for change but discounts them as impossible in the short term for financial reasons – although she does have ideas for the 'just over the horizon' distance. Like the business unit boss at a huge global tech firm who said 'You can't put my name to this', looking over her shoulder in the café to check no one was listening, 'but I'm paying off the mortgage and pre-paying the school fees and then I'm out.' She plans to finish at 55 and throw herself into fund-raising and helping at the school to get closer to her kids' lives. She says she wants to spend time with her kids in their last few years at home before they head to college. As she says this, her voice cracks. Her children will be 17 and 15 by then. She will be reaching for their shadows and she knows it. Another woman's eyes fill with tears when she realises mid-conversation that retirement isn't so far off but that it is also the same year that her youngest son will leave home for college.

When I ask women like this, who admit they are not happy, why they can't change how they work now, they look at me in bewilderment. Despite some of these families being in the top 10 per cent of household incomes in the UK, they always say they can't afford not to work full time. Jane herself shakes her head sadly. 'My husband's biggest worry is that I'll cut back work' she says, 'because he says we need the money and he's right. £8k goes out of our household account every month just on school fees and the mortgage. Only the rich can work a four-day week.' On one level, you can see how she feels trapped but on another level this is clearly bonkers. Particularly as many of the changes Jane could immediately make wouldn't even reduce her salary. She could simply choose to use her holiday time, work less in the evening, limit her screen use, delegate more trips to her team and do some sort of exercise. And that's before she even starts on a bigger analysis of their holidays, housing and schooling.

But her sense of who she is won't allow it. It's a big mental leap: we justify working this hard because the family *needs* things (good education, holidays together, a house they can enjoy) but if we then decide that maybe they don't ... what the hell would the last 15 years have been about? Choosing to downsize these things would undermine the way they live and how they define achievements.

There is a fourth possible reason why we get into these cycles and it is the most depressing.

When I read the descriptions of insecure overachievers and what the search expert says about high-end firms and senior roles, I am struck that they seem to apply to most levels of professional jobs in most companies I've worked at. When I do workshops, or interview professional women in offices, the majority – at all levels and from companies that would describe themselves as 'elite' through to little start-ups – are staffed to a greater or lesser extent by people like Jane. Her engagement and anxiety are at the top end, but not unusual. Across business, her personality type tends to thrive. They meet needs fast and efficiently, they get a lot done, people like working with them and they do well. Companies hire for it (whether we are conscious of terms like 'insecure overachiever' or not), train for it, reward it and it's no wonder we continue doing it even when it no longer serves our needs well.

And the research does show that it's a terrible way to work long term: working sensible hours, taking regular breaks and disconnecting mentally are critical to making better decisions and performing better. In *The Way We're Working Isn't Working* Tony Schwartz, Catherine McCarthy, PhD and Jean Gomes explore how relentless work leads to emotional volatility, bad decision making and burnout.

Researchers at King's College London and Royal Holloway recently found that the most passionate workers are at risk of damaging their careers by failing to take time off and unwind. The study, published in the *Journal of Occupational Health Psychology*, looked a group of just under 200 priests (chosen because their work is a vocation) and found that those with the most intense calling tended to work longer hours and be less detached from work. This increased the risk of fatigue, which impacts negatively on performance, and other risky behaviours and, ironically, made them less good at their jobs over the long term.

What's more, leadership expert and executive coach Noomi Natan has written about how 'overgivers' in organisations are often exploited for their commitment and then, eventually, pushed out. The way she explains this is that, in any relationship, we are highly aware of the balance between what each side contributes and receives. If the employee gives too much, more than is good for them – time, energy, emotion – the employer becomes increasingly uncomfortable knowing that the debt cannot be repaid. How can an employer compensate for a broken marriage due to hard work, for example? The employer tends then to push away the employee as the 'debt' becomes a guilty burden. 'This of course happens completely unconsciously, but the impact is very real,' Noomi says. 'Organisations, like people, develop an awareness of whether the balance of exchange is fair.' I had not heard before about overgivers being pushed out but I recognised it as soon as I read it, and can see the pattern in people I've worked with over the years. There is nothing that their company can give them that would be enough, but they feel unable to resign and walk away because the company 'owes them' so much.

It seems like the grandmothers are right. We have more things and more options but many of us are less happy for it. Perhaps contentment comes from resetting our expectations of what a normal working day should look like and limiting the hours in which we use our phones. It certainly comes from ensuring that the division of tasks at home is in line with how we now work. Otherwise we risk ending up with the worst of the way our grandmothers lived and the worst of modern working practices.

If you're too tired and wired to read the above

- Work out what matters to you: at home, with your kids, in your relationship with your partner, with your family, and work – and your relationship with yourself. If you accept the boundaries others create, you may well be consumed by work. But if you take control you can get much more out of your life. And remember the old advice that, for everything you agree to do, *there must be something that you stop doing to make space for it*. That includes having children.

- Be clear with yourself and your kids about what your values are and what you're teaching by example. If it's hard work, then OK, but are there limits to that? Are there other things that matter? What do you want them to remember about their childhood?

- Take control of your whole schedule. In *Is Your Job Making You Ill?* Dr Ellie Cannon recommends scheduling everything in our lives in the same way we schedule work meetings. Put in social occasions, exercise, rest, playing with the kids and even colour code them so you can see the balance of your week before you start.

- Similarly, for holidays, start by thinking about how you want the holiday to play out for you and for your partner and kids. Is it total time off and you disconnect your work email from your phone? Is it important you are contactable and so agree that one person will get in touch if you need to step in? Or would you feel better if you checked in once a day? Whichever it is, make an active decision before you go and stick with it rather than tumbling into crises and finding yourself spending all day standing on the shallow steps of the pool on conference calls, hoping no one splashes your phone.

- At work more generally, make conscious decisions about what you are motivated by. Is it money, status, developing new skills, pleasing people, taking on new challenges, creativity? Probably a mixture. Take the time and space to review this properly. Get some distance, travel somewhere and disconnect, visit someone who lives differently, do nothing. When you're away from work – away from the addiction of goals, your priorities can quickly change. One woman I interviewed said: 'I went on a yoga holiday and thought "why the fuck am I doing this at work...?" and "if I don't want to be doing it, why do it for another day?" When you're "in it" it's toxic, addictive, gotta fix it, hit the goals, you're being reactive. When you're out of it, it can all look very different. I went home and changed everything and am so much happier now.'

- Read and process all the advice around about how to take control of things like emails/meetings. Tell people you only answer emails between certain times and stick to it. Or have one day where you have no meetings so you can think. Decide and do it. When you feel in charge, you do better. Watch the people you see doing this and copy them.

- A coach I once interviewed advised us to write an imaginary letter to someone important in your life from five years in the future that describes in very practical detail how your life looks. Where you wake up, who you are with, how you feel, what you do. 'Dear X... It's been a brilliant year.... As a family we.... At work, I....' Then work out how you did it, working backwards over the year. It's freeing for the brain to think it's looking back on something that's been achieved and then work out how to make it happen, rather than look at what seems to be an impossible mountain to climb. One person who did this said:

'In my case, years ago, I went freelance, worked out how much I'd like to make in a year, and that I'd like to work 150 days a year, and then what qualifications I might need to get to be able to justify that. I left my big job partly because it was a million miles away from the creative stuff I'd set out to do, and I realised I was drawn into helping other people achieve their goals, and because it was fixed and became dull. I then made a plan in achievable chunks over time – days, weeks, months, years. It's too easy to only live in the now and be reactive.'

- Draw a pie chart of your life and allocate sections according to what dominates your mind: work, partner, home life, kids, hobbies, exercise, friends etc. If you are not happy with what you see, don't ignore it, work out how to change it. In workshops, usually women are unhappy to see that more than two-thirds of their circle is dedicated to work and then realise there is no slice dedicated to 'me' at all.

- Be realistic about the balance of responsibility between you and your partner if you have one. If you are doing all of the housework and carrying all the mental load then what are you teaching your children about equality? What can you do to even that out? If you have the money you may need to be brutal about how much help you need, if you don't then sorting it out may be critical to you both being able to continue working at this pace.

- Consider that two alpha/alpha careers may not work indefinitely with kids. This doesn't mean you have to step back, but that one of you may need to *for some of the time*. Be constantly open to other ways of working: from home, changing hours, taking leave, alternating the pace so each of you has the 'lead' job at different times.

- To that end, spend time observing others negotiating what they want, getting themselves on to the right team and having the relationships that allow them to convince others they can work the way they want. An accountant was denied the right to work nine days over two weeks because it had to go through an approval committee that fundamentally disliked 'part-timers'. But her boss said she could work from home one day a week without any formal approval process. Given that what she wanted was to be at the school gate a few times a week this ended up working better for her.

- Read and act on the research that shows establishing clear boundaries at work will make you *more* successful. Reflecting later in their careers, some mums say they think they would have done better if they had exercised more discipline because they would have been better-respected and more able to think clearly. Review your own insecurity: if you know you are unhealthily motivated by self-doubt then consider addressing it. Read/explore ways to be more assertive.

- Don't neglect your partner. Karen Doherty, who does a lot of her work in 'affair recovery', says that these sorts of crises are often caused by ignoring the relationship, and they often happen at 'the point when one of the couple unconsciously loses their "love" for the other. Left untended this leads to resentment, unmet needs and potentially opens both of them up to interest from others outside of the relationship.' She advises seeking help from a therapist early on and not putting jobs before our relationships. She also cautions that our relationships inform how our children will manage their own romantic relationships later so we need to be aware of what we are unconsciously communicating about love and sex.

- Remember that professors Lynda Gratton and Andrew Scott argue in their book *The 100-Year Life* that many of us will live to be 100 years old. We have a lot of time and we can't all collapse in a heap at 50.

What happened next?

ONE DAY JANE JUST couldn't go in to work. She called in sick and, persuaded by her husband, went to the doctor who said she was burnt out and who wrote her off for two weeks. She used her first Out Of Office ever to tell people she was not answering emails or calls. Her doctor told her to read magazines and watch TV and do nothing else, so she did. Her doctor then extended her sick leave in small chunks for four months. Her feelings at this time reminded her of when she had postnatal depression – something she hadn't thought about in years.

She took the time during this break to sit down with Simon a few times to hammer out what they both need/want from life. Not just in terms of money, but what's going to make the rest of their lives rewarding. What's going to make them look back on their family life and say they did what they wanted, they passed on good values to their kids. During one of these conversations they realised that their kids are part of the same performance culture that is crushing them. They wanted to change for themselves and their children.

Also, while she was off, Jane was recommended a cognitive behavioural therapist (CBT) who helped her work out how to recreate happiness without work validation. She learned techniques to manage her stress triggers in different ways. She realised that she became very anxious if anyone questioned her work so she learned to be assertive rather than aggressive in response. She was taught to only focus on doing three things every day and to give herself time to think rather than just do.

She allowed herself to be connected by friends to other women in the same situation. Initially she found it shameful, because she thought she was admitting she had failed, but the other women helped her to see that the organisations they worked in drove these unsustainable and damaging behaviours.

After four months, she went back full time but works at home on average half of every week and manages her time very carefully. She has taken up a gym membership and either swims or works out every day to train for a triathlon. Now she says the pie-chart balance of her life looks like half work and an even split of the other half between her kids, husband, herself and her health and pleasure and doing things for others. She says she is calmer, more patient and far more engaged with the kids. The kids appreciate that she doesn't fly off the handle any more, and she now knows not just when GCSE exams start and finish but every exam, whether it's Maths A or Maths B today, what book each child is studying and who their friends are. She says that the only person who misses the old Jane is her husband, who's taken to teasing her about spending too much time with her personal trainer.

CHAPTER TEN

Solo

I USED TO BE head of maths at a secondary school, I was ambitious and hard-working and thought I would go on to be deputy head. But, after just five years of marriage it turned out that my husband wasn't with that plan and was having an affair with a younger woman at work. I was devastated. We had marriage guidance and it emerged that he was addicted to porn, sex, alcohol and gambling (yes, all of them). Having a nasty penchant for flogging dead horses, we tried mediation but it ended up in Financial Dispute Resolution and the divorce cost £30,000 (three times as much as our wedding). I found myself, aged 40, single and feeling both ashamed and alone with two very young boys to look after.

I tried to keep working as our relationship fell apart but it was impossible. I was doing a disservice to the children I was teaching and worse still, my boys were visibly suffering. I reluctantly resigned. In court, his lawyer argued that I could easily support the children financially if I went back to teaching. Thankfully the judge disagreed, saying it was obvious that the boys needed at least one of their parents to be available and it was clearly never going to be John. In this I was fortunate because he had to pay full child maintenance and spousal support until our youngest child started school. I have never been financially or materialistically motivated. Although I was not the 'Take him to the cleaners' type, I was pragmatic enough to understand that not having to worry about money would enable me to survive the collateral damage that divorce inflicts on a family. By not having to work, I could dedicate myself to the children and at that time they had to be my priority.

Once the divorce was settled, I decided to relocate our family closer to my sister which meant moving 200 miles up North. This meant a new start for me and the boys, which was important as we had been living in his home town and I wanted to be free of him, our shared past and further away from whatever he did next (which was to marry another younger woman – no, not the one he'd had an affair with, another one – and have babies with her).

The massive downside was that we all had to settle somewhere totally new. The whole process focused my mind on how responsible I was for the children. I went from juggling them alongside my job and everything else including my fucking feckless husband to putting the majority of my mental energy into them. It changed who I was, it changed my priorities, my outlook, everything. On reflection, I feel for the better. Before kids I thought I was tough. Now I know how vulnerable I am. Like my children, I wear my heart on my sleeve. Whatever happens to them, happens to me. I used to think my job was rewarding but it was nothing compared to being a full-time, single mother.

At first, I accepted that my career was the price I paid for ensuring their stability and I made it ok with myself that I was no longer 'employed'. But now they are in school I intend to get 'back out there' in every sense. I need something for myself and our financial stability. I feel like so much has been sacrificed and now it is time to make myself more of a priority, knowing I have given them the stable and secure base they need to be the best they can be.

Marianne, 46, teacher

****

Listening to mums retell the details of a relationship breakdown is like watching slow-motion fight scenes. They cite exact time and dates. The breaking point. The day they told the kids. The day one of them moved out. The day their friend took sides. They cry, they always cry. And they cry even if they were the ones who decided enough was enough.

Some, like Marianne, had to leave because they settled down with the wrong person: 'Because he hit our kids', another shrugs with resigned regret. For others, the wrongness is an emotional mismatch: 'He was needy and I met those needs. But when we had kids, I grew up and, as the kids became less dependent on me, I didn't want to give in to his emotions. I felt a lot more confident than I did before: more capable and stronger. I felt like the mother-lioness. He saw me being strong and independent and it wasn't what he signed up for. So we grew apart.' But the process was devastating: 'It was like being his possession. We would argue and argue and argue and then he would shut down and stop talking or disappear. Then I was the bad person. I was walking on eggshells. I lived for many years in a very heightened state of anxiety and became sick a lot in that time.'

Others are less sure that the end had to be and reflect quietly they would do everything differently if they did it again:

'I'd ban the emails in bed. The wine every night and the boxset and I'd sleep naked. It's just too easy to lose intimacy. If you're naked you don't have to have sex to feel that you connected in a special way. We stopped doing that. All that shit they say about date night? Yeah, we should have listened to that. Because it made it inevitable that, eventually, one of us would meet someone more exciting than a Scandi-noir.'

The alpha/alphas say they spent one or two nights a week each out at events related to work. The rest of the week was frantic and exhausted and left no time for their relationship. Inadvertently setting up a scenario when a third person can create chaos in what seems like moments. 'A moment of flirting, a drink in a bar and I'd stumbled into a crazy affair where the crash of our marriage was unavoidable. It happened before I'd properly thought it through.'

Whatever the scenario, when it ends, everyone suffers more than they expected. 'It's the crushing sense of a failure, for yourself, your kids and your friends and family.' And, for some, a feeling of wincing shame. 'I even feel shame about meeting the priest who married us because I feel I let him down. He had faith in us as a couple.' Another who fell for a man she knew professionally and left the father of her kids said: 'People who know what has happened know perfectly well I didn't put my kids' needs above my own. That hurts.' A therapist agrees with this: 'We have normalised leaving without fully understanding that causes havoc through immediate and extended families for decades to come.' She adds that: 'The adults eventually do move on, but it stays with the children forever. I reckon that nine out of the ten couples I see are in a high-conflict divorce. My main goal is to try and get them to work together but that takes both sides to want to.'

There are of course alternative paths to lone parenting: choosing to have a baby alone – or finding yourself alone through life experience, like being widowed. When asked, some solo mothers by choice say that they would rather have met the right person and had children within a couple, but others strongly reject this and are proud to have actively chosen to parent alone. Either way they had to choose to have kids alone if they wanted them. For many who come to this in their late 30s or early 40s, although challenging, this feels like a positive decision. Some relish the chance to select the father from an online service that allows them to choose the genetic characteristics they value. Others hate the bureaucratic process and prefer to pick someone they know. Whichever way the pregnancy is achieved, those who have been working too hard, over many years, to meet someone can have the advantage of bucking the trend of single mothers being hard up.

But whether you suffered the trauma of losing a relationship, or you left your partner or you accepted that if you wanted kids you would have to do it alone, you invariably find out that you have all the problems that couples do, but none of the support.

The challenges

Interviewing single parents, you cannot escape the fact that the unifying challenge they face is money. Marianne was awarded some by the courts and that helped a huge amount. My own mother didn't have it when her first husband left her and their two small children for someone else. She married again and raised me, her third child, with the words: 'You must always earn your own money so that when some bastard leaves you, you can support yourself and your children.' Because as she knows, for those who do it alone and struggle for money, it is a relentless, exhausting and bloody battle. And it's a very widespread problem: a study by the charity Gingerbread, as part of its Paying the Price project, suggests that 67 per cent of lone parent families are constantly struggling with their finances, and that one in 10 are not coping at all.

This is despite many seeking more work when, on account of the cost and inflexibility of childcare, even the most driven can be pushed off course. The brightest girl in my class at school got pregnant during her A-levels, married and had the baby, but had to decline a place at Oxford as a consequence. After they broke up she found a way to get a degree in French and got a place on a PGCE course as she hoped the structure of teaching would fit with raising her daughter. However, in the second week of the course they posted her to a work placement that was over an hour away, because she had a car. She had childcare during working hours in the day but not before and not after and, despite every effort, they wouldn't change her location and she had to leave the course.

Similarly, those widowed often face enormous challenges, a subject recently explored in depth by Sheryl Sandberg in *Option B*. A woman whose own dad died when she was 10 and who has seen others lose partners young says, 'You find you have to fight for life assurance to come through to be able to pay for your house (it took my friend three years); widow's allowance is now pitiful and restricted to a miniscule period of time; work becomes no longer a choice for most because you have to earn a living because you don't get the alimony you would if divorced; you have to face the prospect of raising the children and maintaining a household all on your own, and think through how to get help/support; how to move onto life after bereavement, to love after bereavement...'

Whatever the reasons for raising your children alone, many seem to reach a similar conclusion about finances: you can eventually thrive *if* you can afford it. The research supports this: lone parenting/family structures don't in themselves cause social problems for kids, but poverty does. One says: 'If you can afford to have a child alone, it's a better option than being in a bad relationship.' It's harder than doing it with a good partner, but they are quick to notice that a lot of other mothers have, in their other half, 'nothing but an extra child.' In fact, some single mothers say they are magnets for those women who are dissatisfied with their relationship and hear more than their fair share of relationship dramas. It's as though other women are looking for a safe place to sound out the possibility of doing it alone.

Money is such a factor that it may define how long we stay in relationships in the first place. Research shows that financial security among women may increase their propensity to push for divorce since they are less likely to tolerate their partners. Under the age of 45 more women ask for divorce than men, but this changes for older groups who are more likely to be financially dependent on the male partner.

By the time couples are in their 60s, Office for National Statistics figures show that in 2014, for example, 9,443 men began divorce proceedings compared to just 5,783 women.

What's more, if you are the more financially successful part of the couple – an alpha/beta dynamic – you may be at more at risk of a break-up. Research from the US suggests that successful professional women are more likely to be dissatisfied with lower-status partners. Especially if those men also fail to contribute to running the households.

The next big problem of lone parenting is the consequences of a difficult break-up. A high-conflict divorce, with the kids torn between warring parents, wreaks havoc on families and kids. A mum who had an amicable divorce but saw friends in different situations reflected on it like this: 'I'm proud that we seem to have got through it and kept things civilised. But I really understand how many people don't manage that. Because conflict is easier than sadness. It would feel easier to fall into fighting to distract you from the pain of everything else.'

Which is part of the reason why networks are even more important to solo parents. Speaking to a mum who is well supported by her ex and works in her community, I am struck by the security she demonstrates. Her parents come once a month, her ex takes the kids once a week, she has lots and lots of friends and interests. It's not perfect – when is it ever? – but she seems vastly happier with her lot in life than some of the married City-based mums I have interviewed over the years. In contrast, another single mum learned the error of her ways and advises others to: 'Work really hard to get in with the mums because if you don't your child suffers. It's not my strength as the sight of insider groups makes me run a mile. But I was too judgemental in hindsight and now realise the benefits and that you get out what you put in.'

Research from the European Society of Human Reproduction and Embryology supports this, concluding that the children of single mothers have no difference in outcomes than the children of heterosexual couples. It says that this may be because they tend to seek and have wider social networks.

Those without local networks struggle, especially in the school years. One who moved to join a new relationship is bereft of her old friends and support crew:

'There's bad traffic and I am literally running a raging sweat at the thought of my kids being last at the gate again. I don't have a bunch of people to call and pick them up for me and it breaks my heart to think of them being last at the gate with their teacher and wondering if I'm coming. My boyfriend is at work too and he doesn't see my kids as his primary responsibility so I couldn't even ask him to go.'

A solo mother by choice says that either her child is with her, or she is paying someone else to take him. 'If I go to the doctors, he comes, if I get a haircut, he comes, if I meet a friend … you get the idea.'

The psychological independence can be even more biting. A woman with a very intense medical job says:

'The hardest thing is to carry all the emotional stuff. It is so difficult because my ex and I don't communicate and I don't know what he is saying to the kids about school or any issues they are worried about. Sometimes there's a piece of me wondering who'll take care of me. I think "I'm sick of this. I want to be taken care of too". I always have to be on-the-ball, no matter how tired, stressed or hungover I am. I went on holiday with some older friends, while the kids were with their dad, to celebrate a birthday. I was the youngest there – and just out of a divorce so they took care of me – it was so wonderfully liberating for the first time in years not to be the responsible one in the house.'

This is compounded by a lack of time to replenish your own mental reserves. Whether a weekly swim, a one-on-one visit to their mum, a mooch around the shops or Friday-night drinks, many lose their own 'islands of sanity' when they do something just for themselves.

A potential upside awaits those who have split childcare responsibility and find themselves suddenly liberated some weeknights, weekends or holidays when their ex takes the kids. For some this is the opportunity to catch up on work backlogs. Others relish these adult escapes with a passion: stories of Tinder, rekindled ex-lovers and a restored commitment to dance nights abound.

But others can hardly bear these breaks from their children, especially at first:

'You lose the sense of owning your kids. I know our kids are on loan to us – we can't keep them forever – but I didn't think I'd have to let her go so soon…. I mean I thought my daughter would be mine when she was five. And it turns out that she's not and sometimes I don't even know what she is doing or who she is with. I never used to miss my kids when they were at school, I used to absolutely love it as I could get on with work and I loved my job…. Now it just seems much less important. I was never great with a prolonged absence from them – I think the longest I ever did was a week for work and I found it tough enough that I wouldn't have done it again. The craving now is that I feel really keenly that it's unnatural not to be there whenever they need me, I can't get used to it. So even though I would say I have more hours with them [a 50:50 time split with their dad] than I did when I was married, a) because it's more like 60:40 with me because of his job and b) because I do all the pick-ups and never go out when they're around, I still feel like it can never be enough, because it might not be me there when they stub their toe on a Tuesday morning. One of the hardest things is dropping off on a Friday morning and knowing you won't see them again 'til Monday afternoon.

It's just exquisitely painful to have to say "see you on Monday" in a playground. I think all divorced parents feel like this. I have a friend who said she never says it out loud because she can't, she just goes "see ya". When I've had a bad one of those drop-offs, sometimes I just mope about the area because I'm nearer where they are. I genuinely don't know if this is a female or unisex response. Or maybe I do know but I've never asked my ex because I would hate to hear the answer.'

Career

Having gone solo, some women choose to stay at their jobs, and work becomes their foundation for creating their new world as a parent. Many report that it was their job that saved them: it gave them control, structure and independence. One woman in finance said that, once her husband left, any guilt she felt about working evaporated. She had to work. He could not be relied upon. Spending any time reviewing that was wasted energy that she needed to spend creating a new structure for her and her sons.

But others, like Marianne, chose to wind back their careers. A single mother by choice says the same: 'Having chosen to have my son, it was only right to give up two years to caring for him. He is everything to me. He is my heart.' She is now looking to go back to work and highly conflicted about it but believes that in the long term it's important that she works to give them stability. This is a frequent observation: even when scaling back for a while makes sense, with an eye on the future, it's important for lone parents to have a work plan.

This might, though, require a deep think about personal priorities. Before the divorce, many women list their priorities as: children, job, self and then, way down the list, their partner. Marianne certainly did. The time her husband took up was mostly spent dealing with his issues rather than them connecting as mutually supportive partners.

Similarly, another mother had got so wrapped up in the baby and her graduate job that she had become more and more disconnected from her partner – just as he remained very wrapped up in the lives of his old local friends which she wasn't much part of. Looking back, she thinks her success threatened his happiness. They were living in different orbits: his local, familiar, childhood networks, and her running, via her graduate trainee role, into a professional world that she saw as the way to escape a difficult childhood.

After divorce, the order of the priority lists read the same but the magnitude of each has changed so much it's really a different list: the children can no longer be slotted in between conference calls. 'They need you like never before, they demand your focus, your attention, your support' says Marianne. It was a steep learning curve for her to create a stable family base for her boys, swinging between moments of being paralysed by her love for them and moments of raging frustration at how to cope with their big emotions alongside her own.

Those still working usually put the job as the next priority. But now, initially, it can feel like a tortuous pincer:

'Establishing this new family structure is the most stressful thing you'll ever do. The whole thing takes so much time and emotional energy. When everything else is so demanding, for me, work is the only thing that *will* give. I spent a third of last year in tears but am not normally someone who cries. Yet, at the same time, money is a huge problem and you can't let your work life fall apart.

'However much you might focus on work normally, it now has to fit around dealing with them and the logistics.'

Because, of course, those battling with their ex-partners focus on two things: access to the kids and money. One woman confessed: 'My lawyer was telling me, "To get the level of access you want to the kids, you need to be really visible". But my lawyer was also billing me relentlessly. In one month alone, I had legal bills of £15k yet she was advising me to be at the school gate every day at drop-off and pick-up to show how engaged I was. Organising play dates, seeing every school play and every sports event. It just wasn't possible with my job. So I realised I had to quit and I set up my own business. Just to have that flexibility. Because I was self-employed I could be flexible. If I'd been working full time I wouldn't have got as much access to my kids.'

Throwing the starting of a new business into a divorce process is, she says, a bastard of an extra burden. When her ex has the kids, she works every waking hour to pay off her divorce debts and keep solvent. 'But I couldn't have done it as an employee. I wouldn't have had the flexibility. I wouldn't have seen my kids. Two afternoons a week I pick them up and we hang out and it makes it all worth it. I wouldn't have been able to do that. I have to be able to set my own hours.'

Another who works in an office says: 'Some of my colleagues have been amazingly supportive, and I will always be grateful for that, but this one HR guy is hounding me. He wants to know exactly what hours I work now. I just can't answer. I've had to move the kids into two different schools, I've not sorted reliable childcare. I am living day-to-day and doing what I can. I have 10 years in the bank with this company and thank God or I worry they'd have given up on me by now.'

For some, work becomes part of the drama. One mum's first partner was someone they knew through work and she was surprised to find her colleagues and professional connections taking sides. For others, it's even more complicated as new lovers are linked through work to their exes or themselves. In the worst-case scenarios, everyone is linked professionally.

'We met at work, he was MD and I ran a large team. He had an affair with someone else at work. Crazy as it sounds we all stayed in the business for years after, but I have no idea why now. I guess I refused to be pushed out by his behaviour but looking back it was foolish because it damaged me and our son.'

Another mum of two had an affair at work with a senior man who was married. He left his wife and they stayed together, but it was made known that one of them had to leave the company they both worked at, so she reluctantly resigned. Eighteen months later he was made redundant in events that seemed unrelated to the affair, but she still suspects it undermined perceptions of him. Both have found the battle to re-establish financial security and merge into their new family unit harder than either ever imagined when they first met for what might have been an innocent drink after an away day. Neither would admit it was a mistake, but talking to them it feels like a lot is unsaid about how hard it has been.

For women with big jobs, traditional social expectations about children staying with their mum after a divorce can be really challenged, especially if the dad is well established as the primary care giver. Some have ended up not only losing custody of their children but also having to pay maintenance to their non-working ex after being portrayed as poor parents on account of their working hours. A mum who is a pharmaceutical researcher describes a gruelling battle to keep her kids living with her. She saw her major contribution to the marriage as keeping the household solvent, despite the fact she would have far preferred to spend more time at home. Her husband had been made redundant 10 years before and didn't want to work again. So, although he nominally ran his own small business, he was really the one doing the washing, ironing and cooking dinner. But she still felt that the critical emotional connection for the children was with her as he was also depressive and, periodically, reclusive. In retrospect, she wishes that she had engaged with getting a mental health diagnosis for him as it would have helped explain their dynamic. After a lengthy and expensive fight, the court awarded her main custody of the kids but she felt punished when, as a compromise, he got the house and she had to scramble to find them a place to live. She had no choice but to move to a cheaper area, away from her friends and the kids' friends and to new schools.

New life, new love

Some leave for someone new and their priority list really does change: the exciting new partner slots in below kids and above work, albeit sandwiched by guilt. Learning from their previous experience and, energised by the thrill of something new, this sounds appealing. But setting up a working relationship with kids in the mix – their own plus perhaps some children of his too – can quickly become another massive energy drain. 'It is *nothing* like starting a new relationship in your 20s.' The logistics of moving houses, schools and integrating step-children is agony. From the big things, such as childcare, down to the smallest details, such as whose potato peeler they can agree to keep.

'With my ex, I just said "I've a work thing on Wednesday so you need to have the kids" and never thought about it. Now life is a lot more complicated.' The problems relate to parenting and the division of responsibilities. Your new lover is just not quite as committed to the well-being of your kids as their other parent was. 'My boyfriend, much as he might love my kids, will never see them as his own. It's hard to say this, but he's just not as interested. If he has a work thing he won't see it as his role to stay home.'

One mum explains how the complication of combining families is adding to the ticker tape or domestic load, asking:

'So do I have to iron his kids' school clothes if they have never been ironed before? Can I send my own kids out of the door crisp and clean, and let his drag out looking a state? Does that reflect on me? Or am I just creating more work? To what extent is it my responsibility if his son smells or has no friends or eats total crap? Because his birth mother is not interested in these things and, while I care about him, I'm not sure how much attention I have to spare right now. Honestly, I often have to remember how bad things were between me and my husband before we broke up to justify this level of stress.'

She is someone who left her partner for happiness with someone else and then found her own needs hadn't gone up her list of priorities, they'd completely fallen off it. Therapist Karen Doherty says: 'When relationships break up and other people are involved, there is often a rush to create new homes and new family units of blended families. It's always harder than people expect. I wish more people would be brave enough to stand alone after their break-up. Keep the kids with them at the same school and in the same area, date their new partner if they want to, but really hold back from setting up a new structure that may also turn out to be fragile.' She adds that the thrilling and explosive chemistry of new romance after a marriage lacking in intimacy can diminish the influence of your rational, thinking brain and won't necessarily guide you to the right new partner.

For those who seek love after their break-up, dating experiences are a very mixed bag. Some revel in nights without kids to explore new possibilities and embrace the world of Tinder and online dating. Others retreat, afraid of making the same mistakes again. A single-parent dad says he gets more offers from women than he ever had as a younger man but it's all too much and he focuses his spare time on doing Ironman competitions. When asked about sex he says simply 'the internet', by which I think he means porn rather than dating. His main energy is split between the kids and his job and that works, he says, for all of them.

The compromise that some women share is to discreetly experiment with dating in a fairly low-key way. They say that having kids comes with more baggage than they expected. 'You hear how men are wary of women with young kids but I see it for myself now…. I do think it's an issue and while I'd never blame my kids for me being single I am pretty sure it's a factor.' But it's worth persevering as it can help with creating some boundaries around the all-absorbing needs of your kids. 'I never wanted the kids to meet a string of "mummy's boyfriends" (how very optimistic that was!) as I give everything I have to them. But when I do date, I keep it to myself. It's really important for me to have something just for me. Something private, that I don't share.'

What works about it?

You can't make generalisations about single parents. There are a thousand ways of making it work. So, I offer a few observations, none universal.

The first is that the quality of life of single parents appears to conform with what we are told about how money makes us all happy. If you have enough money to feel secure, your happiness seems generally less tied to work and professional success than that of many couples.

Many openly talk about their priorities having shifted and their children coming into total focus as the most important thing ever. This perhaps is why they often discuss their kids in such glowing terms: they are more likely to describe the delight they take in spending time with them than many couples do.

Reflecting on all my interviews with parents doing it alone, I've yet to interview one who describes being out of control at work in the way some professionals with partners can be: besieged and drowning in hours and messages. Many say they were like that before, but events have forced them to make conscious decisions about where and how they work. They tend to speak more about finding ways of making it work for them. A mum, for example, talks of spending evenings working at the dining room table while her older kids do their homework at the same time. The way she describes it is as a comforting ritual. She gives no indication of having lost control of how she spends her time and is highly engaged with her kids.

Those who are able to continue with established jobs and roles seem to benefit from extra psychological support if they have a bad period. Others return to work later or retrain with a view to a blended life that is both financially viable and stimulating – with half an eye on pension provisions and life after kids leave home. Having a plan for how to do this seems to offer focus and stability. A mum of young kids explains how she has started taking on freelance remote-working projects – reviving what she calls some rather rusty IT and admin skills – that fit around nursery and the kids' early bedtimes. Her goal is to build on this as they all get into school so she can secure a base that supports all of them if and when her ex scales back his contributions.

Just as with couples – but to the power of 10 – the happiest solo parents also have a solid network of friends and family locally. This helps to support their kids and helps these parents get support for themselves outside of work or the kids.

Years ago, I did a research project for a supermarket during which we tracked 12 families over many months to understand their habits and choices. The most inspiring character we met was a single mother with a teenage son. She didn't work but was studying events management at college. I would visit her during my 50+-hours-a-week job to interview her and accompany her on shopping trips, while my baby was in childcare, and I would leave her flat rubbing my head and wondering what the hell I was doing. Violet was completely engaged with her son – who was doing well at school – and her community and had an active social life. I never remember visiting her and not finding someone else over for tea or lunch. She was always planning a local event, a christening or wedding dinner. Without diminishing her financial challenges – and there were many, she kept her phone and internet with different providers so only one got cut off at a time, and chose meals on a pennies-per-portion basis – I used to leave thinking she knew a lot more about life and active parenting than many of the career mums I know. Including myself.

If you're too tired and wired to read the above

Before you separate

- If you are worried about the stability of your relationship, the advice is consistent: if you want it to survive (and it's not abusive or violent) *try everything* before splitting up. Literally make a list of everything you could do. A twice-divorced dad, reflecting on his break-ups, said: 'Unless you are fundamentally incompatible you should try everything to make it work before you give up. Even if you still do, you have to know that you tried.'
- Advice varies on how to do this, but the talk a priest gave someone before marriage may help:
  Priest to husband-to-be: 'Who is the most important person in your life?'
  H-t-b: 'My fiancée.'
  Priest: 'Excellent. And who will be the most important person if you and your wife are lucky enough to have a baby?'
  H-t-b: <anxious pause> 'The baby?'

Priest: 'No. Your wife. Because if you two are fine, your children will be fine too.'

- If you can't make it work, stay honest if you possibly can. Negotiate the end rather than distracting yourself with an affair. Karen Doherty says: 'My observation is that it's the lies, rather than the affair itself, that irrevocably crushes the marriage.' Tell everyone you can the truth as early as possible. Including your children.
- If you do have a wild, obsessive romance with someone new, don't assume that they will offer a stable basis for a new family life.

Breaking up

Back to Karen:

'Divorce is becoming so normalised that only those who have been through it fully appreciate the long-lasting damage it does to children and families. While the adults move on to new relationships (that don't necessarily work) and extended melded families are attempted, the collateral damage is the children. Their pain, confusion and powerlessness is taken into adult life, and is often repeated with them not being able to manage their own relationships well. My advice is to get lots of help when separating so that you can reach some sort of amiable parental relationship, listen to the real cost of your actions and don't get caught up in the "I don't love you any more" script. The relationship went wrong because neither was listening to the other. Now you need to try and listen to the children and their needs rather than introduce them to new family models before they have really accepted the loss of their families.' Remember that conflict feels easier than sadness.

But, however much you listen to your children, Jenny Franklin, a family mediator who specialises in helping divorcing couples avoid court battles, warns parents not to take everything the children say at face value. Not because they intend to deceive but because children are adept at saying what each parent wants to hear and, ultimately, it is the adults who must come to the right conclusions about how things will be organised going forward.

Going solo

- If you can, keep your job. Keep your job. Keep your job. Do mornings, do three days, do four days, take a sabbatical. But don't walk away at this moment, when it gives you stability and choices, unless you really have to. And if you have a massive meltdown during a break-up, try to talk to your workplace and get support. People have had mixed experiences with this but some report with surprise that they got a better-than-expected response ('I had no idea but it turned out that my boss had been through an awful divorce in her 20s and she really understood what I was going through.').
- If you cannot sustain your job, when you can breathe again, start making a plan for what you will do next. Even having a plan seems to help.
- Give yourself time to be alone. Commit your mental and physical attention to supporting your kids. Don't dash into anything new too hastily. The family has already been through a trauma, don't risk another.
- The mental load of being a single parent is massive ('I take care of everyone but no one ever takes care of me') so you need the best support networks you can get. Work hard to build them

and maintain them. If you share access to your kids, use the time when they are away to build your social connections.

- Go into it expecting years of financial torment and financially prepare for the divorce: be smart and savvy. Save, invest and make sure you get a good financial adviser.
- Get therapy sooner and do more of it.
- Invest in sex toys (yes that is really what they say).
- Consciously try to use time away from your kids to your advantage. Recharge, unwind, enjoy adult company. Your kids need a lot from you and you need to be strong enough to be there for them.

What happened next?

MARIANNE USED SOME OF the divorce money to improve her statistics and IT skills with some online courses and has become a data analyst, working with a small network of freelancers. She works from home while the boys are at school. It has the benefits of being flexible and relatively well paid but without the stress and politics of working in a complex organisation. She consciously spends 45 minutes to an hour a day focused on each child, individually listening to them, reading or doing an activity.

John continues to thrive at work and financially.

Marianne would also love to meet someone new. At a friend's party recently, the husband gently put his hand on his wife's back and asked 'What can I get you to drink, darling?' and she was surprised to find herself choking back her tears. She thinks it's much harder with two kids. She says, though, that her single-dad neighbour is a total 'fanny magnet' – and then laughs raucously.

CHAPTER ELEVEN

Why does dealing with school turn me into a child?

MY HUSBAND AND I have a little girl called Eva, who is six.

Eva started primary school last year and to be honest, I've been quite upset not because she was going to school (although, I was a little nervous about it) but because it wasn't the one we wanted, not even close. One of the many problems is that it's a big school with large classes and I'm worried that Eva's not getting the attention she needs. For example, I can't help but notice that other children from her class are way ahead in their reading, while Eva still struggles. I'm worried she's going to get left behind, she doesn't seem to enjoy it, and I think she would benefit from more attention from her teacher. I've raised my concerns a few times but the school seemed to think there was nothing to worry about.

I email her teacher regularly asking for updates but she never gets back to me. She doesn't ever have time for me at the school gate. She's always chatting with the same group of mums she seems to know better and I can't help thinking that their children are getting more attention than Eva. I'm starting to wonder if I need to play more of an active role in the school and whether this would help Eva get more help from her teachers. I know they need someone to help with their PTA accounts which I could do but it's quite a lot of work and I'm not sure if I really have the time or want to get involved.

My sister says we should move Eva to the local private school. It's academically better and they would definitely give her the attention she needs. But I'm worried about whether our finances will cover it.

Deborah, 40, Accountant

****

There is a fascinating contradiction at the heart of many a career mum – especially the competitive type – and the education of our kids. On the one hand we tend to be driven to ensure our kids do well. Not just 'well' of course. Average isn't the thing. By 'well' we mean 'better than the others': to succeed convincingly at one thing at least. But on the other hand we're also quite busy doing whatever we do at work and are focused on getting that right.

In *The Economist*'s lifestyle and culture magazine *1843*, Ryan Avent writes about high-pressure parenting, noting that in the last 20 years the time parents spend on child rearing has jumped. 'In America in the 1980s, for example, young mothers spent about 12 hours per week actively engaged in childcare while fathers spent about four hours per week ... Mothers without university degrees now spend about 16 hours per week on childcare, while those with degrees spend nearly 22 hours per week. For fathers the figures are seven and ten, respectively. This pattern is repeated across the rich world.' He notes that what is strange about this trend is that these better-educated, better-paid parents are not spending less time at work: they are spending more. Which means that what they are giving up on are their social lives, hobbies and sleep. Avent explores why and comes to the conclusion that increasing income inequality means parents feel they must do more to help their children get ahead.

But these two traits of putting our time and effort into helping our kids and working harder and longer don't sit well together and can cause a lot of angst.

Choosing schools

I invested less time and mental turmoil getting into university than I did getting our kids into what we thought was the right primary school. Ridiculous, but not unusual. The selection and application system for university is reasonably transparent. The selection process for schools is like a battle with the Red Queen in Wonderland. Catchment areas change, criteria for selection change as siblings, special needs, religious status or whatever else go up or down the list. This is before you've even got your head around the relative benefits of local authority schools, free schools, feeder schools and whether you need to give up food for the next 11 years and try private.

From conception, some parents plot their school strategies. The head of an elite school told me that they repeatedly have to decline registering unborn children on their waiting lists, explaining that if the child has no name and no date of birth it's rather difficult to list them. They ask the parents to return after the birth, which some are quite grumpy about. From moving house to renting the flat next door, baptising kids old enough to own their own Heelys to faking vicars' letters. It has all been tried, with a million nights of sleep lost along the way. The scale of this endeavour presents a potential problem for career-focused parents, many of whom, distracted by work and not involved in local networks, may come to the school-gate scramble late and realise they have been out-manoeuvred, exactly as Deborah has been.

Is private an option?

For the vast majority of us, private school is well beyond the realm of possibility. Yet, I have talked to parents who scoured the available school options and, not seeing anything good enough, panic-bought private school. The way they tell it, it's almost an accident.

It starts when, finding no access to good state schools (or, like Deborah, finding themselves in a school they are very unhappy with), they have a quick look at the headline prices for private Reception, do some back-of-the-envelope maths (ignoring their other toddler and the current pregnancy, they'll get to them later) and decide that having a little tour can't hurt. Soon they are admiring the Hogwarts-style dining hall, luscious playing fields, red-curtained theatre and the super-charming head. They are dazzled, imagining their child growing up in this idyll. Thinking 'the very reason we work so hard is to provide exactly this for our kids', they sign up to get on the waiting list and pay a hefty admin fee. After that, cursory visits to the slightly shonky state options look decidedly primitive and confirm they've made absolutely the right decision. Especially since little Jonny is such a very bright child. They can easily justify it because of their jobs: school days are generally longer and more padded at each end with useful clubs and activities. 'Gosh look, there is even a bus that'll pick them up from the end of the road for a little less than the cost of installing our own helipad in the garden.'

Now, if they really can afford it, it will probably work out just fine and they'll be very pleased with their decision. Particularly as one mum who has worked in both private and state schools says one of the biggest differences between the two is the willingness to listen to, sometimes flatter, parents' views.

However, if it's a financial stretch and younger siblings are coming down the track, that little look-see can bite them hard on the arse. The true cost of private school is way higher than the listed fees – when all the 'essential' additions such as uniform, trips and lunches are included. School fees go up year after year as the kids get bigger. Sibling discounts barely take the edge off. Before you know it, you can find yourself neck deep in incoming bills and unable to swallow the bitter step down that moving them to a state school midway entails for you and for them.

Don't underestimate the psychological pressure of school fees. I have always been cautioned by Mrs Moneypenny's account in the *Financial Times* of having to pull three kids (she calls them her 'cost-centres') out of private school after the financial crash of 2008. In my imagination, I picture her raiding old savings accounts, closing ISAs and selling furniture before she makes this call. I also wonder at the pressure it puts on relationships: a high-flying dad said his wife campaigned for their kids to go to private schools when he wasn't bothered either way, and he now feels he has to deliver a massive chunk of salary *just* to cover the school fees. This pressure keeps him awake at night and he resents it.

A potential kicker in this is that, just as you kill yourself paying for school, you also realise your kids are being belittled by the cruel but casual snobbery children specialise in. A mum who scraped to get her kids into a private school with subsidies from her parents was appalled when her son came home one day to moan that his friends had said they were the only people who didn't have a tennis court. She told him he was being ridiculous and vile and then he listed all of his friends and she realised it was partly true. A girl with well-off but not showy parents who went to a private sixth form college said that everyone asked if she was on a bursary because they couldn't understand why she'd been to a comp beforehand. When her new friends saw her family's house they asked if it was their country place. Other parents have admitted that, despite bleeding cash to pay for schools, they've ended up feeling like misers – one dad says his kids constantly make him feel like Bob Cratchit – depriving their kids because they've turned down the ski trip or the Spanish exchange to try to keep a lid on the costs.

The upsides of private schools are all too obvious on practical levels (smaller classes, great facilities, longer days, academic selection, better discipline, holiday clubs, etc). In some professions the social benefits are also important: the location of your kids' education is as important a status symbol as where you live and holiday. Yet there is at least one practical downside for working parents that is rarely noted: the catchment areas tend to be wider, which means you may be signing up to a long daily school run as well as losing out on a network of kids to knock about with, and end up doing yet more driving for play dates. You may also find that the benefits of a longer school day are offset by longer holidays. Although, if you can manage the additional cash, you can of course take advantage of the above-average-price holiday club. You may also consider boarding school, which of course removes childcare worries altogether during the short term times, but comes with a hefty price tag and rather depends on how you and your children feel about the idea.

How much effort should we give this?

The main learning I take from parents of older/grown-up kids is that the school decision probably wasn't worth as much angst as they put into it. Many say, on reflection, that a decent school, conveniently close to home, with friends they can connect with is more than enough, particularly at primary, especially if the child has good family support. Especially if taking this path frees up your own time and energy to help them along the way. A mum who works for a train company bunged her girls into 'a very dodgy primary with metal detectors on the doors' (I'm not sure she was serious about the last bit) just because it was the school on her commute to work, but her girls all did well and got into a selective state secondary, albeit with a lot of help from their parents with the exam preparation. A mother who coached her four children through primary to get into the local grammar school says this:

'Two got into the grammar and two went to the local comprehensive. It seemed like an awful situation at the time. I felt two were getting a sub-standard education and that felt deeply unfair to them. It was also a logistical pain. But now they are grown up, I can honestly say that the two who went to the comp are better adjusted, relate to others more easily and work harder. My grammar-school kids take themselves that bit more seriously and get easily distracted by people around them. My conclusion is that you think you know what is best and you really don't.'

The trouble with education is that, until your child emerges on the other side, you have no idea whether it was the right decision or not. And schools all have strengths and weaknesses: an outstanding school can have a crappy maths teacher and a failing one can have an inspirational head. And the next year both could move, so it all changes again. On balance, I conclude from my research that the right strategy is to take the time out to find the right school for your family. Try not to let it bring on a nervous breakdown. See it in the context of how the whole family lives day-to-day: how much time you spend together, your journeys, friendship groups, your household budget, clubs and activities *as well as* the quality of the actual school. And, don't see anything as unchangeable: many a parent has noted that it can be easier to get into very popular schools in the years after the main entry point, as families move out of the area and spaces become available.

How involved should you get in the school-gate psychodrama?

Whichever school they end up at, the gates of primary school then often form the battle lines between the parents who, at the extremes, either gave up their careers to focus on their kids and those who continued at work full-time. In the middle are those straddling both worlds, who work locally or from home during school hours and in the evenings and often at weekends, but also do the school run and ferry their kids to and from after-school clubs.

Those who keep working full-time often feel disregarded by the 'post-career mums', who they see as the super-competitive tiger brigade. The ones cracking through Kumon maths, ballet and music exams, and three languages, two of which they don't even speak at home. These are the same mothers who are likely to throw their considerable talents into the school. Running the PTA. Becoming a governor. Volunteering for trips and outings.

What is interesting is that, however much effort it takes to get in, as soon as their kids are through the door, many parents express disappointment at their chosen school's lack of perfection. The highly engaged parents often seem to then start campaigning to change the school they have so fiercely fought for – or start to eye up the next 'perfect' place for their child. The first of these options means getting involved and investing their own time and effort fixing it. For them, the upside of this decision is enormous access to the teachers and the kids plus a highly complex network of other women (it generally *is* other women), with a similar amount of time to invest who also share information. Many a working parent has been stunned to realise that a specific group of mothers is carefully tracking what reading level their child is on, their swimming stage and the relative sophistication of their social skills.

One full-time working mother told me her daughter was invited on a play date. She was a bit surprised as she'd heard little about the other child and wasn't aware they were friends, but she agreed. Before the play date, the at-home mother asked her to pack her swimsuit. Which she was fine with – her daughter is a keen swimmer – until she was briefed by another mother that the inviting couple see their own daughter as the best swimmer in the year and actually wanted to see how her daughter did against her. The point, it was implied, was that they wanted to show their 'competitive swimmer' how hard she would have to work to keep up her number-one position. The working mother was utterly exasperated by this as she has no inclination to worry about such things.

Now most of that story is hearsay. We don't actually know what the at-home mum wanted to achieve – she may very well have been inviting the girls to have fun, knowing that they both enjoyed the water. She may have just noticed that they got on and was keen to include someone new into her daughter's friendship group. But stories like this fuel a sense of unease between the various groups of parents that can be very unhelpful. Particularly when it comes with the inference that there is a two-tier parenting structure, and that full-time, absent-from-the-gate working mums are at the bottom of it: as Sara Bennison, then a director at Barclays UK retail bank, said in her interview with me for *Management Today*, 'Most women are really nice but there are some that are tricky. The worst was when my eldest daughter got into a particular school and another mother called to ask how. She was astounded because, as she put it, "you work". The implication was that, as Sara had a big job, she was too busy to take the time to get the kids into the right schools. This inference about being 'second tier' is where, I think, the many complaints about the yummies, the mum-mafia and so on come from.

There is also often a link between these feelings and a flashback to our own school years; Sarah Clarke explains this is called 'rubber banding', when an experience snaps us back into the feelings we had long ago when we experienced something similar. Some cannot bear the return to that vulnerable place where we felt rejected. They park around the corner and send their kids through the gates without them. One woman at a private school even sends her nanny with the child while she waits in the car with the engine running, ideally on a speaker call so that no one is tempted to tap on the window: anything to avoid other parents. But some cannot resist returning to the centre of the fray, either to recreate an environment in which they thrived or perhaps to slay the ghosts of their own socially awkward childhoods.

Deborah has both of these reactions to the school crowd: she is repelled in some ways, but attracted by a desire to help her daughter do well. Initially she held back, keeping herself on the fringes. Later, she found it hard to join in. Like a mother who travels for work who says:

'Some of the other mums are wary and don't come near me. People who have known me from the start know I am wearing odd socks and pretending to make cakes that I've obviously bought. With people who don't know you, there is always a risk of answering a question honestly and saying you're going to Tokyo and it killing the conversation dead. It is tricky because you feel in some ways that you want to be a part of it but you can't break in.'

Some then choose to own their lack of school engagement. Career mums often tell me versions of: 'I don't have the time to listen to what Heidi said to Ayesha in the playground that caused Yaz to be so upset that she told Ollie and she got sent home for the day. They have to learn to sort these things out.' The social lives of children can be complex and, when told like this in long form when you have no idea who the various characters involved are, it's mind-numbing. But the author Catherine Wallace PhD advises us to tread carefully: 'Listen earnestly to anything your children want to tell you, no matter what. If you don't listen eagerly to the little stuff when they are little they won't tell you the big stuff when they are big, because to them all of it has always been big stuff.' Whether we agree with that or not, many find later that their lack of engagement has cost them: especially if they are the kind of people who like to know what is going on.

A mum of two boys in secondary builds on this:

> 'There's something also about the fact that when they get to secondary school and inevitably start pulling away from you and developing an understandable desire for some normal privacy, it becomes harder and harder to find out what's going on in their lives and how they are doing at school. Secondary school staff expect to communicate mainly with the kids, not the parents. So, things can happen that parents know nothing about or only find out too late, for example that the majorly important maths test is tomorrow. BUT if you have a fairly good radar for how your kids have been at school early on, who their friends are, who the troublemakers are etc then you can have a better feel for how it is in the teenage years.'

Deborah is not a tiger parent, but she wants their daughter to thrive at school and had realised that her being a bit more involved might help. If her being visible helps her to achieve this aim, she sees it as her duty. The question is how involved, and, in what ways can she achieve her goal of being supportive and visible without compromising family life or her own sense of well-being. She is thinking through her potential points of contact and how to get the best from the situation.

In most schools, it's the governor role that carries the clout and enables people to make a positive impact, which is why many a career parent is drawn to the role. Some also see advantage in furnishing their CV with something terribly responsible.

A dietician and single mother (currently working one day a week), says:

'I chose to run for the governors because I wanted to contribute to my kids' education and I believe that if you're not part of the solution then you are probably part of the problem. Or that is what I say publicly.... Privately I admit that I also really like that I can have a bigger impact. My daughter was chosen to be interviewed for the local paper and I pretty much know it was because of who I am and what I do for the school. That said, governing is hard work. You get trained. You can't raise personal issues in meetings and you can't promote your own interests. But you can impact on policy. My kids are pupil premium but they are not academically struggling. I realised that their budget was being put towards school trips when it is supposed to be dedicated to the kids who need it. I raised this and suddenly my kids now get free instrument lessons. I also know that if I stop to ask the head a question in the playground, there is 100 per cent more chance she will engage with it seriously than if another random parent asks. The classroom teachers know too and will make that extra bit of effort to help me when I need it. I really like that and it's worth putting in the time for.'

In some areas governor places are very highly sought after. Parents describe campaigns that are as political as the general election, complete with infighting and smears. After hard-fought elections, expectations about the role can be unreasonable and many a head ends up frustrated that nothing can be discussed without an obvious personal interest being triggered. For this reason, many seek out as many governors as they are allowed who don't have kids at the school. But this can be difficult because the roles are arduous and unpaid and it tends to be the parents who are most motivated to try to help. The role is also often boringly technical with a lot of reading and data analysis that must be done as well as meetings that can last for hours. One governor mum told me that she asked to be excused from one meeting over the course of her four-year term as she had a big interview for a new role the next day. Her request was denied and she was furious; particularly as the vicar is often excused to prepare for services and events. She felt the decision was profoundly sexist and may resign over it.

For working parents, the governor role can be useful if you are very clear why you are doing it – to help the school, to support your kids, for your CV – and are able to manage the time commitment. But it is best to have realistic views about what can be achieved. 'Non-experts' in education can only have so much impact on how a school is running and many governors report feeling like rubber stamps who are accountable for mistakes but get zero credit for anything going well. They also have to sit through a heck of a lot of school functions even when their children are not involved.

The next level of service in many schools is the PTA. 'The PTA is full of people who want a finger in the pie and status but who spend all their time chasing people for small change for charity and badgering people to volunteer time' sniffs a governor. But many a PTA team would strongly disagree, arguing that they have a critical role in supporting parents and the school as well delivering much-needed money.

Where PTAs function highly, they are well organised and disciplined, closely communicating with school and delivering useful services, from extra equipment to volunteer support for trips. They create ways for parents who want to and can spare some time and cash to help the school make contributions that support those who can't. They also enable people to use their personal and professional talents in a useful way: from a photographer taking good pictures to a web designer improving the school's homepage. That said, some question whether their existence increases social divisions. One parent reports:

'My kids' primary school had a cohort of super-charged, alpha, middle-class parents who fund-raised like mad so the school was always buying new playground equipment, whiteboards, musical instruments – which meant my tone-deaf kids were obliged to bring home musical instruments to drive us mad with. Meanwhile, schools down the road have massively less money and I'm pretty sure life didn't get easier either for the working parents or the less-privileged parents – who, if anything, I think felt more alienated because the PTA had more of a vibe of a dinner party than a community project. So I'm not sure who really benefits from all of that effort – not the wider community [i.e. those local, less-privileged schools], or stressed-out time-poor or money-poor parents. I think schools and kids only need so much stuff – all of that effort could be channelled so differently – like by campaigning for some of the bigger changes we need to improve education or organising collectively around health/sickness/holiday care and so on.'

Sometimes the PTAs step into real problems though. A PTA mum who had to manage a major issue with the school's struggling headteacher explains:

'You know that state schools are stretched in terms of resources and that actually the parent body is a massive resource that, if harnessed well, can add masses to school life. In schools facing a major crisis the parent body galvanising itself and taking a major lead can be critical. In our case we had to find a way to communicate with large numbers of parents we had never met before when our children were in their first year at the school, which we did by word of mouth and email networking and then we had to hold meetings in our kitchen, appoint a spokesperson and then we had to use the statutory powers in the board of governors constitution to insist that an open meeting was held to which every single parent at the school was invited by letter to air the crisis and decide on a way forward.'

More to the point for Deborah, PTAs create a vehicle by which to build networks among parents and the friends. One head I spoke to flags that primary school is a precious moment for this as: 'come secondary school, parents are not at the gate and the moment to connect is passed.' She encourages all parents to take the opportunity while they have it.

Whatever the upsides, we know they don't make films and sitcoms about the horrors of the PTA for nothing. Everyone has a PTA-rebranded-as-a-PITA (pain in the arse) story if you ask for it. One head I spoke to even closes down the PTA every time she arrives at a new school because she thinks it entitles parents to meddle and make her life complicated, and some of the stories you hear explain why:

'Our PTA was run by a salon manager called Leanne. Leanne had the usual quiet dogsbody sidekick, Becca. The PTA was disbanded after money from the summer fete "went missing", leaving Leanne spitting chips at the injustice of it. She set up an unofficial Facebook group as a way to "support and inform" parents, given there was no longer a PTA, and used her salon appointments to express her views in full. Although the homepage urged that it should not be used for gossip and whinging, that is exactly what it was used for and, although the homepage reminded parents that in the event of a complaint they should go to straight to the head, that didn't happen either. When Ofsted sent out their standard questionnaire, Leanne used the Facebook page – and her network – to remind parents that they could make any complaints about the school directly to Ofsted and gave them the contact details. Which they duly did, and Ofsted had to make an extra inspection to tackle the level of complaints they got. This created a hugely stressful administrative problem for the head and governors – but the school was vindicated and ultimately unscathed by the incident, as the Ofsted inspector said that parental involvement like this was "all too common".

Another mum and former PTA head says:

'There are three main types as I see it. The frustrated manager who uses the PTA to get the control and authority they crave, often those who have stepped back from work to focus on the kids. These are the most likely to take it very seriously. Then there are busy people doing more than they can cope with and trying to combine the PTA with a time-consuming job – sorting second-hand uniform at midnight the day before the end-of-term sale and tearing their hair out. And then there are the lovely, sweet, kind people who do it because it's the right thing to do and always seem to be the poor bastards left after each event washing up every piece of Tupperware and sweeping the floors. The problem that can come from either of the first two groups is that they have an axe to grind, because, if they have kids at the school, they can't be kicked out. Every meeting becomes about their own worldview – we had a mum who saw our school as grubby and cold (possibly true) and spent her time wanging on about antiseptic gels, hand sanitisers and warmer uniforms. It was impossible to engage her on anything without her coming back to these issues, which no one else was very bothered about.'

Less dramatic are accounts of people joining PTAs to help out when you can and finding yourself sucked dry with endless calls for help with cakes, tombolas, raffles, trips, sponsored events, etc. The upshot for working parents is that PTAs can give good access to lots of people and allow you to engage more with school, but are also often time vampires. Approach, but approach with caution.

How to engage with teachers

Then there is dealing with the teaching and leadership team. Many career parents struggle to get the tone of this right. Are the teachers to be deferred to because they are teachers? Or are you equals because you are both professional and all adults with the same intention of getting children educated? Or do they work for you, paid for by you (through tax or fees) to deliver your child a good education? If they work for you, then are they up to the job? Every parent seems to be able to furnish you with a story about a teacher with flawed grammar.

When we were children, our parents put teachers in the same group as doctors and bank managers. To be respected, listened to, deferred to. My mother says that, aged 25, she felt good as a newly qualified teacher driving her little Mini and having a little bit of status in society. Sadly, for those groups it has very much changed and teachers are now used to all sorts of unhelpful interaction from parents.

A mother of two who taught before having her kids describes how she sees the disconnect between teachers/parents like this:

'I was a newly qualified teacher in 1994. I was so keen and so excited by my job, I arrived at school at 7.30am and left at 7.30pm and did more lesson planning at home later. But my fierce commitment meant I was also completely disparaging about parents and what they didn't do. I couldn't understand it when, three days later, they still hadn't responded to my important note in the Home Book. I saw them as totally irresponsible. At parents' evening I was pompous and smug about what they needed to be doing. Now I have two kids and can see the other side so clearly. I am a teacher and I find myself thinking about my

daughter – "Fuck, why is she still on the reading scheme in Year Four?"
As I scratch my head to remember the last time I read with her. I forget
to attend parents' evenings! I completely miss some of them. The kind
of thing that would have horrified me as a NQT.'

A head says that working parents can be particularly disengaged:

'Some professional parents take the "my child's OK approach". They
think it is cool to not fuss over their child and ignore correspondence
in the child's book bag. They then question at parents' evening why
their child is not on the next reading book, when it has lain among
the sandwich crumbs at the bottom of the bag for half a term. They
don't bother to read the weekly update letters, so forget to send their
child in with money for the charity pyjama day, and arrive flustered and
late to the nativity, missing their child's key line, as they only realised
it was happening when their friend texted to say little Eric is in floods
of tears as he can't see them in the audience. These are also the parents
who expect sports shorts and trainers bought in September to still fit
on sports day in July, and wonder why their child doesn't win the race
because it actually hurts to run or they are embarrassed by their tight-
fitting PE gear.'

Some choose this path of non-engagement as part of their parenting
strategy. A secondary school teacher tells of a 12-year-old who asked to
be emailed the parent letters and updates. The school said no, because
the letters are for the parents. But the child got terribly upset, saying
her parents were far too busy at work to read them and that it was her
responsibility to know when she needed sun cream for a trip or had to
sign up for a new club. This ended in an unsatisfactory stalemate on
both sides, with the parents saying it was about taking responsibility
and the school feeling it was about the parents supporting their kids.

In contrast, others put their efforts into trying to fix the school:

'There are these career parents on maternity leave for a second child, or between jobs, who cannot resist trying to organise the school from the gates. Snookering the head who is trying to get the children through the gate on time, they will bend the head's ear with their latest inspiration, which "you could do for the children", while the poor head is shuffling the late-comers into line, and desperately thinking what they have organised for assembly, and how on earth they are going to cover the lessons for the absent French teacher as two other staff are out on a training day.'

Much of this boils down to some fundamental questions about whose job it is to educate our children. Teachers say that parents expect miracles without doing anything at home. One told me about a mother, an engineer, complaining bitterly to him that her Year One child wasn't making any progress in maths. The teacher suggested she got a game of snakes and ladders and played with him in the evenings, saying how quickly children learn to add up dice when they are working out how to avoid those pesky snakes. The mother looked at him like he had two heads. She explained that she didn't have time for that. She rushed through the door at 6pm to race through dinner, bath and bed. The thought of stopping to play board games was incomprehensible. This is a theme echoed by other working parents. 'Every parents' evening the teachers tell us what we need to do with our children. I am like "hang on a bloody moment, I am at work all day doing MY job, YOUR job is to do the education bit, not tell me how I should be doing it".' Which all points to the fundamental mismatch between the work and school days. One mum winced when she realised that her child had perfectly replayed her response to an invitation to a school show at 11.30am two days later with: 'My mummy says that if you put these things on at the start or end of the day, and gave some notice, then people like her with REAL JOBS would come but, as you don't, no, she won't be there.'

How to manage homework

Wars are being fought over homework in every household with school-aged children across the land. Except those who already managed to get it banned for lack of evidence it actually helps. Caitlin Moran wrote a perfect piece in *The Times* on the topic, calling for the biggest dog in the world to come and eat all homework, but sadly she has yet to achieve her goal of ridding us of it. She rightly points out that in reality it's a test of parents and that kids in too-busy or too-chaotic households end up being the most disadvantaged.

Ultimately every family has to choose its own approach. Some parents swear by putting a note in the homework book after half an hour saying: 'he/she did enough and then we stopped'. Others are determined to teach their kids that you have to finish tasks and will push to do all three of the possible questions rather than choosing one, as specified (FYI teachers don't thank you for this, they just have to mark more). Others think homework is a total waste of space when they could be pond dipping and ignore it. Choose your route, communicate with the school, and be happy with it.

The communication tip that working mums often cite is to put effort into keeping good relationships with teachers. Some schools have effective email policies and you can drop them a quick note if the hamster dies or they were up half the night worrying about a troll in *Harry Potter*. Many lag on the technology front though and you are left with booking a five-minute slot, catching their eye at drop-off or sending a note in school bags. The trick here is to be the parent they are happy to hear from because they know you will be sane and treat them with respect; they'll never choose to give their email or mobile number to the parents who harangue them at every turn and see the darkest side of every challenge.

One mum was outraged to learn that the boys at her kids' school were being taken to play football competitively against another school while the girls had been invited to watch. She worked herself into a rage about the message school was sending about sport and competition and composed a ranty note to the teacher about it. But on reflection, she pulled back and said: 'Wanted to ask about football today. May have wrong end of stick, but are the boys playing a competitive match against another local school? Keen – as am sure you are – that we don't accidentally communicate that competitive sport is something just for boys. Am sure you're on this, just wanted to get the full picture.' To which she got back: 'The PE teacher is organising it and this is the first thing I asked him as well! Apparently, the boys are playing versus an all-boys school, hence the gender split. The PE teacher will make sure that the girls play a competitive fixture as well later in the term. Thanks for your concern, I do try to have as feminist a classroom as possible and it's good to have support!' In retrospect, she was relieved she'd used the challenge to build a better relationship with the teacher rather than ripping her head off via email.

Whatever you decide, in the early years, *someone* has to be there after school and the skills required to help with homework aren't too demanding – but teens are a different story. Teenagers are too old for a babysitter, yet need homework help that is sophisticated enough to tackle quadrilateral equations and the tactical mistakes of Hitler's generals. While schemes exist to recruit university students to do a few evening hours and supervise school work, experiences of their success are mixed. The challenge isn't usually the brainpower, it's grit. 'I get in and find the work has been done as fast and shoddily as possible to get to dinner and get the TV on. I am furious and have to get them to start all over again. The problem is, what student has my capacity to force my kids to do their work properly?' demands a mother who would happily describe herself as a tiger. Well, quite.

The combination of the demands of school, the disconnect of parents and the questions about the quality and intention of teachers can lead some to end up perennially angry with school for general incompetence. Parents will regale you with stories about school getting it 'wrong' – on everything from who they employ to how they teach and especially how they communicate – but so too will the teachers. One teacher told me about a five-year-old girl who had a fight with her friend at playtime. She felt sad and wanted to return to the classroom to be on her own but she wasn't allowed to go back in until the end of break because there was no one to supervise inside. She wandered off briefly but came back saying she had to go in because she needed a drink. The teacher gently directed her to the fountain. Then the girl came back again to say that she had a little cough and needed to go inside for her asthma inhaler. The teacher watched her for a minute or two: she had no signs of breathing problems or any cough. So instead she took her hand and went with her to help her make up with her friend.

The next day, she found a searing letter in the girl's bag from the child's mother, one she barely knows as she rarely gets to the gate as she works in town, accusing her of risking the life of her child by denying her access to critical medication. Threatening her with a lawsuit if anything should happen to the child, the letter gave no suggestion that the teacher could have had any good intentions within her. The teacher started and ended that day stressed and demoralised by the tone of the letter. It coloured how she taught and how she felt about herself. She notes that parents she never sees are generally more inclined to be angry and aggressive. This is a very big challenge for all working parents who are, by definition, less present and, in some cases, feel pushed away by schools. It's not uncommon for schools to discourage parents from going into the building at drop-off and pick-up. While there may be good reasons to do this, I wonder whether it increases the risk of disharmony. I don't think there is a 'fix all' solution but do note that parents who have a considered approach to engaging with school often seem happier with the engagement they get.

Another headteacher accounts for a similar scenario like this:

'Often children who have busy or distracted parents discover that they can gain attention by creating a sympathy situation during the evening at home. The tired parent having completed a long day at the office, on hearing of a minor fracas and feeling suddenly guilty that they may be ignoring their potentially "bullied child", then fires off a ballistic email (often fuelled by a large glass of wine) to the poor, unsuspecting class teacher who receives this on entering school the following morning. The enthusiasm of the teacher quickly drains to be replaced by frustration and hurt at the lack of tact and trust, and much of the rest of the day, during the odd free moment, is spent investigating and writing a reply for what was an exceedingly minor playground tiff.

'If parents would just take a small step back and say to their child, "I am sure that made you feel very sad" (acknowledging the child's plea for attention); "we could discuss this over breakfast, but how about having a cuddle and a story now and thinking of lovely things instead". The child is quite likely to have forgotten about the situation by morning and to be eager to attend school the following day.'

One obvious route to being a less-distracted parent is to take the opportunities school does create, be that parents' evening, the system they use to teach children to read or a talk about cyber bullying. Which is probably to advise against conference dialling into parents' evening…. Although if that is all you can manage, it might be better than not showing up at all. A top tip from a working mum on the issue of parents' evenings is:

> 'We always, always, always start and finish each session with each teacher, including the bozos, with "you teachers work so hard, we have no idea how you do it, you're doing an amazing job" because truly they are. I would never do it no matter how much you paid me. You only have to watch *Educating Manchester* for five minutes to be truly awed.'

Then there are parents who intentionally or by accident end up right in the centre of school life. This can be a positive or negative experience for the school and the parents. Some thrive in the involvement, some get crushed by the limitless demands that schools can make on time and resources. Many working mums say that they tried to engage for a while but found the juggernaut express of requests all too much. It is a cliché to talk about mums working all day, putting kids to bed, having dinner, finishing emails and then starting to ice cupcakes. But it is a cliché because many find it easier to provide a cake occasionally than to run the tombola at every event.

Managing school days, holidays and sick kids when working

A bastard of a challenge facing a lot of working parents is the fundamental mismatch between the working day and the school day and – of course – the nightmare of long holidays and kids' sick days. The first two have the advantage that they are at least predictable. Most families develop some strategy based around a 'grid of doom': the complex timetable of after-school and holiday cover.

One mum said that at one point she and her partner were working such long hours that they had their three kids in breakfast clubs and after-school clubs every day – her own mum told her she might as well go the whole hog and have them adopted. This is the reason why the relief of leaving the payment for pre-school care behind (though the new 30 free hours a week is a godsend to many) is heavily hampered by the worry of what to do with so many extra hours when help is needed.

Every kind of strategy has been devised from swapping pick-ups and drop-offs with friends/neighbours, to calling in family or changing working patterns. 'My husband has changed his hours so he now leaves the house at 5am every day and starts work at 7am so he can leave at 2.30pm. I do the morning slot and drop-offs and he does pick-up', says one mum, who admits they're a bit disconnected as a result. Some swear by au pairs or local childminders who will do pick-up for you. Club provision can be the best or worst of times, with reports ranging from kids running feral in gangs all day and watching borderline inappropriate pirate DVDs to jam-packed days of thrilling activities. The latter, naturally, tending to be more expensive than a fortnight in the Caribbean.

A mum in retail sees holidays as the highest pressure point. 'The times when it's most hard are those things outside of the norm – seasonal events like Christmas and summer holidays can send me into a meltdown. They are usually also the busiest times at work. I sometimes feel I could go into a room and cry because it all gets too much. I go and do "smash and grab" shops in a frantic panic and find I have 17 T-shirts and no shorts! It takes the first few days of holidays to wind down.'

An estate agent reflects on this:

'When my kids were at nursery and early primary school age I couldn't wait for the school holidays to end. Basically, holidays meant maybe a few days of "holiday" for the whole family (which really meant just trying to pack up our whole lives and all associated stuff into carry-on bags to be stressed out and exhausted in a different environment for a while) and then a series of childcare headaches – (uncomfortably asking for favours from non-working mothers that I would probably never repay – and they knew that – asking my elderly parents to step in, sending the children to ridiculously expensive "camps" that they hated and protested about going to more than they ever did about school). So the sigh of relief when they got back to school, routine, planned childcare etc was huge.

'But as they've got older I kind of dread their going back. I love the slower pace of life in their school holidays – of course now they're more self-sufficient and can be left to their own devices (at least up to a point). I like the fact that they're still in their PJs at noon and that there's no pressure of homework, sports kits and weekends of football matches and gym competitions. Over the last few years I've noticed how down I've felt going back to work after a family holiday, particularly when the kids are still off. It's almost a kind of mourning – I miss them and I miss that feeling of lolling around together not really doing much. [Major difference between older and younger kids: older kids know how to loll.] Recently, I've tried to build in a couple of buffer days so that I'm not bouncing straight back into work the morning after we get back from holidays – it's just too depressing and too much of a shock to the system, and I don't think anyone in the office wants to hear you moan about how you miss your kids when as far as they're concerned you've just had a blissful two weeks away from work....

'I'd definitely recommend trying to make friends with nearby neighbours with older children – particularly sixth formers – to help with some babysitting as it seems that most kids love these "half grown-ups" and they're usually keen to make money and reasonably flexible on hours. Plus their parents (realistically their mums) are accessible to them by phone if they're not sure what to do and they don't want to bother you – back-up. In holidays the teaching assistants at school can be a good source of reliable help as most are so badly paid they appreciate some extra cash.'

One practical tip on getting the best out of holidays, however short, is to take a little time with your kids to create a bucket list of what everyone would like to do with that time. So, if you do have to work four days of half-term but have three days together at the end you can actively plan that time to include what everyone wants and needs (within reason!). Similarly, for family holidays and Easter/Christmas breaks, taking the time to plan the celebration well can make a big difference. It's so easy to get caught up trying to buy presents or Easter eggs that you forget that what the kids might really love is to draw their own T-shirts for the occasion, go to the special hot chocolate place that puts the marshmallow on top or go for a family swim at the big pool with the slides.

A mum who lives in a village describes how on INSET days (unilateral training days mid-term that schools love to chuck under the wheels of working parents) the mums are all working from home and 'bouncing a gang of 10-year-old kids between their houses in shifts so they can all get work done'. Although a consistent caution from almost all working parents is that seeking to combine work and kids at the same time is, at worst, 'like a slow painful suicide': but to be fair it gets more achievable as they grow up and become more independent. A mum who has always worked during holidays while the kids are downstairs says, 'If you do need to do some work while the kids are in the house, the key is to be very clear with them about how long you will be, and what you are going to do together afterwards. Clarify the situation by saying something like: "I will be working upstairs for two hours, during which time you can play with whatever you want downstairs. After that we will have some lunch together, and then you can choose what we do. If you keep interrupting me during my working time, it will take me longer and we will have less time to do stuff together." It helps if you set them up with sufficient activities that they can easily achieve on their own before you disappear to your desk, and set a time limit on their screen time (if their devices allow this – some do).' Another says that she takes great pride in always booking out her annual leave before anyone else she works with so she gets the best slots and builds her plan for the year's cover – a mix of grandparents, clubs, aunts, parents – from the start of January.

A mum with teens reflects:

'When kids are ill … what a nightmare. I shudder and am deeply embarrassed to remember leaving my son at home alone when he had a bad cold because I just couldn't get out of work and my husband was off somewhere. That was when he was in Year Five (aged 10). I've lied at work about being ill myself in order not to say I'm taking time off because one of the kids has been unwell. Somehow you feel it weakens your position and exposes you as a … what?? … a parent…! to admit that your child *needs you*. I've seen people, usually men, make faces at work, exchange glances, roll their eyes when someone, usually a woman, has taken time off for a sick child and I've been asked "Well, couldn't you get someone else to look after them?" when I've taken time off myself. The question is annoying on so many levels – on a practical level because it was asked by a man with a stay-at-home wife – the implication being that surely, I must have a similar arrangement myself, or if not, a number of keen female relations living around the corner, 1950s style. And on a more values or empathetic level because it ignores the fact that I might want or feel I need to be with my child when they're unwell.'

The fact that women are more likely to stay home with unwell children is a distinct professional disadvantage. At a breakfast meeting recently, two women out of 20 attendees cancelled at the last minute. 'Bloody women' said the organiser, rolling his eyes in mock humour. One had a child who got an operation rescheduled at the last minute. The other was woken by a toddler with a raging temperature at 5am. The attendees who did get there made good connections and a number of them said later it was useful for finding new work opportunities. So it was a double loss for the mums: networking and a reputation hit. A therapist I spoke to says that she advises couples before kids to talk through their deal on career sacrifice after children because she so often sees these default 'mum' answers as a source of conflict.

Parents of children with Special Educational Needs (SEN) can find it even harder. One teacher says: 'Schools are by law required to take children and students with SEN, however Extended Day Activity and Holiday Club providers are not, and some refuse to do so if they cannot cope with the specific needs of the child. Working parents with SEN children have to find carers with additional skills to care individually for their child and collect them from school at the end of the school day. These people are few are far between. In addition, parents do not necessarily have the strategies to cope with encouraging their SEN offspring with homework and find themselves in the Catch-22 situation for wanting to earn to provide quality additional care for their child, but being unable to do so as they have no one to leave them with.' Similarly, children with SEN are less likely to be able to cope with breakfast clubs and after-school provision than other children and are much more reliant on routine and being supported by the same person at home every day, which means you simply can't just palm them off on a changing roster of different people at the school gates – be they paid help or other mums.

A teacher who specialises in SEN adds an extra caution: 'You can pay for extra help for your child with SEN, to cover you outside of school and to help build skills, but you need to be very careful. A huge number of people advertise as having specialist skills but, in reality, have an online diploma. I would advise anyone to check their credentials are from a proper university very carefully.'

SEN children can also pose a problem if you work a long way from the school. A mother whose daughter has autism says 'The chances are that you will be required to drop everything and go in when something goes wrong, sometimes taking the child home with you if things have got really out of hand, like when they punch a teacher or won't stop screaming in class. I was called in every single day for half a term in Year One, thankfully it's got better since. The point is that you need to have a much closer link with the school so you can find out exactly what is happening, how their learning is being supported, and whether they are actually receiving the extra provision that they require. On the social side, they probably need more help making friends, so the onus is on you as the parent to get to know the other parents and set up play dates and supervised social events which depends on your being around. It's also important to communicate to other parents that your child does have special needs, so if they attack or are mean to someone else's child there is at least a degree of allowance made for this. Other parents are generally very understanding and once they know about the issue can be an invaluable source of support for you as well as your child.'

What does work when dealing with schools?

Teachers and heads beg for parents to be engaged, at least to some extent, and broadly supportive. The best marriage advice I was ever given was to assume that anything you partner says or does *begins with good intentions*. Even if that turns out to be wrong, at least you started in the right place. Schools would ask for the same courtesy: start with the assumption they do things for logical and sensible reasons and work from there. Don't jump immediately to the worst-case scenario, don't assume they are 'out to get you' and try to hold off the all-guns-blazing scene until you know what is going on. Don't forget that, like politicians, their job is to look at the needs of all the kids in their care. Not just your needs. Which means that someone will always be disappointed.

That said, never be naïve. Experienced working mothers encourage staying on it with schools. A mother of three in their late teens says: 'Keep a close watch on the education your kids are getting, wherever they go to school. Remember no one cares about your kids as much as you … so don't be too trusting on the progress they are or are not making. Learn to understand the curriculum and make it your business to know what they are meant to be learning. This applies at all stages from childhood to adulthood.' Others recommend engaging fast if you see anything going wrong – from eating disorders to concerns about bullying to worries about special needs. The advice is to be on it enough to spot it early and then do something about it. Don't assume it's a phase and let it drift into a crisis.

This engagement applies to all ages but there is also some specific guidance. In the early years, the daily reading *is* important. Ignore it and risk that your child will start to slip behind the others and at some point, this may come back and bite you. Now, listening to a Reception-age child read is fine, even a pleasure, if you are in the right frame of mind. But, if you've just charged through the door, your pulse buzzing from a frantic day, it will be brain-explodingly painful. 'Cuh. O. Wuh.' says the child as it stares at the picture of the cow and tries to run those sounds together and remember what an 'OW' sounds like. Finally, they get it. 'COW!' they shout. Delight and high fives all round. Then, turn the page, look blankly at the first word, still with a cow picture, 'Cuh. O. Wuh….' They stare at the page utterly lost for an answer and it is all you can do not to scream, 'It's a BLOODY COW, you dozy child. YOU just *SODDING* read it'. As you smile and will them on with your eyes.

Everyone says that you have to find special close moments to read once a day but most mums I spoke to admit that they do it while stacking the dishwasher or packing lunches. It's not ideal but the way I see it, if you're not simultaneously on your WhatsApp and combing for nits, take it as a win.

As the reading progresses, in come the spellings (for most schools, some are too cool for them these days, lucky you) and the times tables. Engagement required. Easier to combine with bleaching the sink or while in the car on the school run, though. Later it all gets much more complicated, especially if their work moves online and you can't view their tasks without remembering all their passwords. Wise parents advise still keeping an eye on it though so they don't get the idea you are no longer interested and so they can be disinterested too.

In terms of how you personally engage with the school, there is a vast spectrum and the riskiest spots are at either end. Not engaging at all – while alluring on so many levels – is laden with problems. However, going full pelt will kill you as schools will gobble as much of your capacity as you allow. If you're a Marmite character who easily falls out with people, you might also want to hold back from full-on engagement, at least in the early years. People can stay around schools for a long time and embarking on an endless psychological war is draining and pointless.

Seek a middle way and manage it as carefully as you would a new job. Don't fall into the trap of undervaluing your own time. If you take a pay cut to do a four-day week, don't make the mistake of devoting your 'spare' day to school and finding that your weekend is packed with all the stuff you wanted to do on that day at home. A university administrator told me that when she was on the PTA she got into big fights with her husband as she'd ask him to be home early from work and look after the kids at all events – which he was fine about doing – except she always ended up coming home late, tired and slagging off everyone on the committee. He ended up shouting, 'Why don't you just do something you want with your time and enjoy it rather than dragging us all into it and ending up furious?' To his possible point, I've noticed that a lot of dads are adept at getting this right. Or, perhaps, have less expected of them so are appreciated for time-defined tasks. They seem better at being clear about what they will and won't do and not worrying about it.

A dad of two who works for a coffee chain explained: 'I've established that my role is to provide the stuff other people can't. I gift a big bunch of coffee and food vouchers for the fair and raffle. On the business side, I help kids get work experience at our headquarters or in one of the cafés and will also do talks about business and management at the school.' These efforts did not, however, protect him from the head of the PTA, who set upon him one day when he was delivering his vouchers and said that parents like him needed to do more than just 'give stuff', they needed 'to volunteer like everyone else'. He laughs when he tells this. Her take didn't bother him at all, he just said he couldn't give it the time and continued to make his contributions. This stands in marked contrast to the armies of women who have invested weeks and months on invisible tasks that no one ever truly seemed to notice.

That said, another mum remarks: 'I notice that the chair, vice chair, secretary and treasurer roles at our parent council are all women. The men would not step up. And these roles have to be done. So, if we all behaved like men, I wonder if it would function at all?'

At the most down-to-earth end, turning up at the primary school gate a few times a week – regularly, but it doesn't have to be every day – seems to be linked to mums especially being calmer and happier. Perhaps because it connects them into school, kids and parents. Perhaps because the rituals of pick-up and drop-off are so psychologically comforting. It is, I believe, the reason why mums with long commutes find them more draining than dads do: it separates them from the community their kids and friends live in. I find that I feel just a little less securely grounded on days when I race to work early compared with those when I've delivered our children, on time and appropriately attired, through the right doors. My husband likes to do this too, but says it doesn't have the psychological resonance for him as it does for me. Another dad says something similar, albeit with some disdain for the humdrum:

'A lot of the day-to-day random chaos of family life – essential though it undoubtedly is that your children are wearing shoes to school in the morning – feels somewhat low value to me. But I think, interestingly, Rita gets much more value out of the random chaos than I do. For me it's just logistics and a lot of whining, for her, getting them to school in the morning with the right shoes on the right feet seems much more of an achievement and a valued part of her day.' I'm definitely with Rita.

Secondary school is a different beast because the daily drop-off is gone: your kids will kill you if you insist on walking them after the first day. Usually the form teacher is the key as they are the first port of call. As above, making nice with whoever it is seems to deliver better results than no relationship or a snippy one: 'I make sure to praise and praise and praise when we meet,' said one mum, 'even though my daughter thinks her form tutor is "constantly premenstrual". She triages me to maths teachers if an exam causes a home crisis etc – there are so many teachers at secondary it's impossible to keep track without having someone as a connector for you.'

The most important thing about engaging with school is to decide how you (and your partner, if you have one), as a family, want to be involved, what you can offer and what your boundaries are. A therapist mum of teens says:

'I had taken on one of Elliot's teachers at primary school who I felt was totally shit – in fact she was clinically depressed, which I felt sympathy with her about but it meant she did not smile at any of her class all day ever for months and was clearly not coping. At a parents' evening I had it out with her and then told my best mum friend the next day over coffee. She totally disagreed with my approach, said it was uncool to have challenged the teacher and that you just have to go with the flow on these things really, those sorts of issues are too intractable, that it would all even out in the end. I was devastated at being criticised for my approach, I was only trying to do the right thing for my child. It took me a good couple of days to recover. Now, with hindsight of course, I can see that she was right but at the time I was absolutely convinced that this conversation with teacher needed to happen. The point being that the wise parent decides *with their partner* on what the approach to the teacher and head is going to be, acts on it and then absolutely does NOT discuss it with other parents.'

Others add caution to this: slagging off a former teacher to parents whose kids are about to get them and calling that 'the lost year' probably isn't very helpful, and they may have a better experience than you did anyway.

If you're too tired and wired to read the above

- Education is a marathon not a sprint. Being madly obsessive about any phase of it is exhausting and, when you look back on it later, will probably seem like a total waste of energy. Yes, even the bit where you moved house to get your kids into the right school. Loads of parents say later they shouldn't have bothered. Stay engaged throughout the process to the level that works for you. Expect ups and downs, be on hand to help sort things out and try to avoid catastrophising each incident. Try to keep your involvement consistent. Don't swoop in full of drama over a crisis and then vanish until the next incident.

- Very specifically, parents advise to never do any of the following: fall out with the school receptionist; ask the school office why they phoned the mother not the father; admit to having ignored a phone call from the school office (just pretend you left your phone at home); check your email, Facebook/WhatsApp while your kid is telling you how they got a Dojo (no, we don't really know what Dojos are either); volunteer to lead the school parents' group; admit you sent your kid in with a fever and stuffed full of Calpol; admit to anyone you forgot about the class mascot that was sent home for Christmas, stuffed it in the cupboard and made up shit it did in the holidays for the fucking book you have to write in; ask the teacher/other parents why the class mascot has to exist when it just creates work for parents who are already too busy....

- As with work, don't close your mind to other options if a school isn't working for you. Yes, you might have to move school but, if it's that important to you, don't get trapped in a hostile relationship long term. That said, if you do move, don't recreate the same dynamic elsewhere.

- *Never rummage in school bags to compare reading stage books when you have kids over to play.* The kid reading *Harry Potter* independently in Reception may have no mates in secondary. On this theme, never show off about the reading stage or mathematical ability of your kid. Other parents will smile politely and then go home and rip the head off a voodoo doll with your face on it.

- If you choose to consider private schools, be sure that you can afford it: not just the headline fee but with uniforms, lunches, trips, etc taken into account too. Especially if you are someone who will be sensitive that your child appears to be 'deprived' compared to other kids there. I hear from so many career parents who regret signing up to the fees but feel they cannot now move their kids without destabilising them. Some realise later that they would have preferred to have had less financial pressure and more time at home with their families. Remember that even if your state school options are not perfect you will have more time to help if you're not as tied to the rat race paying for private, and will be more able to afford extras like tutoring or drama or music lessons if you need them.

- Be aware of your own psychological demons with school and try not to entangle your kids with them. The head is not your boss and you shouldn't be terrified or him/her. Teachers are not your staff and should not be terrified of you. Normal adult/adult relationships are the way forwards. Any parent/child-style interaction that doesn't involve actual children needs to stop.

- Skip the yummy mummy wars and don't see the Stay At Home Mums (SAHM) as the enemy. If you are never there, they don't hate you: they don't think about you because they don't know who you are. Or maybe they've even got a bit of a crush on you and your new Boden coat and are dying to get to know you if only you had time for a Friday-morning coffee....

- But don't be so invisible that you have no idea who anyone is or who teaches your kids. When something blows – and during a whole education everyone has some bad moments – you need to have enough knowledge and contact to sort it out effectively.

- When you do need to sort things out, confront gently. Assume no ill intent. Ask, listen, think. Don't be the parent every teacher dreads to hear from. You'll just end up knowing less and getting less support.
- Actively choose how engaged with school you want to be: being a governor or on the PTA are options, but neither come without significant risks of being drawn into politics and guilted into devoting more time than you intended.
- If you resent how much you are doing for school, then that is the indicator that it's time to change it. But you don't have to see this as 'all or nothing'. Find a middle way. The best route is perhaps to choose something you can contribute that is tangible, visible and time-boxed and consistently deliver this throughout the school years – buying a hamper for the Christmas raffle or being the face-painting ace at every event, or whatever it is you can do without feeling irritated.
- Keep focused on what works for you *as a family*. One working mum nearly collapsed trying to manage three kids in three different schools. She had the revelation that it wasn't just about what school worked for each child, it was about what worked for the whole household. Moving them into the same school has made the week a hundred times easier and smoother, and the whole family feels happier and more stable.
- Also practise having good conversations about school that aren't just you being fobbed off with 'it's fine' or 'I can't remember'. A therapist told me they have a family ritual where everyone talks about their day – the highs, the lows, the trivia. They ask each other questions, laugh and sympathise and, she reports, it's one of the most important things they do.
- Choose your own approach to your kids' education and your own role in homework.

What happened next?

DEBORAH DECIDED TO ENGAGE more with school. She started by inviting a few of the girls in her daughter Eva's class over on playdates and getting to know their parents gradually. Rather than signing up to the formal PTA, she decided to start helping out on a few school trips and events and getting to know the school and teachers better. Her daughter loves to see her mum in school and waves proudly to her when she spots her. She has invested more of her own time in helping with reading and feels it's getting better slowly. For the moment, she's not thinking about private options but secondary is another question…

CHAPTER TWELVE

Help, my teenager is causing problems

WE HAVE FOUR KIDS and are a close family, I've worked, aside from maternity leaves, since I qualified, but as the children have got older and more independent, I've started to think about moving into a bigger, management role. Until now, I've always put the kids first but have started to feel that it's time to get some of 'me' back. Having kids puts your life on hold but there's a time when you need to own it again otherwise when they leave, what are you left with? I think I saw this with my own parents… and they soon spilt after we were all older and independent. I didn't want this to happen to me and our family. If someone was going to love me forever I needed to love myself and be ME, not just Mum and Wife.

All our kids have always been great but very recently our eldest is causing headaches: until now she's been really sensible, very sporty and good at school. Suddenly she is on me all the time, always on my phone, texting, nagging me. Wanting money, waxing, trips, parties and more expensive makeup than I have. I think this is just a typical 14-year-old, as they all seem the same when I speak to my other mum friends, but nevertheless it's tiresome and disappoints me as to how selfish she can be at times. You always think you've brought them up to see things from everybody's point of view but sometimes they can only see themselves.

A few weeks ago she went for a sleepover with a friend from her high school that we don't know. We come from a village where at primary school everyone knows the children and the parents – it's safe and almost like extended family. At high school you lose that control and hope and pray that you've embedded values for them to be able to pick friends and make wise choices as you are often not part of some of those decisions. We called her at 7pm to check in and found she and the friend were on their own at the shopping centre. I don't know what made us call but I'm so glad we did. When asked how she was getting home, she replied 'walking'! Well, it was dark and the route they planned was down an alley called 'the black path' so you can imagine my horror. When asked where the girl's parents were she replied that her dad and his new girlfriend were drinking at the pub. At that point I scraped my husband off the ceiling and sent him to fetch them and drop her friend safely back home.

A few weeks after that, I got a call late one night from one of my close mum-friends who had overheard her child and my daughter talking about how our daughter had sent a Snapchat naked selfie of herself to a boy she'd met at the gym. Luckily my friend knows my daughter well and was able to probe her on this straight away and my daughter felt comfortable talking to her, but it left me feeling hurt as to why she hadn't come to me. She'd obviously been feeling anxious about it which is why she was discussing this with her friend. As it unfolded, we found it had stemmed from a boy asking her to send photos of her naked and my daughter at first refusing. However, the boy got very forceful on instant messages and said if she didn't send them he would beat up her best friend (a boy). With that threat my daughter sent him the pictures he wanted. She's renowned for being a very sensible girl – she's the girl who other mothers always say they wish their own was more like. I am still staggered she would even think of doing something so stupid. She's never had a boyfriend and there have been plenty of discussions about online safety. We talk to her all the time about being in uncomfortable situations and not to ever do anything she doesn't want to – how could she not say 'no' after all the discussions?

Now the whole house is in crisis. I'm completely devastated. She is crying hysterically and refusing to go to school. She feels totally ashamed of herself and is having to deal with her own guilt and I'm left having to deal with mine about letting her down as a parent and a confidante.

The thing is that the kids are older now and I've just started to reclaim myself. I lost four stone last year and feel so much better. I feel so ready to take a management role where I work. I thought the kids would be more independent as they get older, but I actually am starting to think they need me more.

Sacha, 43, Nurse

****

As every mother of a toddler who meets a mum with teens knows, they say: 'Enjoy them now, I know you think they're difficult but, believe me, it's actually *much* harder later on.'

No one with small kids has ever believed this – they just laugh edgily, wondering how it is that people forget so fast. I mean, if your kids can wipe their own arses, sleep in their own beds and never fiddle with their willies in public, what do you have to complain about? The teen mothers see this thought process, wish that all these things were actually true of their teens, and give up trying to explain. They know they didn't believe it either and, in the same way that not knowing about childbirth can be seen as a kindness, wonder if it's perhaps better not to know.

What I get from talking to mums of teens and older kids is that, in the teenager years, traumatic events just seem to happen. However well brought up and sensible your child is, everyone seems to have a crisis. Some have many. They range from unexpectedly failing exams to eating disorders, shoplifting to pregnancy, devastating break-ups, drug misuse and doodling swastikas on pencil cases. You never know where they will come from. A mum who has kids who are now in their 20s says it's best not to even try to predict because, whatever you think the issue will be, it never is. They always surprise you and you just have to deal with them. A mum of five kids agrees, saying that the great advantage of having so many children is that they all have such different crises you can't hold your parenting style responsible for *all* of them.

Psychologists explain that the teenage years are the time when our children learn to separate from us and become independent. It is part of their biological journey to fight for their right to be treated as adults, but many then prove that they are extremely poor at predicting the consequences of their actions and circle back to needing parental support. As Sacha and her family have suddenly discovered.

Somewhat terrifyingly, journalist and mother-of-four Geraldine Bedell puts it like this:

'By the time they're 14 I tend to think your work is done: annoyingly, there's only a limited amount you can do after that! I'm not sure how conscious a process this even is – but it's something to do with conveying to them that you're on their side and you won't throw them out. It's about getting them to understand your bedrock values in a way that means they have some respect for your red lines (whether that's about valuing education or being kind to people or not partying during the week). Not that they'll necessarily stay within your boundaries – but you do want them to appreciate why they matter to you.'

That said, working parents often say that they were astounded to discover that, just at the moment they expected to be able to focus more on work, the demands of their children actually increase. In a recent article, Lorraine Candy, editor-in chief of *Sunday Times Style*, goes as far as to say she should have kept half of her four maternity leaves for the teenage years. Many parents also find that this is a period when they want to be more involved and desire to spend more time with their children because they enjoy it and because they want to be that first port of call in a crisis.

A shift in the power balance

Which isn't to say it's all a joy. Many a parent of teens wonders when exactly someone stole their child and replaced them with a monster. 'Toddlers are all about the logistics. As someone used to organising work you can take control of their needs in an organised way. Teens are big, difficult emotional stuff. You wonder if it's because you work but, when you have a few kids, you realise they are all different and it's just because they are teenagers. It seems to me that all thinking teenagers have dark patches.' This from a mum who works full time and has a houseload of children.

A dentist I spoke to says: 'When they are little and you say "no" then it means no and they accept it. But teens will argue and argue and argue and never give up. I didn't think that I would ever say this, but you do have to pick your battles, because they will fight you on everything and it's just so draining. They'll say they are going to a friend's for tea, you'll say they can't because you are away that weekend at their gran and grandad's house, they'll say you didn't tell them that and it's their best friend and it's their birthday and all their friends are going so they are staying behind … and on and on it will go.'

Not only have you seemingly lost the power you so recently had over their actions but their irritation with you also increases dramatically: 'They just don't care what you think about anything. They just don't care that there are 20 items of clothing on the floor and that every damned surface is covered with shit and clutter. It doesn't register as a problem. But a simple "can I have your washing?" is seen as an intrusion, an interference and then they get *really* grumpy. And you're only trying to wash their clothes and keep their rooms liveable in. Is it because it's their space? Or is it just easier to pick up everything from the floor? I really wish that I knew.'

It's common for parents to say that their teens actively seek to oppose every view they hold, however insignificant. This seems to escalate if it's a subject on which you are knowledgeable. A mum who works in fashion says: 'If you express a view. Say, holding up a jumper and saying "this one is nice, it suits you" you are met with denial. "No, it's awful, I hate it" and then they will never wear it. Never. I've learned that it's best not to express any view on anything.' Yet, at the same time, they frequently pass scathing judgement on their parents: 'My teenage kids are terribly judgemental and abstemious. If I ask them to pass me my glass of wine, they tell me I'll get mouth cancer from drinking it. But then they live in this world of different drugs and different sex and you wonder who is the abstemious one.' Another mother reports that her son regularly asks in sarcastic tones, 'Another glass, mother?', making her feel bad about what, she is adamant, is a very modest drinking habit.

A mother of children who has largely emerged from this stage reflects soberly on its significance to the experience of family life:

'The terrible thing about teens is what they say to you. It's awful. They're not in love with you anymore: not like a six-year-old loves you. They have periods of hating you and it's heartbreaking. They do come back eventually but not the same. An older friend told me that God created teens so that we could bear to let our children go. It's just a process you and they have to go through. If you see them at six you can never imagine you'd let them go. But after the teens you are kind of ready.

When they re-emerge as adults they are nice relatives you love to see for a few days but who then go on their way. It's a process that's a million times worse than childbirth. You suddenly realise you'll never all sit down every week and watch *I'm a Celebrity* together again and it makes you terribly sad.'

The biggest thing parents who've been there say is that you have to be prepared to be tough and stay in the parent role. Everyone has a story about a mum or dad who wanted their teen's attention so much that they bribed, begged and cajoled them to hang out. Especially parents who work a lot and then feel really guilty they are never home, so go all overindulgent to compensate. One who tried it says: 'We worked out that cool parenting isn't very cool if you see it through the frame that they need boundaries not more mates. As we found out, if you loosen your grip, it is a bugger to get your authority back later.'

Big emotions

The emotional roller coaster of the hormonal teens is perhaps to be expected but presents particular problems for working parents.

'I think that the tricky thing with teens is that unlike little ones who need you a-bit-all-the-time, teens really don't need you much but when they do it's at a time of their choosing and it can be quite intense, for example, if they get very anxious about something at school it could well come out at 10pm the night before you have an important breakfast meeting or whatever. It took me a while to get my head around needing to have that kind of flexibility – it's an emotional and mental flexibility rather than a timetable flexibility. Which of course is the bit that you get very skilled at when they're little.' Most agree that picking up on the brief moment when they want to talk is essential for keeping connected.

A mother who was too busy to catch a lot of these occasions realised that her daughter was confiding in her sister (the girl's aunt), which she saw as a good thing but said it also made her feel jealous that she wasn't included. She knew she was becoming more disconnected and resolved to try to engage better. She found that banning herself from delaying tactics, such as saying 'yes darling, we can talk in a minute, just let me finish this email and call Nana first', which she came to accept meant that they never happened. That said, many teens and their parents are extremely grateful to wider family members at this time. Aunts, uncles, grandparents and so on can be exactly what frustrated teens need when their parents are doing their heads in and their parents are overly reactive to them. Quite a few parents have told me that their kids (it often seems to be girls) spent periods of their late teens living with relatives when it all got too feisty at home. One mother says it felt like a crisis when her daughter temporarily moved out but, in retrospect, it was essential for allowing them to shift into a more positive dynamic.

For those in big jobs who can afford it, boarding school is sometimes an option in senior school, perhaps on a weekly basis and some parents I've interviewed have gone down this route. One mother explained how her kids had wanted to attend because she and her husband were out so much in the week they'd rather be with their friends than at home. They had a brilliant experience and they were all happy at the time. But, later, after they had left, she wondered if she had made the right choice. Her children struggled at college (this may not be a coincidence, research from the University of Cambridge in 2015 found that state school pupils are likely to do better at university than privately educated ones who start their courses with similar grades). One child seemed inclined towards taking any drug he was offered and dropped out, and the other self-harmed – and she wondered if they would have been more settled had they and their parents been home more. She will never know. The problem perhaps with not having your children at home is that it creates a focus of blame if things do go wrong. If you are inclined to such thoughts, you might want to consider that in your decision, and perhaps avoid reading the study that indicates that the amount of maternal involvement is particularly critical to good outcomes in adolescents (see References, page 305).

Perhaps part of the risk of teens being away at school or living elsewhere generally is that the moments they want to talk are random – occasional bedtimes, odd moments and in the car. A mum of two says:

'It's not a myth that the best way to talk to them is in the car – they seem to be more willing to tell you stuff when you're concentrating and can't make eye contact! So even though it's entirely appropriate to moan about being a taxi driver, you're best off to make the most of it as it's probably when you'll find out who they're going out with and the latest gossip. Also, if you have a big group of them in the back their banter – 'bants' – can be quite hysterical. Good to tune into if you decide you might one day pack your job in and become a stand-up comedian.' Child psychotherapist Sarah Clarke absolutely agrees with the benefits of 'side-by-side talking', which is less threatening and more constructive. She also recommends cooking as an opportunity for this.

It is also useful to stay connected to other parents:

'Don't be lulled into a false sense of security when your child starts secondary school. It feels quite liberating to no longer have to do the school drop-off/pick-up thing – get to work early, clear your inbox, yay! – but, as I learned, this doesn't mean you can become completely detached from the whole school scene. When my son hit his teens and started to go out more in the evenings I suddenly realised I had no idea who his friends were or where they lived, who their parents were etc. And you can't crash that secondary school socialising scene in Year 10 – too embarrassing to turn up at class drinks and have to introduce yourself to parents who've known each other for three years already! With child number two I'm being a lot more diligent on that front. So when I don't know where she is at 2am at least I'll know who to call....'

This is a message that is reiterated many times in different forms: 'My daughter wasn't home when she should have been, I have made an effort to know the parents of her friends so called a few of them, was told that they'd been spotted at the rec and headed up there to track her down.'

Organisation and logistics

Working parents tend to continue to apply their need for a structured life through the teen years, and, in some ways, this works very well. But it does have consequences.

'It's very tempting to do too much for them because it suits your working life and you need to be really well organised. We have these really busy and complicated weeks so I got used to planning everything: when matches were, social events, what kit they needed every day. I put everything into the central family diary and always checked it so I knew exactly who was due where and when and with what. Because I knew that we couldn't ever drop stuff they had forgotten to school and if they missed a music lesson we were paying for that would drive me into a fury. So that worked for us for a long time. But then you turn around when they are 16, and realise that they can't organise their lives *at all* because you have done all their thinking for them. It's maddening.'

Sacha would say that this was probably her. She had the time and the need to organise her family pretty tightly. So she did take on a lot of the thinking for them. This isn't to say that her children are scatty as a result, but she does now sometimes wonder if they were overprotected and didn't have enough chance to feel the consequences of decisions. When she thinks about this, she usually comes to the conclusion that she will protect them more and not less after this incident.

Others actively seek to impose responsibility on their kids from an early age, letting them forget kit, miss music lessons and fail tests if they don't remember things themselves. Some say it works brilliantly and they have well-rounded and responsible kids. Others say they tried it and it was the most heart-rending, stressful thing they ever did and they gave up quickly. Certainly therapists favour this approach, and encourage us to give our children choices from the earliest years of toddlerhood to build their inclination towards good and responsible decision making.

Sex, drugs and mobile phones

The issues that our teens are up against in some ways feel so familiar. Especially to those of us who aren't 100 per cent sure that we're even grown-ups yet. We read *Romeo and Juliet* and instantly recognise all the angst and self-absorption of youth. We see ourselves in them: 'I might have a responsible role now, with employees who report to me and a budget, but I still feel like a kid in some ways. I still drink too much. Me and my partner love a spliff. It feels like only yesterday that I caused my parents a lot of problems. My father was the head of my school and I humiliated him by running off with a boyfriend at 14, I got caught stealing cigarettes and vomited Cinzano at the end-of-year prom. I try to bear this in mind with mine … but I'm not sure it helps.' Naturally, however wild our pasts, our children think that we're ancient and clueless about everything they care about. And the scary thing is that they might be right because the context of drugs, relationships, gender identity, self-harm and phone use have all changed so much.

The mobile phone and social media are, of course, at the front line of this angst. For working parents the issues range from constant low-level intrusions into their time through to the serious problems Sacha is dealing with.

A wise friend advises:

'Find out about the secondary school's phone policy – I found it really disconcerting when my daughter started secondary school, which is when she, like most of her friends, got her first phone. I was used to dropping her off at primary school and then not having to think about her (in the nicest possible way of course!) for the whole day – but now she can text me/call me whenever she wants and the school doesn't seem to think this is an issue. So I can be at work and get a text saying "I've forgotten my maths book – help", followed by six desperate emojis or "what's for dinner?", or "I'm really upset because so-and-so just blanked me". It feels like she's going backwards in terms of independence and it's distracting – there's not a lot you can do if you're in a meeting and your daughter wants her maths book, which is on the bathroom floor at home.'

This obviously veers into much more tricky territory, which is why many families agree on phone rules – not in bedrooms, not at night, get access to their social media passwords, shut down the household wifi at 10pm and so on. Others go the other way and stress the importance of trust. A lead-parent dad says: 'With teens you have to let go of control and trust them. You have to accept that you can't police them and have to rely on the fact you've brought them up half decent and they have to make good judgements. We just say "write nothing that you wouldn't say to someone's face". This approach does especially require an openness of conversation that ensures they will confide in you if something does go wrong. Another dad said that his approach with his teenage daughter is to say: 'I'll never be cross and I'll never shout, just tell me what happened and we'll sort it out. And then we'll work out how to tell your mum.' I wish I knew what her mother thought of this.

Jonathan Baggaley, CEO of the PHSE Association (it stands for personal, social, and health education and they provide advice on the subject) concurs:

'The choice for parents between allowing their children to "get on with it" online and hoping they are sensible, versus actively monitoring, tracking or limiting their behaviour is difficult but is hardly a new problem. We know that children can very quickly get into trouble and situations can escalate in a matter of hours. The most important thing as a parent is that your child is confident enough to come to you with any problem they have. You want them to be able to walk away from the computer and get advice, whatever has happened. But they are less likely to do that if they expect a nuclear response, which they may worry about if they are banned from social media, or aren't meant to be using the internet.' Which is why the tactic of banning 4G connection and turning off the household wifi can backfire if your kids are able to tap into the neighbours' and then can't seek your help if something goes wrong.

And go wrong it can, with every scenario from paedophiles to group bullying and mortifying sexual experiences. Even the mundane is escalated when you can't ever escape it. Teenage girls were always pretty horrid to each other, but a mum describing how her daughter's classmates were continually re-adding her as 'a friend' in a WhatsApp chat in which they were all being cruel to her does strike you as a new form of torture.

Back to Joanthan Baggaley: 'In truth, there are some basic principles about online technologies that parents should under-stand in order to support their children online. Basically, if you understand that information might stay online forever, be searchable, copied infinitely and could end up "going viral" then you begin to understand the care you need to take online. Similarly, if you also understand that your communications and content might be viewed by people you've never met and may never meet, in contexts you didn't intend and that seemingly private interactions could become very public, very quickly, then you also appreciate how situations can escalate and young people find themselves in trouble.'

Principles that friends Alex and Luke, both 15-year-old boys, might have done better to understand. At Alex's house party, Luke climbed on to the roof of the family car to pose on his bike while all their friends took photographs. It didn't take long for this evidence to get back to Alex's parents – the car owners – who were predictably unimpressed and asked Luke's parents to pay for the damage he'd done scratching it. But then more photographic evidence appeared of a 'worse-for-wear' Alex being very sick on Luke's parents' velvet sofa and carpets. The issue of compensation came to a stalemate. While the boys remain friends, relations between the parents have never recovered.

The problem with teens and digital behaviours is that discipline and self-control are closely aligned with happiness generally. Neither are traits teens are famed for. There are well-established risks with overuse of mobiles, especially late at night and in the brutal teen world of social media. Essentially, you have to decide who is going to be adult in this engagement: if you think your kids should be, so be it. Agree the rules and keep an eye. If they can't manage it then you will have to.

But a teacher notes that your children with SEN are particularly vulnerable: 'In a world where the digital age is upon us this adds further anxieties for parents of SEN secondary students.

Any student with any online access is exposed. SEN students, especially those on the autistic spectrum who take words at face value, are particularly vulnerable. For them innuendo is anathema as they cannot sift out the difference between truth and lies. Constant supervision of their phones and online activity is essential and time consuming especially when your defenceless young person cannot be left on their own.'

On sex, things too are more complicated. 'When we were children the worst thing you could call someone was gay or lesbian. Now any gender or sexual preference is OK so only kids considered be to "geeks" define themselves as straight. That nice girl who's been staying over with your 15-year-old daughter every weekend for the last year turns out to be her girlfriend. It's all quite confusing.'

Modern parents are of course very worried by reports of growing levels of sexual harassment at colleges, of porn-inspired sexual practice – so much so that some say they have completely changed their take on what success looks like: 'When I was young my parents warned me against having a boyfriend and settling down young. Now I am so grateful my daughter is in a stable relationship. I even wonder if it would be so bad if she decided to settle down and have a baby. It would probably be fine. This is completely at odds with what my parents would have thought.' Another mum with two teenage daughters says she worries far less about the one with a regular boyfriend and a low-key weed habit than she does about her party girl who likes her cider.

Drugs are equally problematic. Back to Geraldine Bedell: 'What you hope is that your teens are resilient and can spot potential crises and pull back. You hope your child will be the one who sees they need to pull back from the skunk before they can't get out of bed in the morning. Talking to teens about drugs feels impossibly hard, because they always know more than you. And you want that, in a way: you want them to be informed. I think it's OK to keep asking questions, though, and let them know why you worry – to admit, say, that you're worried by the associations between skunk and schizophrenia. At the end of the day, you cross your fingers and hope that your child isn't the unlucky one that something happens to.'

Many parents worry about how honest to be with their own children about their own wild pasts. One asks 'Should you lie and pretend you were whiter than white? Or 'fess up, which perhaps means they are more likely to be able to talk to you about it (and know that you will be able to spot when they are doing it, having been there, done that)? Obviously, you need to stress the risks and illegality…. On balance, our take is that when the time comes we want our kids to know that we do have experience, but that it is illegal and damaging to your health, and that we will always be available if they want to talk to us about it, especially in an emergency or crisis, rather than them having to try to hide it. We also want them to know that if something happens to a friend they must tell an adult, especially if it's a medical emergency. That's just our take though.'

Anxiety

Teens both inspire and suffer from anxiety. Some parents say that their biggest parenting wish is to protect their children from a highly pressurised adolescence. 'The main priority of child rearing for me: keep them as anxiety-free as possible. The world seems hell bent on fighting me on that one, and I am trying my best to avoid competitive parents, who make me worry that they should be doing 12 clubs on a Saturday and be Grade 9 in something already, but so far, holding firm….'

Geraldine Bedell again: 'Parents sometimes convey to teens the idea that they only have one go at things: one chance to pass an exam or go to such-and-such a school, or be a success. And that creates a lot of stress and makes kids feel that it's monumentally important what decisions they make, and disastrous if they "fail". But that isn't actually how life works: there are often second chances. We do get over things and try again. It isn't catastrophic to fail – adults do it all the time, and we tell ourselves it's a learning experience. Yet with our kids, there's this tendency to imply it's now or never – and that's terrifying for them, and I think may be a factor in the high levels we're seeing of anxiety and depression. If they're not allowed to fail, they can't explore. And then they become unhappy and stressed by the pressure, because exploring (which means making mistakes) is actually what teens are programmed to do.'

Another mum thinks that working through the teen years has many advantages, despite all that anxiety: 'When I see fellow non-working mums who are at the stage of letting go of their 18-year-olds I am so grateful I work. These are women who are bright but who stepped out. They can't go back into work, it's too long ago, and their households have adjusted to them not working. But many of them are probably halfway through their lives and have no idea what they will do now. Two I know have had their husbands leave after long-term affairs. It seems the husbands were waiting for the kids to be out of the house before making their move. It's less expensive for them that way. These women are devastated, they have great holes in their life.

'One final thing – teens are often vilified but all the ones I meet are interesting, a bit bonkers and very, very funny. They like to hear about your job – as long as you don't talk about it in a self-aggrandising way – and I think my kids are (grudgingly) quite proud to have one of the full-time working mums in their classes. I'm less available for maths books that have been left at home, but I would say better company for them as a result. But then I would say that I wouldn't I?'

If you're too tired and wired to read the above

- Just as you thought you were through the worst of it, and started to focus more at work, you found your kids demanding more of your time and mental energy than ever before. Be reassured that this is what every parent of teenagers says. Of this, Karen Doherty counsels:

  'This period of family life is, without doubt, the harshest and most challenging of all. Families tend to hit everything at the same time: teenagers, hormones, 17-year relationship itch, middle age, ageing parents, decreasing sex drives… need I go on? This is the most vital time to get help. Having a safe place to converse with a trained third party on subjects as varied as menopause and its effect on sex, teenage moods and behaviour, different reactions of partners to boundaries and disciplining of kids, and mortality generally is invaluable. These sessions are conversations … but are so effective in breaking down the deadlock that the above can create between two parents who love each other and their families but are facing huge personal challenges, as well as those of the family.'

- Don't disconnect. This is the moment it can go off the rails, as a few mums have described in detail. Self-harm, anorexia, bad sexual choices…. Knowing their friends and briefing yourself on the issues is essential.

- But more important is being open to the random moments when they do want to talk. Usually at midnight when you have an early meeting and are already dog tired. Many parents advise you need to be clear about boundaries. Being constantly bombarded with emotional dramas while you are at work isn't conducive to your own mental health, nor is it the best way to engage. Agree to speak when it's appropriate and then make sure that you follow through with that commitment.

- Teenage issues have moved on. Gender fluidity is everywhere. The drugs have moved on. As for what they see online, who knows. In 'Digital Romance', a report by Dr Esther McGreeney and Dr Elly Hanson for Child Exploitation and Online Protection 2017, they identified what teens wanted in regards to relationship and sex education: it includes open spaces for honest conversations; less judgement and more acceptance of the importance of romances that largely happen digitally; more talk about the good and bad of relationships; and talking about LGBT relationships.

- Sarah Clarke agrees. Her experience working with a 14-year-old client included an interaction that went: '"Do you identify as being gay or straight?", to which "no" was the complete answer. Trying to put this into a wider perspective, I asked whether s/he identified as male or female. I was stared at straight in the eyes and give another "no". I realised that if I wanted to be successful in counselling teenagers I had a lot of work to do in shedding my old-fashioned desire to "box and label" in order to understand.'

- We should take advice from those a few years ahead of many of us. 'I wish I had listened more – even to the "it goes so quickly" stuff because it was right. I was redesigning my house at one point and an older friend said "you won't need lots of shared space, in a few years they will want to go to their rooms. You need to make sure your house is the one they all want to visit so you know where they are." She was so right.'

- Agree household policies before there is a crisis: if you clearly ban sleepovers midweek or with anyone you don't know well and stick to it, they will reduce their campaigning. If each invitation is a negotiation you have opened yourself up to years of battle. Same with mobile phones, if they all go into a cupboard at 9pm – *including yours* – there's not much debate about it.

- If your agreed policy is to trust their judgement, then stay close to them and keep talking. Watch for emotional blips, be prepared to engage if you think something might have gone wrong.

- Find some parent friends who don't drink, says one social mother. Otherwise you'll have years of sober Friday and Saturday nights being the taxi service.

- Be careful of inflicting teens in a difficult phase on your colleagues. One said: 'Never ask your colleagues to give your sulky teenager work experience. And never give your colleague's sulky teenager work experience either.' She also advised against inviting colleagues and bosses round to the house during the difficult years.

- Do try to enjoy it. Everyone says it is over very soon and you miss even this phase. Also, don't wait too long to go on the big holiday or get the dog or whatever because, before you know it, you're into a new phase of life. Very specifically on dogs, one dad advises buying a dog by matching its life expectancy (e.g. 10 years) to when your youngest will leave home (if assumed to be 18, you would want to buy the dog when your youngest is eight) so you will be both petless and childless at the same moment! I wonder whether this advice may in fact escalate an empty-nest crisis but pass it on regardless...

What happened next?

IN SACHA'S WORDS:

'My husband couldn't face or listen to a lot of the conversations my daughter and I had about this, he was in emotional turmoil... the thought of his 14-year-old daughter sending images via Snapchat was just something he'd never thought he'd have to think about, let alone discuss with her face to face. It was just too raw so he left it to me. I talked openly to my daughter about viewing sexual images online of underage children and the fact that it was a criminal offence, we touched on getting the police involved but I was in such a difficult situation I wanted to protect my daughter from any more hurt and shame. When she had finally confided in me I couldn't let her down by spreading this any further, so we decided that it would be best to keep it within the family. However, I did have to let the owner of the gym know for child safeguarding as I did not want anyone else to become subject to what my daughter had. It was another parenting first, one that tested me beyond anything I'd ever had to deal with before and I used to be stressed about not reading with them three times a week when they were at infant school! I wish I could sometimes be back there.

'The thing is the kids are older now and my impression was that they became much more independent, but give me those days back when they were dependent on me for tying their shoelaces or changing their nappies because this is a whole new ball game and is one that is not so easy to navigate. One that you never know whether you are doing the right thing, one which you cannot often ask for advice as the outside influences are different to what they used to be and YOUR confidante – who for me is my mum – hasn't the answers either.

'In the end, I decided not to take on the management role. It was increasingly obvious that the kids needed us around more than ever: not to get them dressed or remind them to brush their teeth but to be near, to be there for them so if anything needed sounding out we were there and they could. It sounds silly but that's all I felt they needed: our presence, because without I was unsure we would miss vital things and conversations that needed to be had. So, after much discussion, my husband and I decided that we needed to be around in the evening for the girls and by him taking on the school runs and me being available after 5pm every day we could achieve that. They need me more than ever and although I want to reclaim myself and be ME, I still had to think of the kids. You can never really be that selfish when you're a mum…'

CHAPTER THIRTEEN

What do the dads think?

I'VE WORKED FULL TIME for 30 years. When I met my wife, she did too – she valued her job and wanted to progress. But after we had kids, she moved to part time. I never really thought about it, it made sense and she's been able to take the lead on raising the kids.

But over the years, I've become disillusioned. My wife works the hours she wants, is under no pressure to earn anything of significance and does upholstery courses and art classes and things she likes. The kids want for nothing and go to loads of clubs and activities. But I don't enjoy my job. I would love to resign or scale back and do something that interests me. But that's not the deal. The deal is that I work and provide everything and don't complain. Maybe I wouldn't mind so much if we lived in the old world, where I got home to a warm welcome and family dinner. But that never happens, the kids are disrespectful and my wife makes it clear she has no interest in my views on parenting. Or, more depressingly, in me really. I'm a very frustrated parent. The pressure to pay for everything means I work long hours that leave no space for me to do the things I want and there is absolutely no sense that this is a deal where my time will come. I'd happily cut back on our life to escape this – selling the family house, anything – but I know it's not even a conversation my wife would have.

If I could go back and do it again, I would work hard to keep us as a team who shared the burden of earning and left space for us both to have meet our own needs. That's what the younger women I work with seem to do. Well I think they do. If I'm honest, I look at some of them with young kids and long hours and wonder if they are just as trapped as I am.

Richard, 52, Management Consultant

Over the years I've interviewed and talked to a lot of 'working dads' (see how surprising that phrase is?). Sometimes the partners of the women I interview. It's probably no great surprise that their views and experiences are as varied as their partners', as are the challenges they face. But there is something I always notice: their experience is *different* to their female partners but they want the same things. Research from America anyway backs this up. The Pew Research Center in America found that fathers were just as likely as mothers to say that parenting was extremely important to their identity (57 per cent and 58 per cent respectively in 2015). The same research found that almost half of fathers felt they weren't doing enough caring.

But let's start with the differences. And the first is that their emotional response to working and parenting is so often *much less highly charged*. Working dads tend to have no/low levels of guilt and lower levels of conflict about the compromises they make with regards to their work and family time. That isn't to say that they don't want to spend more time at home and might regret not doing so – many say exactly that – they very much do. The difference is that they rarely (if ever) say they feel crippled or frozen or anxious about it, and don't generally feel that society is judging them harshly. For example, if I ask a mum how she feels about attending evening events at work, I'll often hear something like: 'I never do more than two evenings a week and I won't do a breakfast on the same day as an evening thing, and I always do the school run the day after so I can catch up and I try to work from home one day a week, and, except for the Christmas period when it all goes mad, I mostly manage that and I do think that my kids see enough of me but I also wish there weren't so many evening events....' Whereas a dad asked the same question is more likely to shrug and respond 'It's part of my job, just the way it is, I avoid those I can.'

In terms of feeling judged and socially included or excluded by other parents, the working dads don't really comment on it, and at-home dads often express either equanimity about being excluded by the mums or positively choose to exclude themselves. Whereas the mums, working or not, often find exclusion by other mothers to be extremely painful, akin to physical pain. Some seem to convert this pain into irritation and actively bitch about the mum gang, which may make them feel better (though I'm not convinced) but it doesn't particularly assure me that they don't care. They often also feel excluded at work for not being part of the late crowd, bonding over the difficult project or being part of the bigger social scene.

The dads – like many mums – place themselves on a spectrum of how committed they are to investing their time and energy at home or at work.

There are some dads, often but not always a bit older, who strongly identify themselves as family 'providers'. Many provider dads are more likely to say that they are happy to be out of the house while their partners lead the childcare (and I suspect that the dad above may well have felt that way when the kids were very young). They are most likely to express the view that childcare is 'routine' and 'boring' and to think that their partners are better at it and/or enjoy it more, while they prefer to focus on specific activities.

'I would like to be more involved but in what I would describe as "quality" time. I think those fathers who feel they would have had a better relationship with their children if they hadn't been tied in to the provider role are talking bollocks. It's about what you do and how you behave in the time you do spend with your children, not the number of hours you put in.'

These dads are more likely to say that they work long hours, distinguish less between home and work time and see those who work fewer hours as at a professional disadvantage: 'We had a colleague whose wife wouldn't let him miss a single parents' evening or nativity play. I think he got the balance wrong and his performance suffered as a result, but I'm sure others would think that's a harsh judgement. He certainly caused a lot of resentment among his colleagues. As did a working mother I had in my team once – she was endlessly leaving early to go to school events, leaving her colleagues to pick up the slack and causing frustration particularly among the women who had made other choices.' These are the dads most likely to say that they were away for key or critical events (a school play or a child being hospitalised for example) and also admitting to inventing early meetings or extra nights away to avoid the madness at home. But there are also the dads, like Richard, who conform to providing but profoundly resent it and wonder how they got left with such limited choices.

At the other end of the spectrum, unsurprisingly, are the dads who are very involved and say that it is the humdrum of day-to-day 'real' parenting that makes the difference to their relationships with their kids. One dad who has taken a career break with three kids says he feels incredibly fortunate to have been able to enjoy so much of their childhoods. He says that, even all these years after giving up work, he still wakes up and feels relieved he's not still getting up at 6am to fly to Glasgow to negotiate with contractors to get home at 9pm and tackle the house and family. He enjoys the sports, the concerts and the day-to-day running of life. He's proud that his kids defer to him on key questions before his wife.

In the middle are the dads who both work and actively carve out chunks of time for family life, at the expense of their careers if needs be. A man in sales told me about his relationship with his daughter. When she was about three she came into the dining room on a

Saturday morning when he was working on a sales document. She asked to play on his computer and he said no, quite crossly because he was concentrating. She slumped her head and her shoulders and trailed out looking sad. As she did so, he thought 'What the hell am I doing? It's Saturday morning, I work all week, why shouldn't we play now?' He vowed not to work at weekends again and she is now 16 and he says he had kept to his word. He reflects though on a colleague who made different decisions: 'He was competitive, always had to be the best, always wanted more money, £30k, £40k, £60k, it was never enough for him.' On one occasion, his competitive colleague invited his family over to their house for dinner and he got talking to the man's teenage son about his desire to join the Navy. A few weeks later he bumped into the son again and had a good chat with him about how the recruitment process was going. As they parted he said: 'Your dad must be so proud of you, you're doing really well'. The boy looked confused and said: 'You know more about this now than my dad does, he's really not very interested.' He found himself defending his colleague loyally while knowing that what his son said was probably true. He wondered whether his colleague had ever thought about what he might have lost through being so committed to success at work.

Like this salesman, many of these dads are very thoughtful and specific about their family time, choosing it over work or other activities. A highly involved dad whose children are now in their 20s says: 'My key parenting activities – day-to-day/week-to week – were spending time with them as they went to bed (this usually meant reading to them in bed most days from the age of two or so through to 12 or 13); being free at weekends, which we planned around doing lots together as a family (or just me and the girls); and doing breakfast many mornings, and most meals at weekends.' A freelancer who is currently working 70 hours a week while his wife takes a career break says: 'Though I would prefer to be spending less time working and more time with my family, I am fairly hands-on as a parent and make it a priority to spend time with my children (including doing school drop-offs, attending school performances, parents' evenings, etc). What perhaps suffers most as a result of working too much is my relationships with other people, including my wider family (of whom I do not see enough, even though they live quite close) and my friends (most of whom I rarely see or even speak to).'

I wonder whether dads who are interested in their kids *choose* to spend more time with them and learn to enjoy them, or whether spending time with your kids actually changes how you see the world. One would perhaps expect the former but interestingly the latter may be true. Research from Northwestern's Department of Anthropology in America from 2011 shows that the male hormone testosterone falls when men have children but, more significantly, it drops most in men who are really involved in day-to-day parenting. This is important because it shows that men are biologically designed to change so that they too can raise children. Lead author Lee Gettler, a biological anthropologist and doctoral candidate, said at the time the report was published: 'If this weren't something that had been normative in humans for the last 100,000 or more years, there would be no reason to expect this decline in testosterone.' What's more, this decrease in testosterone is linked to men becoming more nurturing and better socially connected. Perhaps there's more to the idea of men 'settling down' when they have children than it just being something your granny used to say.

What strikes me reading this research is that in modern society where (despite legal advances aimed in the right direction) very few fathers take anything more than a few weeks' paternity leave, a very natural response to becoming a father is being suppressed. Men who return quickly to work after their first child, many very reluctantly, could actually be missing out on a hormonal change that would help them to be more involved parents. Stretched – possibly too far – it could in fact be a factor in driving a culture of alpha men in the workplace who, in a more traditional society, might have moderated after children. It is particularly interesting to note that Finland, where many dads do take extended paternity leave, is the only country in Europe where dads spend very slightly more time with their kids than mums do on average.

Whether it's hormonal or just practical (mums end up with more parenting experience and tend to take the lead) some dads perceive that the way we organise society excludes them from the parenting role they want. Like Richard the 'frustrated parent' above, excluded from decision making and yet not convinced his wife is getting it right. Recently he has been confiding in his friends about his relationship problems and is amazed that this has unleashed a flood of stories about unfulfilled husbands seeking sex and affection outside of their marriages, be it through affairs or prostitutes or, in one case, an open relationship that allows both partners to pursue their specific preferences. He concludes that the traditional model of marriage has often failed to leave space for men to express their own need for emotional and psychological fulfillment and the modern version seems to be pulling the women into the same trap.

One dad I interviewed built on almost exactly this point:

'My view is that in the attempt to establish equality for women, women felt (and society has come to demand in terms of the need for two incomes) they needed to be more like men. Prove they can do everything. But this has resulted in more stress and work for women. Now both men and women have to have full-time jobs and men are doing more of the "home" work but often not their fair share. This means there is now more pressure and more work and more stress in average families. For example, my wife and I have just taken on a nanny who costs more every month than my wife earns. But it's incredibly important for her (both mentally and in terms of her career) to work, so it's not a decision we've made based on money. But in terms of our daily lives, the result is that we are now both more stressed about work, we both have less money and we both spend less time with our son. So we have reached a form of equality but not a very progressive one.

'For me the missed opportunity in the battle for equality – and an argument I have not heard spoken of before – would have been if equality had been achieved by men being more like women rather than the emphasis being the other way around. By that I mean men changing their outlook on life to be less about going out and earning money and more about spending more time at home. This was a failure of men, not women, I hasten to add. Men lacked the wisdom to see the opportunity and concentrated on getting defensive. Probably as a result of being the product of a Western society that confuses "suffering" with "virtue", but I digress…. The point is, one income used to be enough for a family to live on. Men did all the work out of the home and got money and women did all the work in the home and got no money. So there was a chance for men and women to both work part time to get that single income (but getting half the money each) and have both enjoy the challenge of work and time spent with their children. That would have been a more progressive solution to the battle for equality. The tragedy is that most families I know would leap at this solution if they could today, but a single income is no longer enough to live on so men and women are both stuck.'

I am left wondering whether the cornerstone of changing gender relations in this country starts with ensuring many more men take a decent chunk of paternity leave. If we could also solve the obscene pressure of our housing markets needing dual full-time incomes, we'd really be getting somewhere.

Finally, anthropologists tell us that, traditionally, children learned through participating in male and female adult activity, handling machetes, catching food, preparing meals and so on. For the dads who really see the day-to-day as important but spend much of it at work, they worry that their children are missing out on the balance of gender experiences (see also the majority of primary school teachers being women and so on). One dad suggests this could be addressed by allowing children to be more involved in the workplace:

'The bit I see is missing is not just about dads getting home for bath time, etc, but the vice versa, kids coming out of the home environment and seeing what their parents do when they disappear. I took my daughter to work once a week for two years during nursery and I think it did her the world of good, and me, and our relationship and her world view. Dads would have worked around the home in ways kids would have absorbed and role modelled, and it's only in post-industrialisation that we disappear to become cogs so our invisible benefit pays the way. The relationship as a role model, demonstrating relationships and what it means to work is totally lost. Bring-your-kids-to-work day is the glib end of the iceberg, but what if your kids did their homework from the office, then you go home together? That is the sort of thing I'm interested in.'

The thought of having our kids at either of our offices scares my husband and I but I take his point that the absolute segregation of home and work spaces alienates our children to the future of work and perhaps drives our mental separation of the two.

Ultimately what I take is that the 'old' system whereby dads worked out and mums stayed at home worked fine for quite a lot of dads, especially if they had reasonable hours and were happy enough at work. Many of those at the top of organisations now feel fortunate that they were supported through their careers and didn't have to worry about their kids. But the generations behind them do have to worry. Because their own work is more demanding *and* partners do work and can't/won't shoulder all of the responsibility for their children *and*, even more importantly, dads increasingly really want to be involved. To change it, we all need them to step into the debate and speak up. A final thought from a dad on this:

'Men have a vital role here. More of us need to stand up and argue for changes at work. I have been in too many moments where there is a group of men at work – only men – and one of them makes a misogynist, sexist or biased remark about mothers at work – in general or about a specific woman – and none of the other men speaks up. Or they will criticise a working dad who is trying to adjust how they work to spend more time at home with his kids – and no one speaks up. Until enough men take the risks that many women take and have the courage to speak up, these hidden barriers of prejudice will continue to hold back working mothers.'

What happened next?

RICHARD IS GETTING DIVORCED. He's bruised by the breakdown of his marriage but excited by the opportunity to establish a very different kind of partnership with the women he is meeting through dating sites. They've sold the family house.

CHAPTER FOURTEEN

The questions people ask me

WHEN I RUN WORKSHOPS on careers and children, or just talk to people socially about the work, I get asked what I learned and what we've changed in our house in response to this research.

Q. Why are parents with careers finding it so hard?

A. Essentially it is all the issues covered in the stories here. The mismatch between how our workplaces are set up, our separation from other groups in society and many long-standing social expectations of gender roles – plus the judgement and guilt that goes with that. The mismatch between the working day and the school day, which is getting worse and worse for those who engage with work online and on their phones in the evening. The mental ticker-tape-of-mum, which adds stress throughout the day and night. And the financial pressures everyone is under due to rising house prices.

There is one other thing that I've touched on but not dug through, which is the 'masculine' work culture of many organisations. Be that in terms of abrasive interactions, success being judged on visibility and assumptions that everyone has a partner at home to pick up the slack. It's these cultures that perhaps go some way to explaining why senior women are, on average, more stressed than senior men.

Q. But some professional mums are thriving, right? I mean I know a woman with four kids who works 60 hours per week and she loves it...

A. Yes. If someone is driven, determined and well supported – I often find that women with strong working role models (e.g. their own mother) do better – you can have kids and career and thrive. But it won't be smooth all the way and there is still stuff that you can do to improve that experience. I heard a FTSE CEO at a conference saying she had no life aside from home (by which she meant only her partner, kids and pets) and work and I felt quite sad for her: for me lacking friends and any sort of social life isn't a great way to live. But this is my personal take, she seemed very happy with her situation and, if people are thriving, then good on them.

Q. Who are the happiest working parents?
A. Those who have the right foundations: families who have enough money to survive and get along and support each other and have good support networks. Having local family really helps. Having local friends is, as I say too often, critical.

Beyond that, two big types do well. One: those who psychologically adapt, embracing the new role of parenting, thinking hard about how to enjoy and have a great relationship with their children. This includes being able to continually change to meet the needs of family life. Two: those who make active choices at each point about the practical stuff. They don't accept the way that work/school or housing is, they make choices about it with the whole family's welfare in mind. Especially on childcare: one mum said that before she had kids she thought that childcare was something you sorted once and it worked, but she has had to adjust to the idea that childcare is an ongoing problem to sort. Adapting to manage working hours very well is also key.

If employed, this means putting boundaries around your availability. There are lots of ways to do this: from three- or four-day weeks to working at home some or all of the time, to doing two long days and two short days, working school hours, job shares and so on. This also includes managing your email and social media usage. Turning phones off after certain hours and at weekends, being clear in your decisions. It also includes a holiday-contact policy whereby you decide how and how often you will – or will not – engage with work while you are away.

But shortening the working week isn't a panacea. You have to be sure it's what you want and make it work for you.

The four-day week is a particularly risky area. Many, many women complain that they take a 20 per cent pay hit and get put into a 'mummy track career path' but are still expected to be available and do a full week. This – understandably – breeds deep resentment. This escalates if it upsets your benefits; some get downgraded pension plans. One lawyer said:

'Over the years, I've also seen that most people who do a four-day week are essentially doing a five-day week for 80 per cent of the pay. Even worse, I remember a lawyer who did a four-day week but one year, in absolute terms, was the highest billing lawyer (so had done about 2,000 hours plus); however when it came to her bonus, they then only gave her a 80 per cent bonus. No thanks, not for me – because I know I'd be the muggins who'd be working a full week for part-time pay. Similarly with a three-day week, it is too part time and if you take it, I think you are really considered as someone who has checked out of career/ambition.'

A CEO said he's up for pretty much any option other than a four-day week because it always seems to end in bitterness and the woman leaving.

Those who do make it work are the most disciplined about it: the ones who refuse to be drawn into emails on their at-home day and use the time well. For the very ambitious, it may not (always) be the best way to go. Some have found that working a full week but being based at home for one or two days of it works better. They get to stay connected but also fully paid.

Another mum who stepped out of well-paid and high-status career job put it like this:

'Whether it is old age, wanting to spend more time with my family/husband/have a life, I've decided I would prefer to have flexibility and time, rather than a big job. I am not sure it's worth it – the demands on one personally are too taxing and when I look back to the company I left after 14 years last summer, I just can't think of too many genuinely happy leaders. Those that do seem to enjoy it often have a stay-at-home partner – by which I mean a wife. I've taken a role that pays a quarter of my previous salary but allows me to have a life at home and, although it may not last forever, I think this is the right way for me. But I appreciate that, because my husband has a decent job, I have more flexibility than most.'

The other approach – which is what I have done – is to become a freelancer and/or run your own business. After leaving agency life, I looked at lots of jobs. Finding nothing that suited, I realised that I had to start afresh. Jericho is a communication and leadership consultancy in London that brings together experienced consultants to work on projects that we believe are in the interest of the wider good of society. Part of what works is that we have an entirely flexible working arrangement with no fixed hours or holiday allocations. We get paid for what we work on. It allows everyone to work flexibly whatever their interests. For me, it allows me to speak and write and to work a short office day with a lot of time around home to engage with our family, as well as time to exercise in the week.

But again, this decision is not a cure-all. In fact, quite the opposite as some research suggests freelancers and small-business owners can end up so stressed about earning enough and meeting client needs that they work longer and less social hours than anyone else. There is no 'minimum wage' protection for the self-employed. Turning down an assignment the week you planned to be off for half-term won't suit if you just need the money to get by. Another downside is that tax becomes more complicated and, if you are as useless as me, you spend a fortune on other people to help you sort it all out.

My husband Chris has also gone the self-employed route and runs a travel business called www.villas4kids.com. As the name suggests, it provides holiday villas for families with kids. The advantage is that, like me, he can work from wherever he is and he has spent the last eight years primarily based at home being a very hands-on dad to our three girls. This has made what I have done possible. The disadvantage is that he has to engage with it every single day, come holiday or birthday or weekend away.

The truth is that happy parents have taken *and stuck to* clear-headed decisions about how they want to live. They've accepted compromises (money, promotions, status, new kitchens) and got on with it. There aren't perfect solutions. The key is to be clear about what you are seeking to achieve and figure out how to get there. Yep, easier said than done.

Q. Who are the least happy?
A. Putting aside individual challenges (failing relationships, poverty, family problems, unwell children and so on) those working in large companies, often law firms or consultancies, that bill by hours and appraise people largely on their ability to network and bring in business are often stressed. Very often this packs a triple punch of long in-office hours, an always-on mindset and long 'non-office' hours at networking drinks, breakfasts and dinners. It is very hard for parents who want to be engaged at home to thrive in these circumstances unless they are unbelievably driven and/or unbelievably disciplined.

I observe that the women who do continue to do well in these environments are those like American TV supremo Shonda Rhimes (check out her brilliant TED Talk), before she learned to switch off and play, who still get their buzz – she calls it 'the hum' – from work. Those who find home life boring compared to work. Who find it easier to connect to their colleagues than their kids. Who pride themselves on being above the fray of their daily lives. If well supported by a partner and/or other supporters (grandparents, nannies, au pairs, etc) this can work well for years and some never regret it. But others do. Especially if their kids get into trouble in their late teens and early 20s. One said to me recently, 'My 19-year-old son was so shockingly selfish at the weekend that I shouted at him. I was disgusted. I thought "how could I have brought up a child that is so selfish?" and then realised that I haven't really brought him up. I've been at work.'

In terms of outcomes, some kids will grow up with parents who work like this and be totally fine and tell you that they were inspired by their parents' work ethic and success. Others say it damaged them and they needed more support. Some will say that they will never live like their parents and are planning careers that will enable them to be at home for their kids. Others tell you they want to be a lawyer just like their mum. At some point, many of us will go through the adjustment that Shonda talks about. When our energy moves from being driven by work to being driven by life beyond work. The question – for men and for women – is if and when we allow space for that.

The thing I hold on to is that if you're are exhausted, depressed, alienated from your kids and/or partner, restless at night, drinking to self-medicate or otherwise emotionally and physically depleted by the demands of work, you need to think about making changes. And, however impossible those changes may seem, not doing them will have long-term detrimental consequences for your health, your relationship, your kids and, ultimately, your career. A woman told me yesterday that she had an email from a Chinese colleague that said 'Of course there are always problems but there are always more solutions than there are problems'. I can't tell you if that's true but I can tell you that a lot of working parents are absolutely certain that it is 'impossible' to do anything about the way they work right up until the moment when they do make changes. It's a shame that the trigger for this is often something negative – unwell children or parents, a health problem or other major life event – and that only afterwards do they realise it was their own psychological barriers holding them back.

Q. What parental work/home time split works best if the mother has a career?

A. The truest answer is the one that works for the people in your house: if one parent has a burning drive to be the CEO then a three-day week will never be any good to them. If both parents are highly status-conscious, striving for the best house, car and schools, then part time won't work for anyone. But if forced to make broad generalisations, I would tend to rank them like this. Albeit with a thousand caveats about couples that don't sit within this norm:

1) A reasonable parental balance is a very good option: both parents, say, working a curtailed week or mixing up their hours to cover when the kids are at home. The benefit of this system is an overlap of life experience and perspective. Both parents get to be engaged with their kids and tend not to idealise or demonise either work or being at home. One risk to watch for here is that the work is split like this but one partner (usually the mother) does the vast majority of the housework or admin. This can create a running parental fault line. Another risk is that the budgets are so constrained – perhaps by the cost of childcare – that the parents never get to spend time alone together and the relationship suffers.

279

2) Next up, the alpha/beta model with the mum with the big job and dad largely based at home. If both sides are happy and have realistic expectations, this can work very well as long as chores are felt to be equitably split as well. It comes with some social judgement that everyone has to manage, and requires awareness that our systems were not set up to work this way. But if you can keep mutual respect for what the other contributes and the mother is able to have local relationships as well as working this can be a great course of action.

3) The hardest option, as I see it, is the alpha/alpha option where both parents have big jobs. This can have the advantage of having resources to pay for support and usually is quite a high-status household (the most likely to have the kids in private school, for example). But it is also the most stressful and one where parents can become disconnected from each other and family life and the kids can fall through the cracks. It may work for short bursts but, for the long term, this is a hard way to run life as the day-to-day stuff (cooking, dry-cleaning, dentists, haircuts, fun) can all get lost in the mist of work as whole weekends are given over to sorting out the detritus of the week.

One additional thought – and this is depressing and you'll hate me for it – is that the traditional dad breadwinner/mum largely at home or with 'less important' job still often seems the easiest to manage if it suits you and your partner. Kids and schools get it, it fits with how our world is currently set up and households often run smoothly according to precedents set generations before. Bloody irritating, eh? It doesn't work at all though if the mum is like a caged lion at home raging to get out and get back to work, or if the dad resents being out working while his partner 'luxuriates' at home.

I don't put solo parents into this list because their welfare seems to be so dependent on their own sense of well-being, their networks and their incomes. A well-supported solo parent with a solid income could easily be at the top of the list. A hard-up and lonely one could be at the bottom. Similarly, same-sex couples with clarity of who they are and how they parent could come at any point in the list, while a same-sex couple fighting over how they parent and feeling socially excluded would be in a bad place.

Q. What are the biggest mistakes people share with you?
A. The first is to assume that what worked yesterday will work today and tomorrow. For every career parent who has a baby and flies back to work full of vigour there is a parent, two or three years in, just wishing they could have a bit of time at home. Getting stuck in any fixed sense of who we are and what works is a common mistake. Much as we shape our children, I am more and more convinced that they change us just as much. The saddest parents are perhaps those who do not allow this process to happen because they are so busy working. The happiest are those who adjust as they go, responding to a mix of their own needs and their kids' needs.

The second mistake, which is linked to that, is creating a cost base that demands both parents to work full time. As time goes on, either parent may want to upshift or downshift and having a life that enables that is key to being happy. All the boring stuff about not being too good a consumer and saving money is, I increasingly think, absolutely essential. Not just for us to know. But for us to pass on to our children.

Asking parents what they felt pressure to spend on and then regretted unleashes a long list of stuff you can cut back on: new musical instruments the kids quickly give up (rent them, get second-hand ones, even borrow); electronic toys that are noisy and annoying and take up loads of space (electronic sit-on cars are top of the list); brand-new school uniforms (the second-hand stuff at school will easily cover most needs); highly branded days out/trips (queuing all the hours of daylight with bored and hungry kids when you could have gone camping for a week on the same budget); new kids clothes generally (let people know you love second-hand stuff and thank them generously, even though you know they are just as delighted to clear stuff out); new bikes/scooters/skateboards/playhouses/bunk beds (all stuff that, with a bit of planning, is easily found second hand and therefore less of worry when they break or lose and/or lose interest); and even kids' books, which are so easily found at charity shops (I assume that, as an author, I will be shot for this advice). All of this does require a 'not keeping up with the Joneses' mindset. Something I've had to learn a lot about from my much more down-to-earth husband.

What I notice is that since we chose to buy a crap car, rejected ever considering private schools and stopped spending anything more than we earned, we feel happier and other people ask us how we have time to spend together and with the children (let's not kid ourselves though, I still want a new kitchen). One additional thought on financial planning is that my mind was very much put at rest by creating a long-term financial plan whereby we looked at our incomes and ran the numbers through to a (rather aged) retirement. Although it doesn't change what you earn, it can make it feel more in control.

The third mistake is to allow no time for yourself or your partner. If between work and home you never have time for a workout or a film or lunch with a friend, then you'll be miserable and burn out. The boring old aeroplane advice to put your own mask on before helping others is surely as true here as anywhere. If we're at breaking point, we're shit parents: distracted, petulant and exhausted. And we know what kids are like when they are in that state – we shouldn't be matching them in our own lack of control. Part of the job of parenting is to *take care of ourselves* – mentally and physically – as well as our children: whether that is as small as making sure you have a run with the buggy around a park or doing some lengths when you take them to a swimming lesson, or booking a weekly evening class after dinner. It also includes adjusting your expectations of what socialising looks like when you have kids: adding parental drinks to the pick-up time of a kids' party or having friends over for kids' tea at 6pm and adult dinner at 7.30pm, and knowing everyone will be on their way by 9pm. So many people I've talked to have emphasised the damage that not making time for your partnership and friends can do and it is surely worth putting thought and effort into your relationship.

Q. Are there particular moments when things go wrong?
A. Emotionally, the points when we change our identity and reference points are always difficult.

The first child is, inevitably, the biggest gear change. It can really take time to catch up with how much has altered. There is a lot here about identity and the sense of (not) being in control. I see some parents trying to live life as it was before their baby: eating out, staying in hotels for weekends (the evenings of which end up being spent with one or other parent hunkered down in the en suite while the baby sleeps in its cot in the darkened bedroom and their partner drinks alone at the bar), drinking, partying, working long hours. I relate to them. That first year of staying home can feel an endless prison if you're used to being out and doing things all the time. Not having 'proper' weekends when you can do what you want and relax is miserable until you stop noticing. This period may also change the way you feel about things: a number of mums have reported that, after kids, they became afraid of flying in a way they never had before. Others have said they feel their personalities have evolved: they are kinder or more compassionate than before. These changes can feel disconcerting and need adjusting to.

The second child can also be very difficult. Partly people describe the transition from being wholly focused on their first child to transitioning their emotional energy to the second. Some describe going from being adoring of child one to irritated with him or her if they in any way threaten the well-being of the new baby. Many see then a big shift in family life: from parents dedicated to raising a child to a whole-home mentality. It can also be a moment when people who thought they were doing pretty well as parents question their skills as what works for one child often doesn't work for the next. My observation is that riding one horse, metaphorically, is a very different prospect to riding two. Strangely, once you're used to two, transitioning to ride three and four horses often doesn't seem quite the same dramatic leap, unless you have additional complications (special needs, illness, disability, etc). That said, a few women have told me that their third or fourth was the thing that broke them!

The other increased difficulty with the second child, especially if they are close in age, is the huge financial pressure of childcare between birth and the school years. Pretty much everyone finds this period oppressively expensive unless they have extensive family help. It can help to remember that this is a uniquely expensive few years and it does end. If in that time you're saving nothing, not paying into your pension or settling debts, perhaps give yourself a break. It will get better.

The other big change is when kids leave home. Although many working mums seem to reassure themselves that at-home mothers get it worse, I'm not convinced this is always true. One told me she felt depressed and purposeless for two years, unsure what she was for without her children at home. This was despite, or perhaps fuelled by, a very successful and enormously time-consuming career. Talking to her, she seemed to have nostalgia for her children being young and at home. Based on her own description of her working life, I almost wondered whether that time had ever existed. Sarah Jaggers, MD of Managing Change, agrees this is a risky moment:

'Another stress point we observe is the phase when people combine older children, perhaps teens, perhaps flying the nest, with ageing parents. That can lead to questions of identity and "what did I achieve?". We see that as an opportunity to think about what's possible now and what comes next. It's really important not to suppress your own needs in this situation because it can build into resentment: your children are heading off into their futures while you feel you have missed out on your own opportunities as you've been caring for everyone else.'

A woman who has recently become a grandmother says that she and many of her friends are relishing another chance to enjoy small children because they feel they missed it themselves the first time around.

Q. When you talk to people, what flags worry you?
A. References to disturbed sleep and extreme tiredness, people who mention crying frequently, people who have aches and pains or recurring illness and people who talk a lot about drinking. Plus tension in relationships – how they describe their partner, kids and co-workers. Ongoing financial pressure is a big flag also – people who feel their lives would utterly collapse if they lost their jobs or didn't get their bonus or pay rise.

Unsurprisingly, feeling you have to lie or conceal the truth is often also a worrying sign. Those people doing different hours than they agreed with their boss but trying to hide it – like working from home but actually picking up the kids at 3pm and pretending they are still working or pretending they have meetings when they need to leave early – often seem to cause themselves a huge amount of angst.

Q. What reassures you they are OK?

A. When they tell me positive, happy things about their kids or family life. Not status show-off things but things they do and enjoy, funny things that they say, bits of art or photos that make them laugh. Ideally involving their partners if they have them. When they talk about work positively but also show they have a life at home and interests outside of both work and home. Ideally including some exercise and the kind of complexion that people who eat decently, sleep and move about regularly tend to have.

Q. What should employers do?

A. Let's start by acknowledging that the current system is bleeding critical talent in the form of accomplished women. That, at the very time when we need better thinking and more diverse perspectives to get there, we are still favouring men called John over half of the population. What we need is a seismic culture change along the lines of #metoo where we come to collectively realise that having senior women in work isn't a nice-to-have luxury, it's a massive economic opportunity and one we cannot afford to ignore because it is, as the head of diversity at a City firm once explained to me: 'a boring subject for *Guardian*-reading-liberals that will never interest the men in their 50s and 60s who run this place.' It's not, he clarified, that they are anti-women as such, 'they're just not very interested in the subject at all.' Although the move to publicising pay gaps does seem to have done a good job of increasing senior interest in the subject. Whether this is motivated by a desire for better PR or HR remains to be seen, perhaps it doesn't matter as long as it gets addressed.

In practical terms, managing hours is critical. Karen Mattison, joint CEO of Timewise Jobs, a recruitment organisation that specialises in part-time and flexible work explains:

'Our research shows that this assumption that it's just mums who want fewer hours is wrong: men, Gen X, Gen Y and women – a lot of people want to work less. Over 8 million people in the UK work part time and, of those, 80 per cent choose to. They are not "underemployed", they choose having more time over earning more money. Furthermore, one in four of those working full time now say they would actually prefer to work part time, and wouldn't mind earning less, as long as it didn't affect their career progression.

'Our view is that we have to move beyond the request/response approach to part time and flexibility [by which she means that you have to ask for flexible work and then your employer decides if it's possible or not] – and make flexibility part of our working culture. That is the only way we will move beyond the career progression gap we currently see for many who do work flexibly. The good news is that the evidence shows that companies that embrace flexible working do better.'

She sees two ways this move might happen:

'The first is to say that, although the working day was designed for an era in which men worked and women ran the home, mothers are welcome at work. This is conveyed through, for example, returner programmes after maternity leave and supportive women's networks. For me, this is limited as it keeps the workplace as it is and simply asks women to fit into it.

'The second is a structural change to how we work, that recognises that flexibility is as important as salary. Because those that can't progress through flexible working will leave and take their talent elsewhere. This is why we see the arrival of what we call "disruptor models" (organisations that compete with existing firms on different terms) emerging in so many fields – in law, with those creating flexible and short-term working models, in advertising, in communications, like what you have done with your consultancy. These are models that enable professionals to work at senior levels on their own terms.'

Karen would like to see a move away from fixed patterns of hours, fixed locations and also to mix up networking times so that more people can be included. When I co-founded a women's social group, we set the meeting time as between 4.30 and 6pm rather than later so that everyone can attend and then get home at a reasonable time – or go out and do something else if they prefer. It works really well as people can add it to their diary as part of their working day.

The key is to release the sense that you have to be 'brave' to ask for flexibility because we know women are less keen to come forwards, seeing a choice between being ambitious and the 'mummy track'.

Karen again: 'We need to change that. Critical to changing it is workplace culture: leadership, trust and judging people on their outputs *not their hours in a specific place*. I see the journey of normalising flexibility in the workplace as something like the journey of a bad back. We could carry on with business as usual and eventually things will improve. Or we can take action and accelerate the process. That is what smart businesses are doing and the rewards to them in terms of employee engagement, talent attraction and improved brand are well deserved.'

The point is, we need equality of working hours at a more manageable, flexible level that means both adults in a relationship can work and have a life and not lose out professionally.

Part of driving this change is to ensure more people in the system understand how badly modern working practices sit with family life. To that end, it was fascinating to interview a newly solo dad recently and hear his huge frustration that being out of touch from the office between 5pm and 7pm every week day is profoundly damaging his career. This is clearly something he knew intellectually before, but when it had just affected the women around him he'd never really given it any thought. Now confronted with it, you can feel his sense of injustice being triggered. Which is why we need more men, doing more childcare, experiencing how this works so we can move this on from 'a women's problem' to something much bigger.

Q. What is your biggest personal takeaway?
A. That my energy is finite and that I have to choose where to invest it. Collapsing through the door after a long and manic day, depleted of spirit, beyond coherent speech, and yet tripping on adrenaline leaves nothing for my kids or my husband, let alone my own peace of mind. I notice that on the days when I work to match our school day, doing both school runs plus an intense six or seven hours in the office, I find I am productive and get home still alert with good energy. This is partly enabled by us having a longer-than-average school day: founder and executive principal of Canary Wharf College (the state school our kids go to) Sarah Counter was inspired to set the hours from 8.30am to 4–5pm with extended day activities – to help working parents. Due to government budgets this does mean longer holidays but, on balance, we find it works well. Days when I charge out at 7am to get to a breakfast meeting and drag back in after dark leave me drained for days in a way they didn't do before I had kids.

Being careful with my energy comes back to the old boring maxims. Setting boundaries around my time. Choosing where I invest time and energy. Eating well. Sleeping well. Exercising. Seeing friends and laughing a lot. Seeking out the kind of days that you can realistically emerge from with enough vitality that you're happy to see your children and have emotional capacity for their triumphs and tragedies. And, after that, you can sit and chat with your partner rather than just bitch off every single thing that happened since you raced out of the door.

Q. But did you join the PTA?
A. Oh Lord, I did. I told our Chair right up front that with three kids and two jobs (consultancy and writing) there was only so much I

could do and I was never baking a cake. Yet I still found myself on various Friday nights ineptly sloshing Prosecco, Fawlty Towers style, at school bar nights and being royally taken the piss out of for my incompetence.

At the point of giving up, the Chair (who, to be fair, said she never wanted me for my cakes in the first place) asked me to join a new committee to help get the school more involved in the local community and explore ways in which we might be able to supplement our government funding. Our school is near London's Docks, which are often covered in floating plastic rubbish. I'd seen a video from Plastic Whale in Amsterdam where they took people on boats in the canals with nets to literally fish plastic out of the water and used the plastic to make boats for more plastic fishing. I suggested we brought the idea to the UK.

A year later, working with environmental NGO Hubbub, the world's first boat made out of 99% recycled plastic has been built, launched by a government minister, the kids have been to Parliament to talk about the project, and plastic fishing is a regular school event and a fund raiser. However, although I'd love to tell you that the project has been plain sailing and a total pleasure, honestly, it's been time-consuming, exhausting, frustrating, exhilarating, and cold, filthy and wet, often all at the same time. A year later, though, it's one of the things of which I am most proud in my life. On the back of it, I would encourage anyone so inclined to find something they can contribute to their school or community. But, I've got to tell you, honing some fine bar skills would be a feck of a lot of an easier way to meet a bunch of parents who make you rock with laughter.

CHAPTER FIFTEEN

Conclusions

Where does this leave us?

It leaves us at a juncture, and the first step to moving forwards is to open up more honest conversations about it.

When I interviewed women in *Management Today* about women with big jobs and small children, the comments about the articles were fascinating. On a Facebook chat, one woman wrote of one interviewee that 'She might be powerful but she's no mother', because her nanny cooked the family dinner every evening as she commuted an hour from her office to her home.

For me, this throwaway insult illustrates how we have created the perfect trap. Women are told they can 'do anything', 'be anything' and achieve what men can. Men are led to believe that their role is to provide. So, both pursue work and find that there is no one to care for their children when they have them. If women give up work, many feel they become invisible and are diminished for not 'contributing' to society. If the men step back, we wonder what went wrong with their careers.

As this happens, our politicians speak about families in the warmest terms. We want 'a society that respects the bonds of family, community, citizenship and strong institutions that we share as a union of people and nations; a society with a commitment to fairness at its heart', says Theresa May; David Cameron intones 'if we want to have any hope of mending our broken society, family and parenting is where we've got to start.' Yet, as they say these things, they tinker at the edges of family policies. A bit of paternity leave no one uses (yet). Thirty free hours of childcare a week, from aged three, that some people experience to be complicated to get and keep. Neither of the big two parties are actively campaigning for good-quality, free childcare from the end of maternity leave, nor arguing for equality of maternity/paternity rights at pay levels you can live on nor proposing how we solve the mismatch between the school day and family needs and our working hours culture.

In popular culture, meanwhile, we demonise people who have nannies, and we tax them as if they were a great perk of life, treating those who have them as hugely privileged, while actually the families I talk to who have them are working flat out to pay their bills and often taking home nothing much else at the end of the month. The press loves the 'middle-class crisis' of an au pair shortage, suggesting that women (note the gender) who rely on help for the gap between the school day and the working day are princesses who can't be arsed to make their own beds, rather than families in which both parents work full time and have few other options. Psychologists such as Sue Gerhart – see her excellent book *Why Love Matters* – quietly and consistently caution against the overuse of nurseries, which can lead to small children feeling isolated. So even this 'less political' option of nursery is seen by many to be a selfish choice. Meanwhile, rightful concerns about the badly paid and under-respected – almost exclusively female – carers of small children are an ongoing source of shame. When, in reality, care work is a hugely important net contributor to the economy and a workforce that is deserving of respect, investment and good conditions.

Even talking about these subjects has become mired in risk. For every view expressed, there is a harsh social media backlash. So much so that when I started writing this book a number of friends advised me strongly against even going there. One took me for lunch and said: 'Don't do this, you can't say these things, you'll be torn to shreds.' Somehow even saying what we see has become troublesome, which further diminishes the experience of women.

So we have to allow these real conversations to happen and not let this discourse be dominated either by stratospherically successful women whose experience is, by definition, exceptional, or by those who shout that other groups have bigger problems and so we can't be wasting time worrying about this issue.

What should we aspire to?

What strikes me is that this book isn't really about being male or female, it's about what we need to flourish as humans. To feel in control of our lives, to be strongly connected to others, to feel secure, to live up to the values that we think are important. Which is the opposite of the situation that many working cultures create.

The world I aspire to is one in which we can work and live full lives. With or without children. Where we can bring our skills and good energy to work in a way that is productive – for the medium and long term rather than just this week, month or quarter. To think afresh about where we work and the hours we work, and focus on the outputs far more than the inputs. To value people according to their contributions, not just their staying power. To value the clarity of thought that comes from taking time to reflect rather than just react. It almost certainly means a very big change to the concept of retirement: 30 or 40 years of not working isn't something our generation is likely to access, certainly not as many of our parents have. But, given that we are not going to have all this time after work that is more reason to live full lives *as* we work and not put off the pleasure for a future we may never reach. It will almost certainly mean evolving our skills to meet the future needs of employers and society: a more flexible approach to education and learning throughout our careers rather than a very intense three or four years of studying and partying before we embark into 'the real world'.

I started this book with a story about chasing a toddler round the house in the middle of the night trying to corral her back into her rightful place – her cot – so that we could work the next day. I end up, metaphorically at least, focused on corralling work back into its rightful place – our working hours – so that we can have a functioning family. Because, the truth, as I see it after five years of interviews, is that the happiest working households are ones in which both parents *choose* and are able to *opt out* of modern corporate hours. They work part time, flexi time, do a job share, are freelance or self-employed and actively manage their working hours, locking their phones in drawers when they need to (a good piece of advice from Poppy Mardall). They prioritise time at home with their kids and each other over making more money or becoming the boss or Prime Minister. And they don't trap themselves into financial patterns that cannot be changed: be that running up debts, major renovations or electronics worthy of space travel.

A woman I met at a conference described her life to me like this: 'I used to get carried away at work. At one point, I was working until 1 or 2am every day and getting back in the office at 7am. Then one day I was dressing my two-year-old son and I realised that what I thought were his "new" shorts, which were too big, were actually far too tight for him. He'd grown four inches and I'd missed it. I missed four inches of leg growth. I knew at that moment that it had to stop.'

She resigned and took time off but a former colleague tempted her back and said she could work on her terms. Her terms were that she had no hours or location of work but ran her team and did school pick-up every day. Which meant in reality leaving work at 2pm. Her team was hugely successful – the most successful one in the global company. So they moved her to run a departmental team in a new country. The company didn't want to offer her the same terms in the new market, but they acquiesced when she said it was the only way she would accept the job. Now, she is doing even better in business terms but is slipping back into her old work habits and she is having to reset her old rules all over again. She's learned that this isn't about negotiating once, it's about negotiating again and again and again. And making that same brutal decision every damned day to get up and leave at 2pm. If she doesn't manage it, she'll be another highly talented woman walking out of the traditional workforce because she is adamant that she won't miss big chunks of her children's childhoods. To me, her resolve is inspirational and the rest of us should emulate her.

But my great fear is that if I advise this kind of time management, let alone stepping back from work and holding back for as long as you need to – for men and women – the only bit that will be heard is that women should give up on full-time work to be mothers. And if they do that, we'll ensure that women never reach the top of their professions, and we'll never have anything near equal representation in law, politics or business. At worst, it'll be ignored and at best, it'll be met with rage from those who think I am setting back the cause by decades.

With that in mind, I called some people, fretting about my conclusions: 'I'm a bad feminist, I can't write what I see as the truth without setting back feminism 40 years.' Neal Lawson, chairman of the think tank Compass said, 'Yeah well, you can't be a good feminist in a neo-liberal economy'. Which sounded reassuring but didn't give me an answer.

So, I went to see Sophie Walker, the leader of the Women's Equality Party to ask what she thought, explaining that I see the choice (at its simplest) as between swallowing the advice to professional women that they must 'work harder' at playing a game designed for the other team in another era, or to try to wrest back control and work with the system for ourselves.

She sees it like this:

'We have built structural inequality into every element of our waking lives. It's there through our society, our economy, our culture, through our media. We live and breathe it. Simultaneously, we as women, are all being told that the only thing we have to do to break through that structural inequality – those centuries and centuries of legislative discrimination and oppression and inbuilt bias and sexism – is to *try harder*. If you didn't get the payrise, then you didn't ask right. If there is something wrong with your kids, then you are bad at parenting. If your sex life isn't working, then you're not spending enough time doing enough tantric sex. You should be working, baking, doing yoga, buying sprialisers…. So we've ended up with a generation of absolutely knackered women. They are just surviving. It's exhausting. But it doesn't have to be this way. To change this, we must change society. It's about women and men dramatically rethinking the lives, politics and culture they want. It is our resistance in our linked arms that matters. Because as long as we keep looking at each other in our kitchens and making decisions alone, we will never break free of this. We have been sold the idea that you can solve this through our individual choices but you can't. You have to change society.'

She might well be right and we will come to the structural changes we need, but first we still have to make decisions in our kitchens day-to-day and there is some news that might be helpful.

A plan for living

SO HERE I GO, tilting into the evils of self-help, with my own manifesto for happy professional families.

1) Embrace being a parent. We don't have to suppress our maternal and paternal feelings because we have careers, indeed it may take us a bit of time to find and grow them. We don't have to apologise or feel guilty for being parents and workers or, even worse, hide that we have kids.

2) Open our eyes. When you have a baby it's often the moment you suddenly realise that our society isn't set up to enhance family life, it's set up to increase economic productivity. Know that and use it to defend yourself against every negative thought about not being good/capable/hard-working enough. And never judge your own life against the imagined and idealised life you assume others have. The more we dig, the messier everyone's lives look.

3) Make conscious choices. Be very honest about who you are and what each of you (if you have a partner) believe is important. If your burning ambition is to be CEO, then set up your family and structure to support that ambition. Equally if you want to really be very engaged in the daily lives of your kids, then set your family up that way. But in either case, be honest about who you are and know that it will change as you go and allow space for that change. One early reader of this book called to say that she was feeling guilty for not feeling as guilty as some of the mums I've interviewed do! She is someone who is driven in her career, has great support at home and a happy family. Good on her.

4) Plan work. Actively plan the amount of time and the place that both parents spend working. Don't just tumble into our crazy always-on

workplace with a baby on each hip and hope you make it to their 18th birthday without a breakdown. You might not. Make choices that work for you and your family as a whole and be prepared to move jobs, move home, move schools, change your working structures to achieve it.

5) Plan play and everything else too. Actively plan the time that you both spend not working: when you are caring for kids or other relatives, exercising, having fun, seeing friends or running your home. This includes not just giving yourself permission to do the things that matter to you, but making them a priority. Whether that is reading the newspaper or taking up line dancing.

6) Cut your costs and be the worst capitalist you can be. Constantly seek to reduce rather than increase your spending. Everyone thinks that they need more money. Really everyone, from families struggling on benefits or inadequate pay to those who earn a couple of hundred thousand a year. They can't all be right. So, unless you are genuinely living on the edge, consider what your life would look like if you stopped spending and/or stripped out costs. As a mother of grown children said, 'they don't talk about the Disneyland trip we saved for years for, they talk about the walk we always did on Christmas Day'. Data from the US shows that people have an average of 300,000 items in their homes. The rise of storage facilities shows the UK cannot be far behind. Stop buying stuff you don't even have space for.

7) Turn it off. Take control of your technology and use it in a way that adds to your life rather than minimises it. Which ranges from stopping working all evening on different laptops to turning off Amazon Prime in order to have a chat over dinner instead.

8) Seek to play as one team. See your household as both a team and a set of individuals, and make your decisions accordingly. Having children at different schools, ignoring the five-year-old's

shit sleeping habits or working opposite shifts to your partner so you don't see each other in the week are all fine, so long as they don't bring the household to breaking point. Make choices that actually work day-to-day for everyone. If they don't work, don't resolutely battle on with grim determination. Make a plan to change them.

9) See your choices in the context of *The 100 Year Life*, as explored by Professors Lynda Gratton and Andrew Scott. They expect us to have working lives that evolve through a much longer career path than we have seen in the past. In moments of doubt, I bring to mind women like Hobbs CEO, Meg Lustman, who didn't return to full-time work until her youngest child was 13. She describes the idea of having it all at the same time as 'bonkers'.

But Sophie Walker is right, you can't fight this alone. Society is stuck between the old world where women were home and dads worked and the children were cared for, and a new world where most parents work longer and longer hours and children must be cared for during and around work.

It is time we made decisions that enable this transition not to feel like a crisis in every working family across the land. Not just because we are all individually trying to solve this and, in so many cases, feeling like we personally are failing as we do it, but because it isn't even working economically. We've had the worst decade for productivity growth since the Napoleonic Wars. Which is quite an achievement: more people, working longer and longer hours, more stressed and less satisfied but with nothing much to show for it. That failure may be linked to how we make decisions and another reason we must address this. Research that shows that teams that make the best decisions are half men and half women (for one example, have a look at the work of Anita Williams Woolley at Carnegie Mellon University, reference at the back of this book). If we want to be more successful in industry or as a country, we need the very best teams making the best decisions possible and that means having both genders well represented at all levels. Let's face it, it's not like the single-gendered teams we've created to date have covered themselves in glory (the banks, the priests, the tech giants).

There are some signs that things are changing. The best corporates are embracing job shares and flexible work as never before. We are witnessing the rise of working practices like Jericho Chambers in the communications and leadership world, Halebury in the legal sector and The Fawnbrake Collective in the advertising sector that demonstrate that professionals are looking for ways of working that do really work. What's more, the clients we work with find it works for them, too.

And yet we have a very long way to go. I interviewed a banker not long ago who had been promoted and got a new team to manage. He's not even 40 and is a genial enough bloke, with a couple of kids of his own. He'd found out that one of his new team works a 12-hour day in the office on two days a week, works school hours from home on two days a week and doesn't work on Fridays. 'Well she'll have to go' he said, meaning he would sack her because she wouldn't deliver. But six months later he told me she was the best and most organised person in the team he inherited. He is a convert to flexible work because he's seen it in action.

This is the crux of change we need: for men, as well as women, to viscerally understand the inherent biases of the system. Not on an intellectual level but on a human level. Like that newly solo dad, suddenly getting that being offline between 5pm and 7pm every day is crushingly debilitating to his career prospects. And, informed by that experience, to see that there are better, less traditional ways of working that would serve both men and women better.

It's time to change society

It is time we made proactive, thoughtful choices about how we want our society and economy to operate. That includes driving through a huge cultural shift, akin to the seismic change in perceptions and reporting of sexual harassment.

1) Completely shift our expectations and assumptions about work. To a system that enables people to work in ways that actually work for them and their families and allows anyone who wants to contribute productively to be able to do so in different ways, at different times of their lives. This is going to become more and more important as we compete with machines. As my colleague, the author Margaret Heffernan puts it:

> 'The positive premise of the so-called Fourth Industrial Revolution is that machines (automation and AI) will eliminate millions of jobs without reducing revenue. In theory, this should mean everyone *could* work less and living standards not fall — in which case, everyone can spend lots more time with their families. In practice, this will require that governments finally honour their rhetorical support of family values, because it will mean that the revenue is distributed across populations and not concentrated on the few with jobs or investments. So economically technology could retrieve family life; politically whether it will do so is a choice.'

It will indeed be a big choice, and one that our politicians will have to grapple with as, left to companies, the savings will be captured by the 1 per cent at the expense of everyone else.

2) Take a cold, fresh and joined-up look at our early years, school, college and university provision. I would like to see this thought through by a cross-party group of MPs, informed by experts, with

a view to planning the next 30 or 40 years, learning from the best school systems in the world and breaking through the boring debate about bloody grammar schools. Bearing in the mind the working day, school day, holidays, outcomes and the future needs of our economy. This should include the provision of good-quality free childcare from early years: the quality is just as important as the quantity. It should also include the removal of taxes on nannies and other private childcare.

3) Properly equalise rights about parental leave so that parents can choose which of them takes leave. This has to be appropriately funded, not at a rate that is half of the minimum wage. If people are going to work to 70, 80 and more, we have to give them support relatively early in their careers to have their children without tipping the household into poverty. Equalise parental leave benefits, so that parents – single, adoptive, couples, gay – can share and use the time as suits their family best. This is also important to ensure that hiring women of 'a certain age' is no more disadvantageous that hiring men. The benefits of parental leave should reflect the need we have as a society for people to have children and should not diminish parents into poverty.

4) Reform our relationship with electronic devices. I am not the first to say that we've stopped doing things in favour of communicating about them. We have to drive a culture change through organisations that favours proper thinking, action and team work over sending a gazillion messages and PowerPoints that eat time and deliver precious little. Some surveys have shown that email takes up over half the time in modern work. Half of it! The *constant* interruption of electronic devices is a huge problem: a digital distraction researcher at the University of California, Gloria Mark, says that it takes about 23 minutes and 15 seconds to fully refocus on a task after being distracted, depending partly on how complicated the task is.

More than 20 minutes of distraction for every message. It cannot be beyond us to take control of our distractions and focus on what we actually need to get to done for far shorter – and less stressful – periods of time.

5) Do everything we can to drive change. By being honest about our own experiences, supporting each other, improving our organisations, raising the issues with business leaders, politicians and influencers. Essentially using our power to change society for the better. This obviously includes delivering 50/50 representation of the genders at the most senior levels of business and politics as soon as possible to ensure that our structures reflect the reality that the whole population lives: not just the older bit of one half who mostly think things worked out fine for them.

6) Have faith in the next generation. Let's take hope that they seem to be learning from our mistakes and refusing to be oppressed by work in the way we have become. I am greatly heartened by a banker telling me that they just can't find graduates willing to work 18 hours a day any more.

We will not succeed alone as individuals. The real drivers of change, will be the businesses that sit between us as individuals and the needs of society. I don't believe there are silver bullets to solve this problem: every organisation depends on attracting and keeping the best people and has to figure out their own plan to adjust their ways of working to allow different people to gain more control over how they fit family and job together. Which starts with reviewing their own challenges and goals and then making their own plans to achieve them.

But it'll take action not just words. So, I urge you to go out and show how a different way of working can work yourself and use whatever influence you have to drive organisational and wider societal change.

To take and encourage others to take career breaks and scale work up and down as suits you and your family. Push for flexible hours or part-time hours, job shares, four days, three days, freelance, whatever you believe is right. Be a role model, promote other role models, show it works.

It's the only way we'll change the world to make it better for our children. And their parents.

References

Research by Eve Harris, Associate, Jericho Chambers

General Resources

According to a 2018 Report by CIPD, *UK Working Lives*:

30% of workers find their workloads 'to some extent' unmanageable and 63% of employees working more hours than they would like to.

UK employees work longer than their European counterparts and typically work five hours per week more than they would like. Commuting time typically adds 3 hours 45 minutes each week to this.

The UK stands out as having one of the biggest shares of long-hours jobs in the EU and the longest average working week, with a mean figure of 42.3 hours (Eurostat 2018). This compares with 37.8 hours in Denmark, which is the shortest. The average (median) employee works five hours per week more than they would like.

https://www.cipd.co.uk/knowledge/work/trends/uk-working-lives

The prevalence of involuntary long hours in a job is also a factor. Working longer hours increases the risk of occupational illness (such as stress and mental health problems). A culture has also grown up of unpaid overtime, with a recent national study suggesting that roughly half of workers were not paid for overtime. https://assets.publishing.service.gov.uk/government/uploads/system/uploads/attachment_ data/file/627671/good-work-taylor-review-modern-working-practices-rg.pdf

Fourth Work Life Balance Employer Survey 2013 https://www.gov.uk/government/ publications/fourth-work-life-balance-employer-survey-2013

Work It Out (http://workitout.org.uk), the place for working parents and parents-to-be to get support and find solutions to the many challenges we encounter. Set up by Anna Whitehouse ('Mother Pukka', http://motherpukka.org.uk)

Pregnant Then Screwed (http://pregnantthenscrewed.com)

Mental Health Resources

Mental Health Foundation (http://www.mentalhealth.org.uk)

Information on postnatal depression and perinatal mental health can also be found via Mind (http://www.mind.org.uk or https://www.mind.org.uk/information-support/types-of-mental-health-problems/postnatal-depression-and-perinatal-mental-health)

Introduction: The parent crunch: why I've written this book

The average working day has increased… '15 per cent increase in people working more than 48 hours a week risks a return to 'Burnout Britain', TUC Analysis of ONS data, September 2015

https://www.tuc.org.uk/news/15-cent-increase-people-working-more-48-hours-week-risks-return-%E2%80%98burnout-britain%E2%80%99-warns-tuc

The smartphone has added another two hours… 'Smartphones and tablets add two hours to the working day', *The Telegraph*, 2012, based on a study by Pixmania

https://www.telegraph.co.uk/technology/mobile-phones/9646349/Smartphones-and-tablets-add-two-hours-to-the-working-day.html

Even on holiday, more than a third of us keep up with email… Study by Travelbag.co.uk, May 2016

http://www.mobilenewscwp.co.uk/2016/05/23/brits-spend-two-days-of-their-holiday-expecting-work-related-calls-and-texts/

Commutes have got longer… TUC Analysis, based on analysis of ONS Labour Force Survey, November 2017

https://www.tuc.org.uk/news/average-worker-now-spends-27-working-days-year-commuting-finds-tuc

House prices have almost quadrupled… Allagents.co.uk, House Prices from 1952, 2018

https://www.allagents.co.uk/house-prices-adjusted/

A million more mothers have entered the workforce… ONS Data, Families and the Labour Market, England, September 2017

https://visual.ons.gov.uk/more-mothers-with-young-children-working-full-time/

The most stressed group at work is professional women aged between 35 and 44… HSE study, Work-related Stress, Depression or Anxiety Statistics in Great Britain 2017 http://www.hse.gov.uk/statistics/causdis/stress/stress.pdf

Most of the top jobs are filled by men... High Pay Centre/ CIPD, Executive Pay: Review of FTSE 100 Executive Pay Packages, August 2017
https://www.cipd.co.uk/knowledge/strategy/reward/executive-pay-ftse-100

Financially, it's not working either... Resolution Society analysis of ONS data, January 2017
http://www.resolutionfoundation.org/media/blog/the-gender-pay-gap-has-almost-closed-for-millennial-women-but-it-comes-shooting-back-when-they-turn-30/

Women of teens earn 33% less... Monica Costa Dias, William Elming, Robert Joyce, The Gender Wage Gap, IFS and Joseph Rowntree Foundation research, August 2016
https://www.ifs.org.uk/publications/8429

80% of us who have children... ONS Survey, Participation rates in the UK – 2014.2.Women, 2014
http://webarchive.nationalarchives.gov.uk/20160106100617/http://www.ons.gov.uk/ons/dcp171766_398888.pdf

800,000 children have mental health disorders... The Children's Commissioner's Report on measuring the number of vulnerable children, July 2017
https://www.childrenscommissioner.gov.uk/2017/07/04/shocking-report-by-childrens-commissioner-reveals-millions-of-children-in-england-living-vulnerable-or-high-risk-lives/

Chapter 2: I love my job but is it time I settled down and thought about kids?

78 per cent of women would not question a potential employer about maternity benefits... Glassdoor, Maternity Benefits Survey, 2014
https://www.glassdoor.co.uk/blog/uk-women-fearful-maternity-benefits/

Chapter 3: Wow, I feel like I've totally lost control and don't know who I am any more

68 per cent of parents said they felt isolated, Action for Children poll, November 2017
https://www.actionforchildren.org.uk/news-and-blogs/press-releases/2017/november/charity-reveals-devastating-impact-of-loneliness-on-uk-parents-children/

Chapter 4: Right, I need to get back to work

Returning to work comes with risks… EHRC research, Pregnancy and maternity discrimination in the workplace: Recommendations for change, 2016 https://www.equalityhumanrights.com/en/managing-pregnancy-and-maternity-workplace/our-recommendations-tackle-pregnancy-and-maternity

One in nine mothers report they were let go in some way… BBC Victoria Derbyshire programme, 'I was forced from my job for giving birth', 3 October 2017 http://www.bbc.co.uk/news/uk-40586451

Six in 10 businesses believe a woman should disclose whether she is pregnant during her recruitment process… EHRC analysis, based on an online YouGov survey, 2018 https://www.equalityhumanrights.com/en/our-work/news/employers-dark-ages-over-recruitment-pregnant-women-and-new-mothers

Slightly over half of the women who had flexible working requests… EHRC research, Pregnancy and Maternity-Related Discrimination and Disadvantage, 2016 https://www.gov.uk/government/publications/pregnancy-and-maternity-related-discrimination-and-disadvantage-final-reports

Some evidence suggests that about six months is the longest… Harvard Business Review, Off-Ramps and On-Ramps: Keeping Talented Women on the Road to Success, Sylvia Ann Hewlett and Carolyn Buck Luce, 2005 https://hbr.org/2005/03/off-ramps-and-on-ramps-keeping-talented-women-on-the-road-to-success

The good news is that… Great at Work: How Top Performers Do Less, Work Better, and Achieve More, Morten T. Hansen, Simon & Schuster, 2018

Recent research suggests these women are no less ambitious… The Power of Flexibility: A Key Enabler to Boost Gender Parity and Employee Engagement, Bain & Company, 2016 http://www.bain.com/publications/articles/the-power-of-flexibility.aspx

Chapter 5: I've always been able to cope with everything, so why do my kids make me so crazy?

As the Australian author and child psychologist…

Raising Boys: Why Boys are Different – and How to Help Them Become Happy and Well-Balanced Men, Steve Biddulph, Harper Thorsons, 2010

Quoting RainWildsGirl: 'I use the "label dot" method:… Mumsnet discussion, 'Clothing', December 2015 https://www.mumsnet.com/Talk/larger_families/2528218-Clothing

Chapter 6: How come I feel lonely even as I'm surrounded by people all the time?

Sarah Hesz, founder of mum-networking app Mush... 'The Apps helping mothers wave goodbye to loneliness', *The Times*, July 2017
https://www.thetimes.co.uk/article/the-apps-helping-mothers-wave-goodbye-to-loneliness-ct2x3js5l

Chapter 7: Help, I think I've done a crap job of raising my child

A piece in the New Yorker magazine... 'Spoiled Rotten: Why do kids rule the roost?' Elizabeth Kolbert, New Yorker, July 2012
https://www.newyorker.com/magazine/2012/07/02/spoiled-rotten
In fact a research project published in the American Journal of Sociology...
Social Policies, Parenthood, and Happiness in 22 Countries, A briefing paper prepared for the Council on Contemporary Families, Jennifer Glass, Robin Simon and Matthew Andersson, June 2016 https://contemporaryfamilies.org/brief-parenting-happiness/
Rachel Carrell, founder of nanny-share company Koru Kids explains... https://www.korukids.co.uk/

Chapter 8: Alpha/Beta, the pros and cons of dads as lead parents

This would explain the results of a uSwitch survey that found almost a third...
'Money worries forcing new mums back to work early', uSwitch research, 2012
https://www.uswitch.com/blog/2012/09/07/money-worries-forcing-new-mums-back-to-work-early/
This isn't just anecdotal:... 'Spousal Breadwinning Across 30 Years of Marriage and Husbands' Health: A Gendered Life Course Stress Approach',
Journal of Aging and Health, 2017 http://journals.sagepub.com/doi/abs/10.1177/0898264317721824
There is an unhelpful cultural norm around dads who are primary carers of their children... Performing American Masculinities: The 21st-Century Man in Popular Culture, Dr Elwood Watson, Indiana University Press, 2011
http://www.iupress.indiana.edu/product_info.php?products_id=487356

The Global Gender Gap report rated Finland the second most equal country in the world in 2016... Global Gender Gap Report, WEF, 2016 http://reports.weforum.org/global-gender-gap-report-2016/

...and the Economist recently rated it the third best country to be a working mum... The best – and worst – places to be a working mum, *The Economist*, March 2016 https://www.economist.com/blogs/graphicdetail/2016/03/daily-chart-0

According to Cornell sociology doctoral...

The Effect of Relative Income Disparity on Infidelity for Men and Women, Christin L. Munsch, Cornell University, 2010

And it's not just the thinking... Leisure Time in the UK: 2015, ONS https://www.ons.gov.uk/economy/nationalaccounts/satelliteaccounts/articles/leisuretimeintheuk/2015

This is compounded by the fact... 'Women Are Working More Than Ever—Inside The Home And Out', Huffington Post (US), October 2016, based on a survey by Whitman Insight Strategies
https://www.huffingtonpost.com/brittany-l-stalsburg-phd/women-are-working-more-th_b_9878996.html

The former editor of Loaded, *Martin Daubney...* 'Why don't more dads choose to stay at home? Because they get bullied by yummy mummies', *Daily Mail*, August 2016
http://www.dailymail.co.uk/femail/article-3733657/Why-don-t-dads-choose-stay-home-bullied-yummy-mummies.html#ixzz5ACSPY4tO

Martin Madowitz, an economist at the Center for American Progress... *Calculating the Hidden Cost of Interrupting a Career for Child Care,* Michael Madowitz, Alex Rowell and Katie Hamm, June 2016
https://www.americanprogress.org/issues/early-childhood/reports/2016/06/21/139731/calculating-the-hidden-cost-of-interrupting-a-career-for-child-care/

Chapter 9: The alpha/alpha couples

Interestingly, some research from America suggests that blue-collar... 'Why the White Working Class voted for Trump', *Harvard Business Review*, November 2016 https://hbr.org/ideacast/2016/11/why-the-white-working-class-voted-for-trump

A study cited earlier in the book revealed... 'Smartphones and tablets add two hours to the working day', *The Telegraph*, 2012, based on a study by Pixmania https://www.telegraph.co.uk/technology/mobile-phones/9646349/Smartphones-and-tablets-add-two-hours-to-the-working-day.html

So perhaps it's no great surprise that the 2014 report Gender, Job Authority, and Depression… Gender, Job Authority, and Depression, T. Pudrovska and A. Karraker, 2014
https://www.ncbi.nlm.nih.gov/pubmed/25413803

US data shows that they actually seem to grow up later… The Decline in Adult Activities Among U.S. Adolescents, 1976–2016, Jean M. Twenge, Heejung Park, 2016, September 2017 https://onlinelibrary.wiley.com/doi/abs/10.1111/cdev.12930

As expert on consumer psychology and behavioural design Nir Eyal explained in the Guardian recently… '"Our minds can be hijacked": the tech insiders who fear smartphone dystopia', The Guardian, October 2017 https://www.theguardian.com/technology/2017/oct/05/smartphone-addiction-silicon-valley-dystopia

The first is that some of us are specifically hired for it… Leading Professionals: Power, Politics, and Prima Donnas, Professor Laura Empson, Oxford University Press, 2017

As Michael Fishbein writes in an article titled… 'If working less is so productive, why is it so hard?', Medium.com, August 2017 https://medium.com/zero-infinity/overworking-6d082fed56d6

In The Way We're Working Isn't Working… *The Way We're Working Isn't Working: The Four Forgotten Needs That Energize Great Performance*, Tony Schwartz, Jean Gomes, Catherine McCarthy, Simon & Schuster, 2010

In 2017, researchers at King's College London and Royal Holloway found that the most passionate workers are at risk of damaging… '"It's tough hanging-up a call": The relationships between calling and work hours, psychological detachment, sleep quality and morning vigor', Michael E. Clinton, Neil Conway and Jane Sturges, Journal of Occupational Health Psychology, 2016 https://pure.royalholloway.ac.uk/portal/files/26250310/Final_JOHP_Hanging_up_a_calling_Open_Access.pdf

In Is Your Job Making You Ill? *Dr Ellie Cannon recommends scheduling everything… Is Your Job Making You Ill?: How to survive and thrive when it happens to you*, Ellie Cannon, Piatkus, 2018

Chapter 10: Solo

And it's a very widespread problem: a study by the charity Gingerbread… Paying the Price: The long road to recovery, 2014 https://www.gingerbread.org.uk/policy-campaigns/publications-index/paying-price-childcare-challenge/

By the time couples are in their 60s, a study by the think tank International Longevity – UK showed, for example, that in 2014… 'The Rise and Rise of the Silver Splitter', International Longevity Centre (survey), 2014 http://www. ilcuk.org.uk/index.php/publications/publication_details/the_rise_and_rise_ of_the_silver_separator

Research from the US suggests that successful professional women are more likely to be dissatisfied with lower-status partners… 'When She Brings Home the Job Status: Wives' Job Status, Status Leakage, and Marital Instability', Alyson Byrne, Julian Barling, *Organization Science*, 2017 https://pubsonline.informs. org/doi/abs/10.1287/orsc.2017.1120

The children of single mothers have no difference in outcomes than the children of heterosexual couples… 'Children in single-mother-by-choice families do just as well as those in two-parent families: Family social support services are valued', *European Society of Human Reproduction and Embryology*, July 2017 https://www.sciencedaily.com/ releases/2017/07/170705095332.htm

Chapter 11: Why does dealing with school turn me into a child?

In America in the 1980s, for example, young mothers spent about 12 hours per week actively engaged in childcare while fathers spent about four hours per week…
'High-pressure parenting', Ryan Avent, *1843 Magazine*, February/ March 2017 https://www.1843magazine.com/features/highpressure-parenting

Chapter 12: Help, my teenager is causing problems

Research from the University of Cambridge in 2015 found that state school pupils are likely to do better at university than privately educated ones… 'The role of the A* grade at A-level as a predictor of university performance', Zanini Nadir, Vidal Rodeiro Carmen, *Cambridge Assessment UK*, 2015, https://www.srhe.ac.uk/conference2014/abstracts/0083.pdf

Researchers identified what teens wanted in regards to relationship and sex education… Digital Romance, a Study by Brook CEOP NCA, Dr Ester McGeeney and Dr Elly Hanson, December 2017 https://www.brook.org.uk/data/DR_REPORT_FINAL.pdf

Chapter 13: What do Dads think?

The Pew Research Center in America found that fathers were just as likely as mothers to say that parenting was extremely important to their identity... Pew Research Center survey of parents with children under 18, 2015 http://www.pewsocialtrends.org/2015/12/17/parenting-in-america/

Research from Northwestern's Department of Anthropology in America shows that the male hormone testosterone falls when men have children... Longitudinal evidence that fatherhood decreases testosterone in human males, Lee T. Gettler, Thomas W. McDade, Alan B. Feranil and Christopher W. Kuzawa PNAS September 2011, http://www.pnas.org/content/108/39/16194

Chapter 14: The questions people ask me

I observe that the women who do continue to do well in these environments are those like American TV supremo Shonda Rhimes... 'My year of saying yes to everything', TED 2016, Shonda Rhimes https://www.ted.com/talks/shonda_rhimes_my_year_of_saying_yes_to_everything/discussion?ga_source=embed&ga_medium=embed&ga_campaign=embedT

Sarah Jaggers, MD, Managing Change... http://www.managingchange.org.uk/

Chapter 15: Conclusions

Psychologists such as Sue Gerhardt... Why Love Matters: How affection shapes a baby's brain, Sue Gerhardt, Routledge, 2015

Neal Lawson, chairman of the think tank Compass... http://www.compassonline.org.uk/about/people/

Sophie Walker, the leader of the Women's Equality Party... http://www.womensequality.org.uk/sophie_walker

Data from the US shows that people have an average of 300,000 items in their homes... 'For many people gathering possessions is just the stuff of life', *LA Times,* 2014 http://articles.latimes.com/2014/mar/21/health/la-he-keeping-stuff-20140322

It takes about 23 minutes and 15 seconds to fully refocus on a task after being distracted, depending partly on how complicated the task is... The Cost of Interrupted Work: More Speed and Stress, Gloria Mark, University of California, 2015 https://www.ics.uci.edu/~gmark/chi08-mark.pdf

Thank you

To all the women and men, paid and unpaid, who have helped to look after our children while we've been at work.

To Rev George Pitcher, who passed my proposal to Bloomsbury. To Charlotte Croft, my editor at Bloomsbury, who emailed back to say she wished she'd read this before she had kids. To Jane Eden, for her brutal, witty and wise reviews of many drafts. To Eve Harris, for her endless meticulous research and emotional support. To my colleagues, who have kept the Jericho Chambers ship sailing while I've been in east London hammering my keyboard and drinking tea. To Sarah Clarke, Karen Doherty and Dee Armstrong for generously sharing their robust insights. To my great friends for restoring my sanity and making me laugh every day: Alex, Clare, Danielle, Elaine, Josie, Gillian, Jill, Rebecca, Sarah, Sukhi and Vicky (plus a few who specifically requested not to be named!).

To Chris, my husband, for being the best decision I've ever made and never mentioning the irony of writing a book about parenting while leaving the lion's share of the parenting to him. And to our three girls, who remind me daily that being their mother is more important than any job.

Index